Central Control
and Local Discretion in China

Studies on Contemporary China

The Contemporary China Institute at the School of Oriental and African Studies (University of London) has, since its establishment in 1968, been an international centre for research and publications on twentieth-century China. *Studies on Contemporary China*, which is edited at the Institute, seeks to maintain and extend that tradition by making available the best work of scholars and China specialists throughout the world. It embraces a wide variety of subjects relating to Nationalist and Communist China, including social, political, and economic change, intellectual and cultural developments, foreign relations, and national security.

Series Editor

Dr Frank Dikötter, Director of the Contemporary China Institute

Editorial Advisory Board

Central Control
and Local Discretion in China

Leadership and Implementation
During Post-Mao Decollectivization

JAE HO CHUNG

OXFORD
UNIVERSITY PRESS

OXFORD

UNIVERSITY PRESS

Great Clarendon Street, Oxford OX2 6DP

Oxford University Press is a department of the University of Oxford.
It furthers the University's objective of excellence in research, scholarship,
and education by publishing worldwide in

Oxford New York

Athens Auckland Bangkok Bogotá Buenos Aires Calcutta
Cape Town Chennai Dar es Salaam Delhi Florence Hong Kong Istanbul
Karachi Kuala Lumpur Madrid Melbourne Mexico City Mumbai
Nairobi Paris São Paulo Shanghai Singapore Taipei Tokyo Toronto Warsaw

and associated companies in Berlin Ibadan

Oxford is a registered trade mark of Oxford University Press
in the UK and certain other countries

Published in the United States
by Oxford University Press Inc., New York

British Library Cataloguing in Publication Data
Data available

Library of Congress Cataloging in Publication Data
Chung, Jae Ho, 1960–
Central control and local discretion in China : leadership and implementation during
post-Mao decollectivization / Jae Ho Chung.
p. cm.—(Studies on contemporary China)
Includes bibliographical references and index.
1. Agriculture and state–China. 2. Privatization–China.
3. China–Economic
policy–1976– I. Title. II. Series.
HD2098.C39 2000   338.1'851—dc21   00-037521
ISBN 0-19-829777-7

1 3 5 7 9 10 8 6 4 2

Typeset by Best-set Typesetter Ltd., Hong Kong
Printed in Great Britain
on acid-free paper by
T.J. International Ltd, Padstow, Cornwall

For My Parents
My Wife Hye Kyung
and My Daughter Yu Jean

Preface

Politics is about people. Politics is also rooted in territory. Territorial dimensions of power and politics are particularly pertinent to the study of China whose history has been replete with centrifugal challenges from local governments, clans, and militia. Looking at its central–local implementation dynamics by 'unpacking' the encompassing concept of state, I believe we may get closer to the real meanings and implications of China's reform, transition, and governance. The present volume explores the norms, structures, and agency in efforts to delineate the boundaries of central control and local discretion in China. More specifically, with the case of the decollectivization reform of 1978–84, this book seeks to explain the scope and reasons for the provincial variations in the pace of adopting the household responsibility systems nationally as well as in three case provinces.

This book grew out of my doctoral dissertation for the University of Michigan. I must, therefore, begin by thanking the members of the dissertation committee. I am profoundly indebted to Kenneth Lieberthal who, as the committee chair, was very generous with his time, knowledge, and experiences of China and assisted me in more ways than I can possibly recount. My sincere gratitude is also due to Michel Oksenberg, now at Stanford University, who, as a teacher, friend, and colleague, introduced me to the wonderful world of Sinological research. I am also grateful to Lawrence Mohr who has been not only an energetic teacher of organizational theory but also an extremely affectionate friend, without whom the entire process of writing could have been painfully dull and dry. I owe a special thank-you to Samuel Barnes, previously of the University of Michigan and now with Georgetown University, who constituted an important source of enlightenment and inspiration. I would also like to express my appreciation to Robert Dernberger for his insightful comments, which, in retrospect, were crucial in improving the overall quality of the book.

In the process of additional research and revision for this book, I had the privilege of obtaining invaluable help and support from many individuals. Thomas Bernstein, Bruce Dickson, Joseph Fewsmith, David Goodman, James Kung, Dorothy Solinger, Frederick Teiwes, Tsui Kai Yuen, David Zweig, and two anonymous readers for the Oxford University Press meticulously read earlier drafts at various stages and provided excellent comments that were of immense help in refining the theoretical arguments, analysing empirical data, and improving the style of the book. Nearly three dozen Chinese officials, researchers, and academics in Beijing, Anhui, Shandong, and Heilongjiang were very generous in sharing their insights with me through many long interviews. It is a shame that they should remain anonymous, yet my gratitude to them remains the same. Many individuals also provided logistic support and warm encouragement. They include Du Yuxin, Li Xiao, Wen Tiejun, Zhang Ronghua, Peter Tsui, David Man Tai-wai, and Mr and Mrs M. G. Lee. I am particularly grateful to Kuan Hsin-chi and Jean Hung of the Universities Service Centre at the Chinese University of Hong Kong, who made my stay there so comfortable and productive. I also owe a special thank-you to my former research assistant at the Hong Kong University of Science and Technology, Roy Man Chi-keung, who assisted me unsparingly.

Several institutions provided financial support for this project. The Department of Political Science of the University of Michigan offered a teaching fellowship for three years (1987–9 and 1991) during which concrete ideas for this project were originated. I am grateful to the Center for Chinese Studies of the University of Michigan which awarded me two endowment grants in 1987 and 1990. My research at the Universities Service Centre of the Chinese University of Hong Kong and a field trip to China during 1991–2 were supported by a Doctoral Dissertation Research Grant (grant number SC-6104) from the Pacific Cultural Foundation and by a Rackham Dissertation Research Grant from the Horace Rackham School of Graduate Studies of the University of Michigan. Another interview trip to China in the summer of 1994 was supported by a Direct Allocation Grant for Faculty Research (grant number DAG-HSS11) from Hong Kong University of Science and Technology.

Finally, I am profoundly indebted to my family to whom this book is dedicated with utmost gratitude. My parents have never ceased praying for me since I initiated this journey into the world of China back in 1981. My intellectual and personal debts to them extend far beyond the pages that follow. My wife, Hye Kyung, served neither as typist nor as proof-reader, but her contribution to the book can be found on every single page. This book is also dedicated to Yu Jean, my daughter, with the hope that she will see the world around her more positively and perhaps more beautifully.

Jae Ho Chung

Seoul National University
Korea
February 2000

Contents

List of Tables

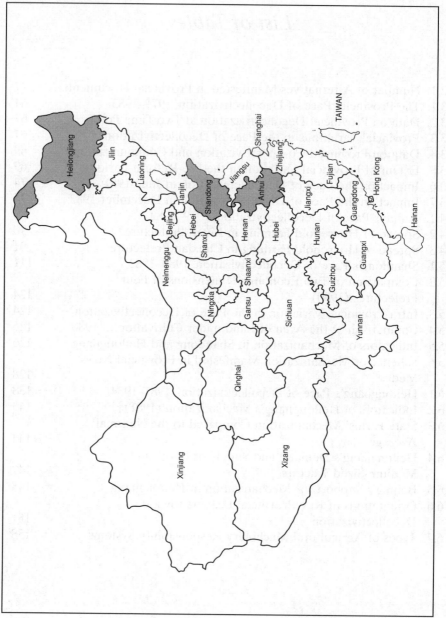

MAP 1. *Location of the Three Case Provinces*

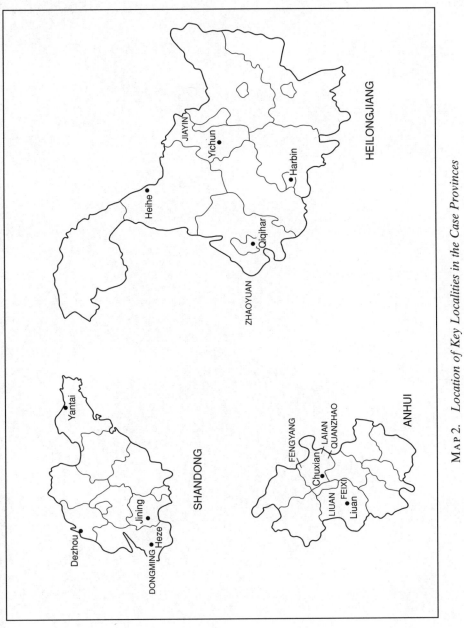

MAP 2. *Location of Key Localities in the Case Provinces*

1

Introduction

Politics, in large part, evolves around the making and implementation of authoritative decisions. The classic imperative of 'who gets what and how' attains a real meaning only when pertinent decisions are actually executed. Implementation thus constitutes a very crucial dimension of politics as its processes and outcomes may often produce critical effects on the legitimacy of the regime as well as on the political fate of its leadership. Such high political stakes associated with implementation point to an intuitively sensible conclusion that, in order to ensure effective implementation of policy, any political system must operate with some degrees of consent and support from the controlled. And there emerges an acute need for certain rules of co-ordinating disagreement and generating consensus with regard to the way crucial policy decisions are implemented.

Several macrolevel conceptions have been developed in efforts to understand the rules of consensus building. In political terms, democracy has been conceived as a mechanism of generating popular consensus by way of voting; authoritarianism as manipulating consensus by resorting to the threat and use of violence; and totalitarianism as imposing consensus through ideological indoctrination. In economic terms, the market has long been regarded as the core institution of consensus building in capitalist systems; and planning as the indispensable tool of imposing consensus in socialist systems. These macro views, however, are largely concerned with systemic relationships between government and people (or, alternatively, between state and society), falling short of explicating what transpires within the government organized in a hierarchical fashion with intervening levels of local administration.

This hierarchical structure of territorial power, designed for effective management of political control, economic development and social welfare, as well as for administrative efficiency, may often pose serious problems for the national-level government when sub-national units become unwilling to comply with central directives. While most of the time certain rules and norms are effective enough to induce central concession or local compliance, the central government may often find it very difficult to prevent recalcitrant behaviour by local authorities.[1] The significance of local recalcitrance is particularly manifest in that the locality is not only legally subjected to the centre but also institutionally placed under a hierarchically structured channel of communication. For discontented localities, therefore, the choice of 'exit' or 'opting out' is largely unavailable except for the extreme cases of secessionist movements. Even the 'voice' option can be costly in non-democratic systems where ideological norms and party discipline tend to stigmatize deviations from central guidelines, leaving discontented localities to suffer in silence. Considering such structural and normative constraints on local recalcitrance, the occurrence of noncompliance is in itself sufficient to damage the 'sovereign image' of the centre, which will in turn seek to contain local deviation for the sake of regime governability.[2]

While implementation slippage and local recalcitrance may be ubiquitous in all political systems, they are more likely to produce severe impact on developing countries and reforming socialist systems with few effective institutions and little experience to handle decentralized structures of interest co-ordination and policy execution. This problem of 'governability' has been recently highlighted in association with such concepts as state capability, regime legitimacy, and authority erosion.[3] Interesting is the fact that scholarly attention is increasingly shifting toward local levels of government and their roles in the complex policy process. Similar concerns have also been voiced with regard to the state capacity and governability of China in recent years. This brings us to the issue of how to assess the impact of post-Mao decentralization on China's central–local policy dynamics.

Scholarly work on China's reforms has clearly demonstrated the important role that decentralization has played in promoting local initiatives since the late 1970s. But the term 'decentralization' is often used rather too mechanically, suggesting that a decision by the centre to decentralize administrative authority *ipso facto* produces local discretion properly keyed to local conditions. But that notion begs an important question: does decentralization *actually* allow localities to utilize discretion in the fashion intended? The findings of this book—derived from the research on the decollectivization of agriculture in the early 1980s—suggest that the earlier efforts for administrative decentralization produced rather diluted effects on the scope of local discretion and that the relationship between decentralization decisions and central–local policy dynamics was by no means straightforward but entailed complex interactions of various factors.

More specifically, this study tackles two questions. First, under what circumstances and to what extent can administrative decentralization *actually* expand the scope of local discretion in the implementation of central policy? Regarding post-Mao decollectivization, did the first-wave decentralization succeed in promoting local discretion, enhancing the levels of provincial variation in the pace and pattern of implementation? Or did the provinces demonstrate swift compliance in a highly standardized manner as before? Second, what sort of implementation patterns are generally available to local governments and under what circumstances do some patterns become more widely adopted than others? As for post-Mao decollectivization, why did a majority of provinces opt for a highly cautious stance eventually to 'jump on the bandwagon', while others either actively pioneered or staunchly resisted the controversial reform?

With regard to the first question, this book suggests that outcomes of decentralization may often differ significantly from its intended goals. Failures of decentralization are by no means unusual, particularly in systems where bureaucratic inertia remains so strong that, despite stipulated measures of decentralization, both central and local officials may continue to operate under 'totalitarian mentality' (i.e. norms of centralized control). Strategic efforts are needed to weaken these dominant norms of centralization. However, such efforts may face serious difficulties in systems where key local officials are appointed by the centre and, therefore, the problem of 'bureaucratic careerism'—a tendency of career bureaucrats not to associate themselves too closely with potentially controversial policies when there is even a slight chance of policy reversal—is pervasive. In the context of post-Mao decollectivization, a majority of the provinces chose to 'bandwagon': that is to say, they did not implement household farming too fast or too slowly, since pushing ahead with the controversial reform or lagging too far behind meant potentially enormous political risk. Once Beijing's preference appeared to be firmly fixed, however, they all quickly 'bandwagoned' by popularizing the policy as swiftly as possible, very often without due regard for their local conditions and needs.

As for the second question, this study suggests that implementation of public policy entails a particular mix of three patterns: in addition to 'bandwagoning', there are two other patterns of 'pioneering' and 'resisting'. 'Pioneering' refers to going far ahead of others in carrying out a given policy throughout the process of implementation. 'Pioneer' localities very often operate as faithful agents of the centre, which in turn controls and protects them through intricate clientelistic networks. 'Resisting', on the other hand, denotes local non-compliance by way of delaying the implementation of central policy or bending it to serve parochial interests. Organizational adjustments and norm changes may facilitate a new 'mix' of local policy implementation. *Ceteris paribus*, successful administrative decentralization may produce a relatively evenly distributed mix among the three, and, as a result, an increased level of local variation may be observed. Post-Mao decollectivization, however, was largely a failed effort in this regard: a majority of the provinces opted for bandwagoning and only a small number of provinces chose other alternatives only to submit to Beijing later. In many respects, provincial implementation of decollectivization approximated the Maoist practice of forced compliance.

The remainder of this introductory chapter consists of five sections. The first provides conceptual discussions of administrative decentralization and bureaucratic norms associated with implementation dynamics. The second presents a theoretical synopsis concerning the three patterns of local policy implementation and their particular 'mixes' in the context of decentralization. The third section examines the determinants of local variation, principally structural factors, leadership characteristics, and the 'centralizing paradox' as the variation equalizer. The fourth section discusses the book's research design with regard to the theoretical and empirical rationales for the selection of post-Mao decollectivization as the case policy, data-collection methods, and modes of analysis. Finally, a brief section delineates the overall structure of the book.

ADMINISTRATIVE DECENTRALIZATION, POLICY DISCRETION, AND BUREAUCRATIC NORMS

In recent years, many formerly highly centralized unitary states, both developed and developing ones, have been decentralizing. The significance of decentralization has been further underscored by a series of efforts in this direction by many 'post-communist' economies and reforming socialist systems, most notably China.[4] What then is meant by decentralization? Decentralization is an umbrella concept as well as a shorthand for a variety of structural arrangements for the allocation of power and other resources. This study takes decentralization to mean *intergovernmental devolution* of authority. More specifically, 'devolution' refers to the downward transfer of power to lower-level units, while 'intergovernmental' denotes the scope of devolution to be limited within the governmental structure. Thus, this study is concerned with the 'downward transfer of power and authority between different levels of government'.[5]

There may be several rationales with which decentralization decisions are made. Politically, decentralization constitutes a neat strategy to relieve the regime of various burdens of excessive centralization accumulated during the period of state formation (such as high taxes, regional suppression, cultural stagnation, and fears of ethnic extinction).[6] Economically, decentralization has potentials to promote efficiency by recognizing local diversities and variations and acquiring bottom-heavy information.[7] Organizationally, decentralization may rationalize interest articulation and decision-making by way of reducing communication overloads and permitting local participation and discretion in the policy process.[8]

The organizational dimension is particularly pertinent for our discussion of administrative decentralization as it delves into the issue of central control and local autonomy. The core question boils down to the extent to which local discretion is allowed in implementing central policy. The most centralized policy structure presupposes that only one individual, group, or unit is put in charge of making decisions for all policy areas. Such a system not only lacks the necessary time and information to make sensible decisions, but it is also highly unlikely to possess viable means to ensure that as many decisions are to be implemented as originally intended.[9]

In order to adapt to spatial heterogeneity and flux, therefore, multilevel policy-making is preferred, which measures of administrative decentralization are likely to promote. Even if local inputs and participation were not sufficient in the policy-making phase, 'policy-remake' could be carried out during the implementation phase. Only with such an administratively decentralized structure, what North has termed as 'adaptive efficiency' can be achieved.[10] In this regard, local discretion is deemed indispensable in interpreting and executing central policy, particularly with regard to the policies that are 'bottom-heavy' in terms of their informational requirements, resource allocation, and execution.[11]

Whatever the potentials of administrative decentralization may be, its goals and outcomes may often be very different. Examples abound with regard to the failures of decentralization programmes due to the active intervention and interference by central and local forces which sought to promote different sets of priorities and interests.[12] Similarly, the failure of decentralization is not unusual in non-democratic systems where legal and administrative stipulations of decentralization very often proved insufficient to prevent the chronic reassertion of the powerful centre, eventually nullifying the entire efforts toward the change.[13] The problem boils down to bureaucratic inertia. Bureaucratic inertia refers to the behavioural characteristic that, despite the efforts toward structural and procedural changes through the measures of administrative decentralization, part of the central and local government apparatus and its officials continue to operate under the norms of centralization. Under these circumstances, the impact of administrative decentralization on expanding the scope of local discretion is likely to be minimal at best. Consequently, the centre's preferences would prevail over local interests.[14]

Genuine intergovernmental devolution of authority must be accompanied by concerted efforts to weaken the dominant norms of centralization which take uniform local compliance for granted. That is, administrative decentralization entails more than simple structural and procedural readjustments, and the transformation of bureaucratic norms is an indispensable component of decentralization.[15] Efforts to transform bureaucratic norms, however, may face serious difficulties if a majority of key local officials are appointed by the centre rather than being popularly elected. In these systems, the problem of 'bureaucratic careerism'—a tendency of career bureaucrats to become highly opportunistic as their highest priority is on the advancement of their careers determined largely by how compliant they are perceived to be by their central superiors—is particularly pervasive. Thus, unless there is a firm belief shared among local officials that decentralization is an irreversible trend, they may continue to act upon bureaucratic careerism.[16]

The symptoms of bureaucratic careerism can be pushed to an extreme in socialist systems where all personnel decisions for top local leadership positions are controlled exclusively by the *nomenklatura* system, and advocating local interests against the centre's priorities may easily be interpreted as following an 'incorrect' ideological or political line.[17] Under these fears of persecution, however important local interests might be, they could never become as crucial as the careers of the officials themselves. Thus, when bureaucratic careerism becomes the widely shared norm of local officials, administrative decentralization is unlikely to succeed, since most local officials would prefer to play safe by doing precisely what they were told by the central officials.

Norms—whether of (de)centralization or bureaucratic careerism—change very slowly. The slow pace of norm change is due mainly to the time-consuming process of organizational learning that entails the interpretation of past experiences and reflections on current practices. The exploration of the impact of administrative decentralization on the norms of local officials thus requires an additional perspective—that of time. That is, after measures of decentralization have been stipulated, local officials need time to see if the centre's commitment to the programme of decentralization is indeed credible and durable. The crux of the matter is to convince the localities that this time the centre's commitment is genuine and trustworthy. In order to create and sustain an 'atmosphere of trust', the central government should frequently remind local implementors that they may exercise their newly granted policy discretion without fears of persecution.[18]

PATTERNS OF LOCAL POLICY IMPLEMENTATION: A 'TRIPLE MIX' TYPOLOGY

If administrative decentralization is *successfully* executed, what sort of outcome may we expect in local policy implementation? One expected outcome would be varied implementation—as opposed to standardization—reflecting differing conditions and needs of different localities. In conceptualizing the patterns of local policy implementation, we may think of a spectrum overarching the two opposite ends of complete compliance and total non-compliance. Complete compliance refers to an ideal situation where all localities implement central policy without any delay, distortion, or resistance. Total non-compliance, on the other hand, denotes another extreme situation where no locality executes the policy adopted by the centre. These two situations seem more theoretical than real since implementation of any policy is bound to entail certain variations in cross-sectional and longitudinal terms.

Most of the actual cases of implementation, therefore, fall between these two extremes, representing particular 'mixes' of three patterns. The first is 'pioneering' which refers to a type of behaviour by local implementors who go far ahead of others in carrying out central policy. Two rationales may explain the pioneers' behaviour of 'compliance-in-advance'. First, pioneering may simply represent voluntary (and often spontaneous) local innovations which are later captured by the central government in search of a nationally applicable solution to a serious policy problem.[19] Second, alternatively, pioneering localities may possess local conditions most favourable to experiment with the proposed policy. That is, the central government seeks to raise the possibility of success by designating them as experimental sites.[20] In the former case, the decision to pioneer may be rooted in personal convictions of local leaders and/or popular demands for change. In the latter, the risk of pioneering is shared by the central government which controls and protects them through intricate networks of clientelism.[21] In both cases, however, pioneers implement central policy much faster than other localities, thus creating an impetus for its swift popularization.

The second pattern is 'bandwagoning': local officials maintain extreme caution by not implementing central policy too fast or too slowly. Since pushing ahead with an uncontested policy or lagging too far behind may mean enormous political costs to localities without central patrons (unlike a few well-connected pioneers), they usually choose not to be conspicuous and carefully monitor the centre's evolving position on the policy concerned. In addition to holding on to the 'wait-and-see' attitude, another key characteristic of 'bandwagoning' is that once the centre's preference appears to be fixed with no apparent signs of further change, these hitherto cautious localities all quickly bandwagon to popularize the policy as swiftly as possible. Historical memories of frequent policy oscillations and political persecution may contribute to the institutionalization of bandwagoning as an opportunistic but safe option for local implementors. As the core rationale for compliance resonates with the imperative of political survival rather than policy effectiveness, the prevalence of bandwagoning tends to create difficulties in problem-solving. And such problems may be more prevalent in systems where permitting local discretion is a rarity and, therefore, local implementors live in chronic fears of punishment in the event that their efforts for flexible implementation are perceived to be deviant and non-compliant.[22]

The third pattern is 'resisting': local implementors do not comply with the centre by way of either delaying the execution of a given policy or bending it to serve parochial interests.[23] In the absence of consensus on the desirability and effectiveness of the given policy, local implementors may perceive it as a potential threat to local interests and seek to circumvent its diffusion. This is called a 'negative agent disposition', and it is usually facilitated by combinations of the following conditions.[24] First, the more threatening are the changes proposed by the new policy to local interests, the more actively may localities resist to protect their vested interests. Second, resisters may have their own clientelistic linkages with those at the centre who do not support the proposed policy.[25] Third, resisting may also require 'heroic' local leaders who sincerely view representing local needs and sentiments to be more important than saving their own necks.

Implementation of public policy is likely to entail a certain mix of these three patterns. With the addition of a time dimension, the pace of national implementation depends on (1) the number of pioneers—the larger its number, the faster the implementation; (2) the timing of bandwagoning—the earlier the timing of bandwagoning, the faster the implementation; and (3) the number of resisters and the duration of their resistance—the larger the number and the more enduring their resistance, the slower the overall pace of implementation. Relatedly, *ceteris paribus*, a higher level of local variation in the pace of implementation is associated with a relatively even distribution of these three types of implementors. On the other hand, a sudden drop in the level of local variation may be attributed to a 'big bang' in which a majority of local implementors bandwagon to popularize the policy very swiftly, as well as to the uniform submission by 'resisters' to the political pressure from the center.

Administrative decentralization and accompanying norm changes may facilitate a new 'mix' in the pattern of local policy implementation. If the norms of administrative decentralization—designed to allow local implementors an expanded scope of discretion in interpreting and implementing central policy in line with varied local conditions—are widely accepted, we are then likely to discern at least three characteristics of the implementation process. First, in the initial phase, we are likely to have a relatively evenly distributed mix among the three patterns.[26] Second, as the key consequence of this new mix, the degree of local variation is likely to increase as compared with, say, the implementation of similar policies prior to administrative decentralization. Third, the duration of nationwide implementation is also likely to lengthen as local compliance becomes more gradual—i.e. in the absence of the centre's political pressure and the subsequent 'big bang', local implementors get to have more time for adaptive implementation.

DETERMINANTS OF LOCAL VARIATION

If successful, it has been argued, administrative decentralization can change the cost-benefit calculus of the implementation game so that local implementors may become less restrained by centralist norms and, therefore, more willing to perform as local representatives rather than mere agents of the centre. An important question remains, however: how to explain local variations—that some act upon changed norms, while others continue to behave as cautiously as before? In other words, would the effects of administrative decentralization be indiscriminate on all localities? Not so, because local interests vary with different policies and because each locality's political relationship with the centre as well as their leadership characteristics may also differ.

Endogenous and Exogenous Determinants of Local Variation

In accounting for local variation, we may adopt an endogenous-exogenous criterion. Endogenous factors refer to varied local conditions, which define the stake of each locality differently and, therefore, make local officials respond to the same central policy in differing manners. On the other hand, exogenous factors denote each locality's political relationship with the central government.[27] First, regarding the endogenous determinants. Since, most of the time, central policy-makers cannot formulate a policy that satisfies all of the local implementors involved, whether the policy affects some localities more than others produces variance in terms of 'salience' they attach to it. When the policy is beneficial to all localities, they would have no incentive to resist and prefer to comply although their pace of compliance may vary depending on the perceived size of potential benefit. When it benefits some localities but penalizes others, or when it affects all localities adversely, the situation becomes more complicated. In cases of severe conflicts of interest—i.e. both central policy-makers and local implementors attach a high level of salience to the policy—localities would seek to slow down its implementation through resisting or bandwagoning unless the political costs of doing so is set too high.[28]

In the prevalence of centralist norms, all other things being equal, bandwagoning is the safest option for local implementors regardless of local interests. Every locality would pay close attention to the evolving position of the centre and to how other localities react to central policy. As a consequence, few opt for pioneering or resisting. Hence, little local variation. The introduction and internalization of decentralized norms may enhance the significance of local conditions and interests, which would induce implementors to venture out to the hitherto unaccepted realm of discretionary implementation. Those who view the policy as highly beneficial would opt for pioneering, while those who regard it to be damaging would resist. Some with neutral preferences would bandwagon, while others whose preferences coincide with those of pioneers or resisters may still choose to bandwagon out of fears and bureaucratic inertia. Hence, the level of local variation is raised.[29]

Exogenous factors may also contribute to local variations. Given that implementation is inherently political in nature, the strategic relationship between central leaders and local implementors constitutes a crucial determinant of local responses. With regard to the high-risk types of local response—such as resisting and pioneering—certain clientelistic networks stable and strong enough to allow local implementors to overcome fears of being perceived as deviant may be a prerequisite. Since central patronage is usually at a premium, not every locality can afford to have one. Therefore, localities lacking such networks would prefer to bandwagon even if they wished to pioneer or resist on the basis of their local interests.[30]

Local Leadership Matters: Agency versus Structure

It has been suggested so far that, in order for local implementors to overcome the constraints of the centralist structure and norms, their perceived benefits or damages to be produced by the proposed policy should be sufficiently large. Generic local interests defining the magnitude of issue salience constitute a crucial determinant of local variation, while central–local clientelistic networks may work as a critical catalyst for pioneering and resisting. In the final analysis, it may all come down to the issue of leadership. Assessing local conditions, gauging the impact of central policy on parochial interests, and interpreting the implementation issue within the context of political clientelism are all carried out by local implementors who must come up with a choice concerning how to respond to the centre.[31]

To understand the choices local implementors make, we need to know where their frame of reference lies. Objective rationality ignores the characteristics of the choosing organism and instead focuses on constraints imposed by structure, while bounded rationality acknowledges the informational limitations of the choosing organism. Given that the future is uncertain and the thinking process incomplete, local implementors are most likely to make decisions that may not be optimal but satisficing within the cultural framework widely shared among themselves.[32] What then is this framework? If the structure commands centralization, the cultural frame of reference induces local implementors to opt for standardized compliance as the non-optimal but safest option. In systems where local officials are not popularly elected but appointed solely by the centre, local implementors are not vote-maximizers and their primary concern is not with the local constituencies but with the centre. Thus, under this structure, the room for local implementors' independent action is highly restricted.

Administrative decentralization may expand the room for agency in two ways. First, the devolution of decisional authority to lower levels of government enhances the accountability of local implementors. Since local implementors are now permitted to take part in policy-remake during the implementation phase, they need to reflect local interests more sincerely than before. Thus, local constituencies begin to have an impact on the calculation of choices by local implementors. Second, the expanded room for local-level decision-making may also allow local implementors an opportunity structure where they can attempt a shift from the 'transactional leadership' to the 'transforming leadership'. That is, local implementors who have hitherto worked exclusively within the stable confines of a fixed set of goals defined solely by the centre may now begin to set their own goals, articulate local interests more concretely, and identify new missions. Consequently, they may break out of the cast of 'bandwagoning' and venture into the uncontested terrain of pioneering and resisting.[33]

There is another dimension of leadership: personalities. Generally speaking, the links between personal qualities and leadership capacity remain vague. As Wildavsky notes, '[T]he trait approach [to leadership research] seemed ill conceived from the start. . . . Exit the "hero in history".' It is nevertheless worth noting that administrative decentralization, if successfully institutionalized, tends to reduce the centre's incentives to resort to coercion as its implementation strategy, and the prospect for intergovernmental co-ordination and adaptive implementation looms large. In these complex processes, personal characteristics of individual local leaders may often surface to constitute a crucial determinant of local variation, although their systematic and rigorous generalizations may be difficult, if not impossible.[34]

The Centralizing Paradox as the Variation Equalizer

However undetailed it may be, a policy programme is bound to have minimum demands for the pace and outcome of local implementation, which the centre reviews from time to time. While local variation is an ideal outcome of decentralization, the centre may often interpret it to be overly deviant. Hence enter the 'centralizing paradox'. The centralizing paradox refers to a dilemma wherein the centre is torn between two incompatible preferences: whether to continue to tolerate local variation for the sake of decentralization, or to reassert central control at the expense of decentralization. The toleration option is appealing when adaptive implementation is deemed crucial for overall policy performance. At the same time, however, the central government is concerned with its image as the effective 'regulator' and, thus, the intervention option also becomes very tempting.[35]

The centralizing paradox stems largely from two factors: a 'difference in focus' and a 'divide in perception'. The difference in focus refers to the situation where local implementors focus almost solely on parochial interests, while the central government is bound to have a national concern. The divide in perception refers to the cognitive discrepancies that local variation usually appears to the centre as having gone out of control, while local implementors almost always perceive their boundary of action as overly constrained. The larger the gap between these foci and perceptions, the more likely is the centre to intervene to regulate local implementation behaviour.[36]

There is a crucial constraint on the centre's choice of intervention, although it is rarely noticed or acknowledged. Once the centre intervenes to regulate local behaviour, relaxed norms of local implementation may immediately become tightened again so as to cast doubts on the centre's commitment to decentralization. As localities collectively constitute an 'audience' that closely monitors the centre, central intervention may produce at will highly adverse effects on the overall norms of implementation. Particularly when the decentralization programme has just been initiated so that a majority of localities remain highly uncertain about the centre's intentions, their fears of policy reversal would be quickly confirmed if the centre treated deviant localities harshly.[37] As administrative decentralization is a political decision which specifies who are to participate and be excluded in policy-making, it is very likely to be contested even within the central government. Therefore, the weaker the centre's commitment to the programme of decentralization, the faster will it revert back to habitual interventionism. After all, decentralization is so often used by the regime as a publicity stunt without any substantive measures.[38]

The threshold at which the centre decides to intervene is almost impossible to predict. We may nevertheless specify certain circumstances. First, issue salience: the centre's patience may run out quickly if the policy concerned is a national priority with high stakes for the regime. Second, the centre becomes tempted to intervene if the policy concerned is of a governance-encompassing nature (that is, the policy involves little tangible resources to be exchanged between the central and local governments, and it is directed at all localities). The implication is that governance policy, as opposed to resource policy, generally demands much stricter compliance since its implementation is dictated mostly by political values rather than economic rationales. Encompassing policy generally induces stricter compliance since it is likely to be more standardized than selective policy with a smaller number of policy targets.[39] Third, when continued local resistance is deemed detrimental to the survival of the new policy as well as to the image of the centre, it is likely to intervene to equalize local variation.

The crux of the matter is that the centre almost always reserves the right to set the rules of the implementation game.[40] It is the centre that decides on decentralization. It is the centre that defines the boundary of acceptable local discretion. It is also the centre that determines the timing of equalizing local variation by supporting pioneers, pushing bandwagoners, and coercing resisters.[41] Although the centre may seek to accommodate some local interests by offering inducements, its agenda is not limited to dealing with recalcitrant localities. It has to consider overall control, planning, and other political priorities. The longer the process of conflict resolution drags on, the more is it likely to deprive the centre of incentives for toleration.[42] The centre's changing priority may also drastically alter the nature of the game. The adoption of a 'superordinate goal'—the total utility of which far surpasses that of the given policy—may transform the overall pay-offs, which then induces the centre to intervene to equalize local variation and obtain uniform compliance. When a political rationale dictates that the centre shortens the overall duration of implementation, its choice of instrument may also escalate from mild and co-ordinating mechanisms to heavier and more coercive ones. The resulting outcome would be a 'big bang' by which hitherto cautious implementors all 'bandwagon' and resisters quickly succumb to the centre's pressure.[43]

In the final analysis, while it may be a truism that administrative decentralization is likely to expand local discretion to varying degrees, the centre's control capacity may not necessarily be reduced by it. As long as the central government remains the 'centre' of power, the antinomy of decentralization also stays with it.

THE CASE OF AGRICULTURAL DECOLLECTIVIZATION IN POST-MAO CHINA: DECENTRALIZATION, STATE CAPACITY, AND CENTRAL–LOCAL POLICY DYNAMICS

This book takes the position that operational effects of administrative decentralization should not be simply taken for granted but need to be demonstrated empirically for each policy issue. In assessing the impact of post-Mao decentralization in China, therefore, this study adopts a critical mindset ready to challenge the popular notions that the centre's capacity for local control is bound to fade under administrative decentralization, that local discretion necessarily expands across the board, and that central–local bargaining and negotiation become more prevalent than before. This study instead suggests that the balance between central control and local discretion depends heavily on the particular policy of concern and that the centre may continue to retain a considerable level of influence over local implementation processes with regard to national priority issues.

Decentralization was not an unfamiliar experience in China during the pre-reform era (1949–76). In fact, Maoist China constantly oscillated between centralization and decentralization with the swings of the policy pendulum facilitated by elite dissensus over the goals and means of development.[44] No concrete evidence is available to suggest, however, that such cyclical repetitions produced an expanded scope of local discretion over the years. Despite intermittent measures of decentralization, rigid ideological control and political propaganda dominated the policy process, depriving local leaders of incentives to risk their political fate for parochial local interests. Consequently, compliance became the norm and discretion a dangerous luxury.[45] Local leaders thus had to be content only with performing as the centre's agents, ignoring the role of local representatives. In fact, it was not that local leaders were not allowed to revolt but that they were not even permitted to be unhappy with the centre. In sum, however decentralized it was in theory and intention, the administrative *modus operandi* during Mao's China was generally for strengthening central control at the expense of local discretion.[46]

While Maoist China was overly ideology-oriented and excessively centralized to allow room for local discretion, the post-Mao era witnessed a drastic reversal in that de-ideologization was stressed to 'liberate' localities from the centralist norms of blind compliance, and decentralization was adopted to promote local participation in economic reform. In its efforts for the 'emancipation of mind' (*sixiang jiefang*), the post-Mao leadership offered candid criticisms of various malpractice and wrongdoing of the Maoist era, consoled their victims by granting official pardons, and injected a variety of 'rational' elements into the policy process.[47] Accompanied were drastic measures of decentralization in a wide range of sectors including planning, agriculture, industrial management, fiscal relations, foreign trade and investment, personnel management, law-making, and so on. Most importantly for this study, local initiatives, discretion and variation were stressed in line with the renewed emphasis on the principle of 'implement according to local conditions' (*yindi zhiyi*).[48] Under the circumstances where local adaptation and variation were promoted, some localities sought to maximally exploit their newly acquired discretion while others for some reasons refrained from doing so. In turn, the centre often intervened to regulate local claims deemed unjustified or deviant. Hence the initiation of a conflictual phase of central–local relations in China.

Scholarly assessments of central control capacity and local discretionary power in post-Mao China differ rather considerably. Many have argued that China's state capacity has steadily declined over time to produce a wide range of local deviations. On the basis of such assessments, many point to the possibility of China being split up, although they differ significantly on the format and nature of the division. Some contend that China has already been undergoing regional fragmentation, the outcomes of which involve political regionalism and 'duke economies' (*zhuhou jingji*) that are not easily susceptible to central control. Others suggest that China may well be on its way to political and even territorial disintegration.[49] Still others take a much more cautious perspective that economic regionalism needs to be distinguished from political independence and that the concept of state capacity needs to be differentiated from the centre's capability to control local governments.[50]

How may we generalize about local discretionary power *vis-à-vis* central control capacity in post-Mao China? Has Beijing's power really waned so much that fast across the board? Or, alternatively, wouldn't it be possible that the impact of post-Mao decentralization has varied significantly among different types of policies? Our conceptualizations of central–local policy dynamics in China may perhaps have been biased due mainly to their mostly one-sided attention to some policy issues but not to others. Since most of the studies on China's central–local relations and post-Mao decentralization are concerned with fiscal, budgetary and planning arrangements, our view of the central–local dynamics may also have been shaped rather predominantly by these important studies, without due regard for their system-wide generalizability.[51]

Some recent studies have found that even in fiscal and investment arrangements, central control remained fairly intact and sufficient enough to induce local compliance.[52] Despite the time lapse since the initiation of economic reform and decentralization in the late 1970s, it seems that Beijing retains considerable power to impose its priorities by successfully overcoming local resistance. This brings us to an interesting thought experiment: what if we go back to the late 1970s and early 1980s to explore the immediate impact of post-Mao decentralization on central–local relations concerning the decollectivization reform as a governance policy without resource ramifications? If decentralization were successfully executed, we would see the prevalence of local discretion, variations and deviations. Otherwise, we would expect to see a much stronger centre, highly opportunistic local implementors, and prevailing tendencies for the 'centralizing paradox' to set in.

Post-Mao Decollectivization: Peasant Power, the Evaporated State, and the Missing Link

The selection of post-Mao agricultural decollectivization as this study's case policy is based on the following considerations. Theoretically, there is an ongoing debate concerning the role performed by the state and peasants. One influential perspective, which may be termed the 'peasant-power school', views the decollectivization reform as a highly decentralized bottom-up process in which peasants asserted themselves over the state, eventually overturning the verdict on collectivization.[53] Several critical questions beg to be answered. First of all, where did the power of peasants come from, which, according to this school, was strong enough to challenge and override the state?[54] Was China's administrative system already sufficiently decentralized to allow peasants so much say that early? Second, due to this school's heavy reliance on the state-society paradigm (mainly that enunciated by James Scott), very little is discussed about the role of sub-national governments as key middlemen. Are such images of the 'evaporated local state' and the fixation on peasants alone justifiable given the very 'strong state' that China was during the period concerned? Third, to what extent is this 'peasant-power' thesis generalizable for China as a whole? Although there is no doubt that local innovations and peasant push for radical changes were a significant part of the reform, brief sketches of a few areas well known for their early zeal for household farming may not suffice to provide a persuasive picture of such highly complex processes that unfolded in a country as large as China. Most importantly, if peasant demands and power had been so uniformly widespread, how can we account for the variations in the pace and pattern of decollectivization around the country?[55]

Two perspectives challenge the 'peasant-power' school in that while there may have been key occasions of peasant innovation and the centre's co-optation of it, it was still the central government and the intervening levels of bureaucratic administration which had set the tone for the overall reform, defined the boundary of permissible practices, and guided the diffusion of household farming. One perspective—say, the 'central-imposition' school—views decollectivization primarily as a totalitarian process where local adoption of household farming was closely guided and very much imposed by the central government.[56] Total rejection of peasant power may also be a fallacy since the centre had initially been divided, confused and lacked a viable solution to the rural economic problems. It seems that the peasant-power perspective fits better for the earlier period of 1978–81, while that of central-imposition better accounts for the later period of 1982–4.[57] Yet, both the peasant-power and central-imposition perspectives ignore the crucial roles performed by sub-national governments.[58]

The other perspective, which can be termed the 'local-variation' school, provides the missing link by focusing on sub-national governments and local cadres as key intervening variables.[59] It views the implementation of decollectivization as having entailed varying degrees of local variation. The 'local-variation' school thus challenges the notion of uniform implementation facilitated either from above or below. Instead, it argues that while the centre and peasants played a key role, the provincial and sub-provincial levels of governments also performed equally, if not more, important roles in facilitating local variation in the reversal of collectivized agriculture. While studies of this school have filled a crucial gap in the literature by shedding light on central–local dynamics and local variation, they nevertheless largely failed to provide a nationwide picture of the decollectivization process and systematic explanations for local variation. Furthermore, few studies have examined the norms and incentive structures that governed local leadership responses to decollectivization.[60] Thus, exploring the decollectivization reform from an intergovernmental perspective seems both theoretically meaningful and empirically worthwhile in assessing the impact of the first-wave post-Mao decentralization on central–local policy dynamics.

An additional consideration for the selection of decollectivization is that a drastic 'reformist' policy—as opposed to a routine policy—permits us to identify more easily the centre's priorities as well as variations in local preferences for and reactions to the scope and direction of change proposed by it. That is, decollectivization as a drastic reformist policy allowed no 'zone of indifference' so that both significant and explicit interactions between the centre and localities could be observed. More importantly, a predominant majority of issues explored by the studies of China's central–local relations either had a very small number of targets (i.e. 'selective' policy concerning project location, preferential policies, foreign direct investment, and so on), or dealt with tangible resource relations (i.e. 'resource' policy regarding the transfer and distribution of fiscal and material resources). The decollectivization reform—with all of China's twenty-nine provinces as its target and with little tangible resources for the central and provincial governments to compete for—constitutes a potentially crucial case from which different theoretical implications may be drawn compared with the earlier studies of central–local relations in post-Mao China.[61]

Decentralization and Decollectivization: The Triple-Mix Framework and the Levels-of-Analysis Issue

This study takes the position that the actual implementation of decollectivization was neither so decentralized as to allow peasants that much power to override the state, nor was it so much centralized throughout the process. It argues, instead, that there was an intervening event of administrative decentralization that stressed the *yindi zhiyi* principle and that different localities responded selectively and differently to Beijing's changing priorities depending on their varied endogenous interests, their political relationships with the centre, and their respective leadership's calculus of benefits and costs associated with compliance, caution, and deviation.[62] In sum, the effects of the first-wave administrative decentralization during the period concerned were largely volatile. While fairly considerable degrees of local variation in the pace of decollectivization were identified for 1979–81, it was not very closely related to their endogenous interests. It appears that bureaucratic norms of compliance remained strong, opportunistic behaviour prevalent, and central–local clientelistic networks mattered. And, eventually, the centralizing paradox emerged to put an end to local variation in 1982–3.

This book suggests that the process of decollectivization consisted of changing mixes of the three types of local implementors: 'pioneers', 'bandwagoners', and 'resisters'. The peasant-power school contends that almost all localities were pioneers who always stayed ahead of state policy. The central-imposition school views them as compliant all along. The local-variation school acknowledges that the whole process was much more complex than the other two schools would make us believe and that local implementors played crucial roles in creating variations. Yet, few studies of the local-variation school differentiate the pace and pattern of local implementation in any systematic manner. Their key case studies are devoted predominantly to Anhui and Sichuan while mentioning others *in passim* and anecdotally, largely devoid of comprehensive local implementation data and concrete comparative frameworks.[63] This study offers nation-wide trends of decollectivization as well as detailed case studies of three provinces, Anhui, Shandong, and Heilongjiang, each of which represents the three implementor types.

A crucial question remains as to which level of analysis this study rests on. Primarily, the province constitutes the main level of analysis through-out the book for the following reasons. First, the province was—and remains so even during the 1990s—the highest and most authoritative sub-national government in charge of supervising prefectures, cities, and counties. With the considerable power to determine plans, personnel, and budgets for sub-provincial units, the positions of the provincial authorities must have been most crucial to the formation of local responses. Second, the most immedi-ate impact of administrative decentralization would be produced first on the provinces, since it was the provinces that in turn decided the scope of devolution for prefectures, cities, and counties. In accounting for local vari-ation, therefore, the province is deemed an appropriate level of analysis possessing both a sufficient number of cases as well as similarly sufficient explanatory power.[64] Third, while there are several studies on the village-level process of decollectivization and inter-village variations, a critical question remains concerning to what extent their findings can be readily generalizable for China as a whole. Similarly, given the large number of pre-fectures and counties—170 and 1,850, respectively, as of 1980—the issue of selecting representative but comparable cases with sufficient external valid-ity poses a formidable challenge.[65]

While this study adopts the province as the principal level of analysis, it nevertheless acknowledges the limitations imposed by such an exclusively province-oriented perspective. With the recognition that local variation could have also been facilitated by sub-provincial levels, this book utilizes several 'layered case studies' that investigate determinants of the pace and pattern of decollectivization in the three provinces as well as in a few of their prefectures and counties.

Data Collection

The research for this book consisted of a combination of documentary survey and field work.[66] The documentary research was conducted mostly at two institutions: the Universities Service Centre of the Chinese Univer-sity of Hong Kong and the Asia Library of the University of Michigan. In addition to statistical yearbooks, provincial newspapers, economic and agri-cultural journals, and sub-provincial publications, particular attention was also given to specialized publications that included several internal docu-ment compilations and field reports, memoirs, chronologies, and speech collections related to the decollectivization reform.[67] The documentary

research produced a large set of provincial data on the pace of decollectivization by China's twenty-six provinces (excluding Hainan and three centrally administered municipalities) for 1979–83.[68]

'Studying China at a distance' was complemented by interviews within
China in 1992 and 1994.[69] Given its inherent limitations concerning intergovernmental and interpersonal dynamics, interviews very nicely complemented the documentary research. A lot of previously unavailable
information on the decollectivization reform was obtained through interviews with central policy-makers, policy advisors, and researchers in Beijing
as well as with those who took part in the implementation of the controversial reform at the provincial level and below in Anhui, Heilongjiang, and
Shandong. Since the reform of decollectivization was 'completed' well over
a decade ago, most of the interviewees were willing to talk about their roles
and experiences. Particularly those who had retired by the time they were
interviewed, regardless of whether they had previously supported decollectivization or not, were very candid, often to the author's surprise, in
sharing their information and insight on the process of the making and
implementation of the decollectivization policy.[70]

*Modes of Investigation: Combining Aggregate Analyses with
Comparative Case Studies*

This book investigates the operational effects of post-Mao administrative
decentralization on the scope of local discretion and variation in provincial
implementation of decollectivization. While decentralization is designed to
rearrange the structure of authority and incentive relations, its operational
effects are manifested mainly in the perceptions and behaviours of policy-
makers and implementors. Such a dual focus on structure and behaviour
poses a serious methodological dilemma for empirical research. As one
scholar has well pointed out, '[s]tructural explanations do not fare well in
case studies precisely because many important structural variables may
change very slowly, if at all, within a single case. . . . [On the other hand,]
wide-ranging cross-sectional studies obscure human agency. . . . Ideally, a
combined strategy should allow the investigator to consider both structural
factors and factors reflecting historical processes and human agency.'[71] On
the basis of this prescription, this study adopts a hybrid method of combining aggregate multivariate analyses with comparative case studies. In
implementation research, which usually concerns the issue of variation—
that is, to identify both overall and individual degrees of deviation from the
expected outcomes—multiple-case design is the most preferred strategy of
research.[72]

More specifically, cross-provincial statistical analyses are employed
to investigate whether the provinces actually acted upon the norms
of decentralization by exercising discretion in the implementation of

decollectivization and to what extent the manifested interprovincial variation can be ascribed to differing provincial conditions.[73] In accounting for
the strategic responses by the provinces, the 'triple-mix' imagery is utilized
to determine under what circumstances a particular pattern of implementation is more likely to be chosen by local implementors. In assessing the
relative weight of endogenous and exogenous factors, comparative case
studies are used, with Anhui representing the cases of 'pioneers', Shandong
constituting a key example of 'bandwagoners', and Heilongjiang exempli-
fying the category of 'resisters'.[74]

THE STRUCTURE OF THE BOOK

Chapter 2 begins with an overview of central–provincial policy relations in
Maoist China (1949–76), focusing on the decentralization experiences
during the Great Leap and the Cultural Revolution periods. Then it pro-
ceeds to compare the rules and norms of provincial policy implementation
between the Maoist and the reform eras. More specifically, such conceptual
criteria as statutory precision, oversight, modes of inducement, and systemic
norms are utilized to capture the similarities and differences between the
two periods with regard to the conditions by which the scope of provincial
discretion and the magnitude of interprovincial variation were determined.
The chapter also provides a detailed discussion of post-Mao changes in
the administrative environment as they were related to the period of
decollectivization.

Chapter 3 first delineates in detail Beijing's evolving positions on the
decollectivization reform during 1978–84. Then, it presents a large set of
provincial implementation data, with which three statistical analyses are
conducted. First, an intra-policy comparison is made of the levels of interprovincial variation between the two time-points of June 1981 and December 1982 to gauge the impact of Beijing's political push for compliance—i.e.
to see whether administrative decentralization made the provinces any less
sensitive to the pressure from the centre. Second, an inter-policy comparison is conducted of the levels of interprovincial variation between post-Mao
decollectivization on the one hand, and co-operativization in 1956 and
communization in 1958 on the other—i.e. to determine whether post-Mao
administrative decentralization was any more genuine than those of the
earlier periods. Finally, multivariate regression analyses are performed to
identify key sources of interprovincial variation in implementing decollectivization—i.e. to see whether the interprovincial variation was caused by
differing endogenous interests or by exogenous political factors.

Chapters 4 to 6 provide detailed case studies of three provincial implementors on the basis of the 'triple-mix' typology. Chapter 4 on Anhui begins
with a discussion on the behavioural characteristics of 'pioneers', followed

by an exploration of how earlier peasant innovations were facilitated and survived bureaucratic intervention, eventually to be diffused into the entire province. The vital importance of 'experimentalism' permitted under administrative decentralization and the local–provincial–central networks of support and protection explain much of the making of a 'pioneer' province. Chapter 5 provides an in-depth case study on Shandong as a representative of 'bandwagoners' that a majority of the provinces chose to be in implementing decollectivization. It shows how irrelevant the stipulations of administrative decentralization could be to many local implementors who had neither protective networks nor trust in what the centre announced and, therefore, continued to behave opportunistically without due regard for provincial interests. Finally, Chapter 6 on Heilongjiang investigates a rare case of explicit provincial resistance to central policy. More specifically, this chapter illustrates how determined provincial implementors could become to defend their crucial interests even in the absence of protective networks, as well as how astute a discontented province could be in devising and employing tactical actions to contain the spread of the controversial policy. It also details the complex process in which the centralizing paradox emerged to discount the overall utility of decentralization, eventually coercing the province to accept Beijing's priorities.

The concluding chapter first presents a summary of the findings that the impact of post-Mao administrative decentralization on provincial implementation of decollectivization was both diluted and volatile. While the measures of decentralization initially facilitated varied implementation, producing higher degrees of provincial discretion and variation than the Maoist era, the prevalence of bureaucratic careerism and the strong inertia of centralized control eventually worked as its antinomy. The findings are then reflected on the post-decollectivization period (1984–) to identify crucial continuities and changes in terms of political institutions cultivating bureaucratic careerism and the competing forces of centralization and decentralization in Chinese politics. The chapter is concluded by making some general observations concerning structural constraints, agency discretion, and norm changes in central–local policy dynamics.

NOTES

1. In this study, the term 'central government' is used for the national-level government, although the 'centre' may also often be employed. When the term refers to the Central Committee-related units of the Chinese Communist Party, the capital initial (i.e. Centre) is used. Throughout the book, the term 'local' denotes all tiers of sub-national government administration, although it usually means 'provincial' when juxtaposed with 'central.' Whenever it is necessary and possible, efforts are made to specify whether the term 'local' denotes the province, prefecture, county, or below.

2. The sphere of activities to which such constraints are applied is of quite variable size, depending on regime types.

3. See Atul Kohli, *Democracy and Discontent: India's Growing Crisis of Governability* (Cambridge: Cambridge University Press, 1990); Joel S. Migdal, *Strong Societies and Weak States: State–Society Relations and State Capabilities in the Third World* (Princeton: Princeton University Press, 1988), ch. 7; Robert W. Jackman, *Power without Force: The Political Capacity of Nation-States* (Ann Arbor: University of Michigan Press, 1993); and Barbara Geddes, *Politician's Dilemma: Building State Capacity in Latin America* (Berkeley and Los Angeles: University of California Press, 1994).

4. For a peculiar trend that federal states have increasingly opted for more centralized control, while hitherto highly centralized unitary states have chosen to decentralize, see C. Lloyd Brown-John, 'Centralizing and Decentralizing Trends in Federal States,' in C. Lloyd Brown-John (ed.), *Centralizing and Decentralizing Trends in Federal States* (Lanham, Md.: University Press of America, 1988), 1–8. For the importance of decentralization in socialist economic reform and post-communist transition, see Robert W. Campbell, *The Socialist Economies in Transition: A Primer on Semi-Reformed Systems* (Bloomington: Indiana University Press, 1991), 144–6; and János Kornai, *Highway and Byways: Studies on Reform and Postcommunist Transition* (Cambridge, Mass.: MIT Press, 1995), 5, 14, 35–6, 47.

5. The focus is on what Richard J. Samuels has termed 'vertical, tutelary, and corporatist linkages' between different levels of government, thus leaving out 'horizontal, extra-governmental, and pluralist linkages'. See *The Politics of Regional Policy in Japan: Localities Incorporated?* (Princeton: Princeton University Press, 1983), 13–17. In Franz Schurmann's term, we are concerned primarily with 'decentralization II' as opposed to 'decentralization I' involving delegation of authority to production units. See *Ideology and Organization in Communist China* (Berkeley and Los Angeles: University of California Press, 1968), 2nd enlarged edn., 175–6. By adopting the above definition, we exclude several dimensions of the concept. First, we depart from normative judgements that the more decentralized political power is, the more democratic is the political system. Second, this study does not deal with the 'transfer of managerial responsibility to organizations that are *outside the regular bureaucratic structure*'. Nor are we concerned with 'popular participation' by which 'power is decentralized to individuals, groups, and organizations outside the government'. For a study stressing the democratic dimension, see David Slater, 'Debating Decentralization', *Development and Change*, 21/3 (1990), 501–12. For various sub-concepts of decentralization, see Moses N. Kiggundu, *Managing Organizations in Developing Countries: An Operational and Strategic Approach* (West Hartford, Conn.: Kumarian Press, 1990), 234–8.

6. Ann Schultz, *Local Politics and Nation-States: Case Studies in Politics and Policy* (Oxford: Clio Books, 1979), 14; and Mark O. Rousseau and Raphael Zariski, *Regionalism and Regional Devolution in Comparative Perspective* (New York: Praeger, 1987), 17.

7. See Rousseau and Zariski, *Regionalism and Regional Devolution*, 13–22; and Norman Furniss, 'Northern Ireland As A Case Study of Decentralization in Unitary States', *World Politics*, 27/3 (1975), 393–8.

8. See Kiggundu, *Managing Organizations in Developing Countries*, 243–5; David B. Walker, 'Decentralization: Recent Trends and Prospects from A Comparative Governmental Perspective', *International Review of Administrative Sciences*, 57/1 (1991), 114–16; and Harold Wolman, 'Decentralization: What It Is and Why We Should Care', in Robert J. Bennett (ed.), *Decentralization, Local Governments, and Markets: Towards A Post-Welfare Agenda* (Oxford: Clarendon Press, 1990), 30–4.

9. For the problems associated with single-level decision making, see Fritz W. Scharpf, Bernd Reissert, and Fritz Schnabel, 'Policy Effectiveness and Conflict Avoidance in Intergovernmental Policy Formation', in Kenneth Hanf and Fritz W. Scharpf (eds.), *Interorganizational Policy Making: Limits of Coordination and Central Control* (London: Sage, 1978), 65–6.

10. For the 'policy-remake' function during the implementation phase, see Steven Maynard-Moody, 'Beyond Implementation: Developing an Institutional Theory of Administrative Policy-Making', *Public Administration Review*, 49/2 (1989), 137–43. And for 'adaptive efficiency', see Douglas C. North, *Institutions, Institutional Change and Economic Performance* (Cambridge: Cambridge University Press, 1990), 80–1.

11. Agricultural policy is a key example in this regard as the case studies of post-Mao decol-

lectivization will demonstrate in later chapters. For the 'bottom-heavy' dimension of public policy and its implications, see Frank Thompson, 'Policy Implementation and Overhead Control', in George C. Edwards, III (ed.), *Public Policy Implementation* (Greenwich, Conn.: JAI Press, 1984), 7.

12. See Stephen G. Bunker, 'Policy Implementation in an Authoritarian State: The Case of Brazil', *Latin American Research Review*, 18/1 (1983), 33–58; Dennis A. Rondinelli, 'Government Decentralization and Economic Development: The Sudan's Experiment with Devolution', *Journal of Modern African Studies*, 19/4 (1981), 140; Sidney Tarrow, 'Local Constraints on Regional Reform: A Comparison of Italy and France', *Comparative Politics*, 7/1 (1974), 1–36; and Ernest Aryeetey, 'Decentralization for Rural Development: Exogenous Factors and Semi-Autonomous Program Units in Ghana', *Community Development Journal*, 25/3 (1990), 206–14.

13. See Douglas Durasoff, 'Conflicts between Economic Decentralization and Political Control in the Domestic Reform of Soviet and Post-Soviet Systems', *Social Science Quarterly*, 69/2 (June 1988), 381–98; and Samuel Humes, IV, *Local Governance and National Power: A Worldwide Comparison of Tradition and Change in Local Government* (New York: Harvester Wheatsheaf, 1991), 245–6.

14. See Brian C. Smith, *Decentralization: The Territorial Dimension of the State* (London: Allen and Unwin, 1985), 92, 189. In the case of China, the State Planning Commission (the Chinese equivalent of Gosplan) allegedly maintained a very lukewarm position toward various reform policies. See Wang Lixin and Joseph Fewsmith, 'Bulwark of the Planned Economy: The Structure and Role of the State Planning Commission', in Carol Lee Hamrin and Suisheng Zhao (eds.), *Decision-Making in Deng's China: Perspectives from Insiders* (Armonk, NY: M. E. Sharpe, 1995), 59–64.

15. For the importance of norm changes, see Brian C. Smith, 'Measuring Decentralisation', in G. W. Jones (ed.), *New Approaches to the Study of Central–Local Government Relationships* (Westmead: Gower, 1980), 141–2; and Richard Vengroff and Hatem Ben Salem, 'Assessing the Impact of Decentralization on Governance: A Comparative Methodological Approach and Application to Tunisia', *Public Administration and Development*, 12 (1992), 476–8.

16. For the issue of bureaucratic careerism, see Migdal, *Strong Societies and Weak States*, 239–42.

17. For the constraint imposed by the *nomenklatura* system, see Ferenc Feher, Agnes Heller and György Markus, *Dictatorship over Needs: An Analysis of Soviet Societies* (New York: Blackwell, 1983), 108.

18. For the importance of a 'time perspective', see Andries Hoogerwerf, 'Policy and Time: Consequences of Time Perspectives for the Contents, Processes and Effects of Public Policies', *International Review of Administrative Sciences*, 56/4 (1990), 671–92. For the centrality of credible commitment, see Vengroff and Salem, 'Assessing the Impact of Decentralization on Governance', 476–7; and Daniel Diermeier, Joel M. Ericson, Timothy Frye, and Steven Lewis, 'Credible Commitment and Property Rights', in David Weimer (ed.), *The Political Economy of Property Rights: Institutional Change and Credibility in the Reform of Centrally Planned Economies* (Cambridge: Cambridge University Press, 1997), 20–42. For the need to create an 'atmosphere of trust', see Brian W. Hogwood and Lewis A. Gunn, *Policy Analysis for the Real World* (New York: Oxford University Press, 1984), 212–14.

19. For a detailed analysis of this bottom-up process, see Keith Boeckelman, 'The Influence of States on Federal Policy Adoptions', *Policy Studies Journal*, 20/3 (1992), 365–75.

20. The experimentation of a new (and potentially controversial) policy in a limited number of localities is deemed sensible since it presupposes a relatively low cost in case of policy failure and the endeavour as such tends to produce fewer disagreements than the one involving a large number of localities. See Lawrence J. O'Tool, Jr. and Robert S. Montjoy, 'Interorganizational Policy Implementation: A Theoretical Perspective', *Public Administration Review*, 44/6 (1984), 492.

21. It is also possible that the decision to pioneer originates from local implementors' expectations of the guaranteed promotion to a higher position in the event that pioneering is successful to the extent that it precipitates nationwide popularization. For the importance of central support for the diffusion of local innovations, see Maynard-Moody, 'Beyond Implementation', 139–40.

22. For 'bandwagoning', see Eugene Bardach, *The Implementation Game* (Cambridge: MIT Press, 1977), 242–3; and Hogwood and Gunn, *Policy Analysis for the Real World*, 203, 205, 213–14. For 'institutionalized rules' in implementation, see John Echeverri-Gent, 'Between Autonomy and Capture: Embedding Government Agencies in Their Societal Environment', *Policy Studies Journal*, 20/3 (1992), 354–5.

23. For various forms of 'implementation slippage', see Paul Berman, 'The Study of Macro- and Micro-Implementation', *Public Policy*, 26/2 (1978), 168–9.

24. For the concept of 'agent disposition', see Barry M. Mitnick and Robert W. Backoff, 'The Incentive Relation in Implementation', in George C. Edwards, III (ed.), *Public Policy Implementation* (Greenwich, Conn.: JAI Press, 1984), 66, 69.

25. Keith J. Mueller, 'Local Implementation of National Policy', *Policy Studies Review*, 4/1 (1984), 88; and John W. Thomas and Merilee S. Grindle, 'After the Decision: Implementing Policy Reforms in Developing Countries', *World Development*, 18/8 (1990), 1173.

26. In reality where bureaucratic careerism and suspicions of policy reversal remain, bandwagoners perhaps may continue to outnumber the other two patterns. The main point is that there has to be a strong presence of both pioneers and resisters in order for the mix to produce a high degree of local variation. For the impact of administrative decentralization on increasing the possibility of 'innovative pioneers' by reducing the distance new ideas have to travel, see Paul C. Light, *Thickening Government: Federal Hierarchy and the Diffusion of Accountability* (Washington: The Brookings Institution, 1995), 70–1.

27. The *locus classicus* on endogeneity and exogeneity are Douglas D. Rose, 'National and Local Forces in State Politics: The Implications of Multiple-Level Policy Analysis', *American Political Science Review*, 67/4 (1973), 1162–73 and Douglas Ashford, 'Theories of Local Government: Some Comparative Considerations', *Comparative Political Studies*, 8/1 (1975), 95, 99. Also see Michael J. Goldsmith, 'Local Autonomy: Theory and Practice', in Desmond S. King and Jon Pierre (eds.), *Challenges to Local Government* (London: Sage, 1990), 29–31.

28. For issue salience (or, alternatively, 'preference intensity') see Douglas R. Bunker, 'Policy Science Perspectives on Implementation Processes', *Policy Sciences*, 3/1 (1972), 76–8. For local variations associated with different types of policy, see Max O. Stephenson, Jr. and Gerald M. Pops, 'Conflict Resolution Methods and the Policy Process', *Public Administration Review*, 49/5 (1989), 465; and James S. Wunsch, 'Institutional Analysis and Decentralization', *Public Administration and Development*, 11 (1991), 434–43.

29. Under centralist norms, *ceteris paribus*, the cost to local implementors (C) is the smallest when they choose to bandwagon, followed by that of pioneering and resisting (i.e. $C_b > C_p > C_r$). Under administrative decentralization, two contingencies may be conceived of. First, when there is a serious conflict of interest between the centre and localities, bandwagoning may still be the utility-maximizing strategy, while resisting may be better than pioneering (i.e. $C_b > C_r > C_p$). Second, when there is no conflict of interest—central policy benefits local interests—pioneering may be the utility-maximizing option, while resisting is off the option list (i.e. $C_p > C_b$).

30. See Luigi Graziano, 'A Conceptual Framework for the Study of Clientelistic Behavior', *European Journal of Political Research*, 4/2 (1976), 149–74.

31. Merrilee S. Grindle and John W. Thomas, *Public Choices and Policy Change: The Political Economy of Reform in Developing Countries* (Baltimore and London: Johns Hopkins University Press, 1991), 2–16.

32. Herbert A. Simon, 'Human Nature in Politics: The Dialogue of Psychology with Political Science', *American Political Science Review*, 79/2 (1985), 293–304; and Aaron Wildavsky, 'Choosing Preferences by Constructing Institutions', *American Political Science Review*, 81/1 (1987), 3–21.

33. See Bryan D. Jones, 'Causation, Constraints, and Political Leadership', and Erwin C. Hargrove, 'Two Conceptions of Institutional Leadership', in Bryan D. Jones (ed.), *Leadership and Politics: New Perspectives in Political Science* (Lawrence: University Press of Kansas, 1989), 3–14, 57–83.

34. For the impact of decentralization on intergovernmental co-ordination, Scharpf, Reissert, and Schnabel, 'Policy Effectiveness and Conflict Avoidance in Intergovernmental Policy Formation', in Hanf and Scharpf (eds.), *Interorganizational Policy-Making*, 103–4. The quote is from Aaron Wildavsky, 'A Cultural Theory of Leadership', in Jones (ed.),

Leadership and Politics, 88. And for the influence of personal characteristics on leadership, see Jean Blondel, *Political Leadership: Towards a General Analysis* (London: Sage, 1987), 115–47.

35. See Lawrence S. Graham, 'Centralization versus Decentralization Dilemmas in the Administration of Public Service', *International Review of Administrative Sciences*, 46/2 (1980), 231.

36. John Stewart, 'Dilemmas', Stewart Ranson, George Jones, and Kieron Walsh (eds.), *Between Centre and Locality: The Politics of Public Policy* (London: Allen & Unwin, 1985), 27, 33.

37. For such fears of abrupt policy change, see Hogwood and Gunn, *Policy Analysis for the Real World*, 213.

38. For the inherent instability of decentralization, see Joel Samoff, 'Decentralization: The Politics of Interventionism', *Development and Change*, 21/3 (1990), 514, 522, 524.

39. See Susan Barrett and Michael Hill, 'Policy, Bargaining and Structure in Implementation Theory: Towards An Integrated Perspective', Michael J. Goldsmith (ed.), *New Research in Central–Local Relations* (Aldershot: Gower, 1986), 50–2; and Ruth Hoogland Dehoog, 'Competition, Negotiation, or Cooperation?: Three Alternative Models for Contracting for Services', in Miriam K. Mills (ed.), *Conflict Resolution and Public Policy* (New York: Greenwood Press, 1990), 155–76.

40. This may not apply to many federal states with constitutional stipulations that prevent arbitrary rule changes by the central authorities. See, for instance, David Feldman, Jean H. Peretz, and Barbara D. Jendrucko, 'Policy Gridlock in Waste Management: Balancing Federal and State Concerns', *Policy Studies Journal*, 22/4 (1994), 589–603.

41. One of the core assumptions in game-theoretic models of bargaining regarding the symmetry of bargaining power does not hold for central–local relations. For such criticisms, see L. N. Rangarajan, *The Limitation of Conflict: A Theory of Bargaining and Negotiation* (London: Croom Helm, 1985), 8.

42. For the 'hierarchical' solution in cases of co-ordination failure, see Gary J. Miller, *Managerial Dilemmas: The Political Economy of Hierarchy* (Cambridge: Cambridge University Press, 1992), ch. 2.

43. For the 'superordinate goal', see Robert A. Baron, 'Conflict in Organizations', in Kevin R. Murphy and Frank E. Saal (eds.), *Psychology in Organizations: Integrating Science and Practice* (Hillsdale, NJ: Lawrence Erlbaum Associates, 1990), 211. For the escalation of control instrument over time, see Hoogerwerf, 'Policy and Time', 681–2. For a variety of sanction instruments at the centre's disposal, see Michael Howlett, 'Policy Instruments, Policy Styles, and Policy Implementation: National Approaches to Theories of Instrument Choice', *Policy Studies Journal*, 19/2 (1991), 1–21.

44. See, for instance, Byung-joon Ahn, *Chinese Politics and the Cultural Revolution: Dynamics of Policy Processes* (Seattle: University of Washington Press, 1976); and Edwin A. Winckler, 'Policy Oscillations in the People's Republic of China', *China Quarterly*, 68 (1976), 734–50.

45. See Victor C. Falkenheim, 'Peking and the Provinces: Continuing Central Predominance', *Problems of Communism*, 21/4 (1972), 75–83; and G. William Skinner and Edwin A. Winckler, 'Compliance Succession in Rural Communist China: A Cyclical Theory', in Amitai Etzioni (ed.), *A Sociological Reader on Complex Organizations* (New York: Holt, Rinehart and Winston, 1969), 2nd edn., 410–38.

46. David Zweig aptly characterizes the paradox between intentions and outcomes of decentralization during the Maoist era: '[A]lthough Mao's actions created a highly centralized bureaucratic state, his and the radicals' purpose was to develop a decentralized economic and political system. . . . [T]he state-centric model was more of an outcome than a goal of this developmental strategy.' See 'Agrarian Radicalism as A Rural Development Strategy, 1968–1981', in Wiiliam A. Joseph, Christine P. W. Wong, and David Zweig (eds.), *New Perspectives on the Cultural Revolution* (Cambridge, Mass.: Harvard University Press, 1991), 66.

47. See Hong Yung Lee, *From Revolutionary Cadres to Bureaucratic Technocrats* (Berkeley and Los Angeles: University of California Press, 1991), chs. 7–8; Richard Baum, *Burying Mao: Chinese Politics in the Age of Deng Xiaoping* (Princeton: Princeton University Press, 1994), 75–7. For the rationalization of post-Mao China's policy process, see Michel C.

Oksenberg, 'Economic Policy-Making: Summer 1981', *China Quarterly*, 86 (1982), 192; Carol Lee Hamrin, *China and the Challenge of the Future: Changing Political Patterns* (Boulder, Colo.: Westview, 1990), 30–53. And for the post-Mao leadership's efforts to separate economic policy from politics and ideology, see Jae Ho Chung, 'The Politics of Agricultural Mechanization in the Post-Mao Era, 1977–1987', *China Quarterly*, 134 (1993), 273–6, 289–90.

48. See David M. Lampton, 'The Implementation Problem in Post-Mao China', in David M. Lampton (ed.), *Policy Implementation in Post-Mao China* (Berkeley and Los Angeles: University of California Press, 1987), 3–24.

49. For studies pointing to the weakened state capacity and possibilities of disintegration in China, see Shaoguang Wang, 'The Rise of the Regions: Fiscal Reform and the Decline of Central State Capacity in China', in Andrew G. Walder (ed.), *The Waning of the Communist State: Economic Origins of Political Decline in China and Hungary* (Berkeley and Los Angeles: University of California Press, 1995), 87–113; Edward Friedman, 'China's North-South Split and the Forces of Disintegration', *Current History*, 575 (1993), 270–4; Maria Hsia Chang, 'China's Future: Regionalism, Federation, or Disintegration', *Studies in Comparative Communism*, 25/3 (1992), 211–27; Arthur Waldron, 'Warlordism versus Federalism: The Revival of a Debate', *China Quarterly*, 121 (1990), 116–28; Changsheng Lin, 'Guangdong: China's Slovenia?', *Global Affairs*, 8/3 (1993), 141–55; and Jack A. Goldstone, 'The Coming Chinese Collapse', *Foreign Policy*, 99 (1995), 35–52.

50. For more cautious approaches, see Jae Ho Chung, 'Central–Provincial Relations', in Lo Chi Kin, Suzanne Pepper, and Tsui Kai-yuen (eds.), *China Review 1995* (Hong Kong: Chinese University Press, 1995), ch. 3; John Fitzgerald, 'Reports of My Death Have Been Greatly Exaggerated: The History of the Death of China', in David S. G. Goodman and Gerald Segal (eds.), *China Deconstructs: Politics, Trade and Regionalism* (London: Routledge, 1994), 21–58; and Yasheng Huang, 'Why China Will Not Collapse', *Foreign Policy*, 99 (1995), 54–68.

51. General problems with fiscal indicators are noted in Ronan Paddison, *The Fragmented State: The Political Geography of Power* (Oxford: Blackwell, 1983), 39–40; and Peter Ferdinand and Wang Yongjiang, 'Central–Provincial Financial Relations in China and the Role of the Ministry of Commerce', in John Child and Martin Lockett (eds.), *Advances in Chinese Industrial Studies: Reform Policy and the Chinese Enterprise* (Greenwich, Conn.: JAI Press, 1990), i. 16. The crux of the problem originates from the excessive reliance on fiscal measures as the sole indicator of central–local dynamics. When using fiscal measures (e.g. central–provincial revenue-sharing ratios, respective shares of central and local investment, and so on) expressed mostly in percentage terms, we are likely to adopt a dichotomous conceptualization of winner versus loser, which may often reinforce the zero-sum view of central–local relations. This view seems erroneous, or highly debatable at the least, since fiscal and budgetary arrangements do not tell everything about the delicate balance between central control and local discretion. For the predominance of studies on China's fiscal dimensions and their potential problems, see Jae Ho Chung, 'Studies of Central–Provincial Relations in the People's Republic of China: A Mid-Term Appraisal', *China Quarterly*, 142 (1995), 492, 499–500.

52. See Yasheng Huang, *Inflation and Investment Controls in China: The Political Economy of Central-Local Relations During the Reform Era* (Cambridge: Cambridge University Press, 1996); and Jae Ho Chung, 'Beijing Confronting the Provinces: The 1994 Tax-Sharing Reform and Its Implications for Central–Provincial Relations in China', *China Information*, 9/2–3 (1994/5), 1–23.

53. See, most notably, Daniel Kelliher, *Peasant Power in China: The Era of Rural Reform 1979–1989* (New Haven: Yale University Press, 1992), chs. 1–4; and Kate Xiao Zhou, *How the Farmers Changed China: Power of the People* (Boulder, Colo.: Westview, 1996), chs. 1 and 3.

54. The 'peasant-power' school finds two answers to this question. In macro-terms, China's economic crisis necessitated the state to be benign and passive toward peasant innovations. In micro-terms, peasants allegedly made individual deals with cadres who found them hard to turn down due to extreme poverty. See Kelliher, *Peasant Power in China*, 30–2 and Zhou, *How the Farmers Changed China*, 53–4, respectively. Immediate reactions would be that: (1) strong states facing economic crises do not necessarily forfeit their

control voluntarily and may still impose their own priorities regardless of societal interests; and (2) Zhou's presentation of cadre–peasant deal-making is highly anecdotal and
lacks detailed discussions of such deal-making processes as well as of the reasons for
cadres' willingness to receive bribery particularly given their past memories and experiences of severe persecution.

55. Zhou, for instance, touches upon the complex dynamics involving Beijing, Anhui, Sichuan,
Gansu, Guizhou, Hebei, and Shandong (Dezhou) in ten pages, citing mostly the examples
in support of decollectivization. See *How the Farmers Changed China*, 60–9. Kelliher, on
the other hand, is less sanguine about such an all-China generalization. While his main
stress is still on the power of peasant demands for decollectivization, Kelliher nevertheless provides brief discussions of Hubei as a deviant case where provincial authorities
obstructed the diffusion of household farming, and of Manchuria as another deviant case
where decollectivization was imposed on the peasants against their will. See *Peasant Power
in China*, 65–9, 106.

56. See Helen F. Siu, *Agents and Victims in South China: Accomplices in Rural Revolution*
(New Haven and London: Yale University Press, 1989), ch. 12; Jonathan Unger, 'The Decol-
lectivization of the Chinese Countryside: A Survey of Twenty-Eight Villages', *Pacific
Affairs*, 58/4 (1985–6), 585–606; Kathleen Hartford, 'Socialist Agriculture Is Dead: Long
Live Socialist Agriculture! Organizational Transformation in Rural China', in Elizabeth J.
Perry and Christine Wong (eds.), *The Political Economy of Reform in Post-Mao China*
(Cambridge, Mass.: Harvard University Press, 1985), 31–61.

57. See David Zweig, 'Context and Content in Policy Implementation: Household Contracts
and Decollectivization, 1977–1983', in Lampton (ed.), *Policy Implementation in Post-Mao
China*, 264–74. Also see Chapter 3 for details.

58. Comparative studies of decollectivization, too, tend to be silent on the issues of local
governments and regional variation. See Frederic Pryor, 'When Is Collectivization
Reversible?', *Studies in Comparative Communism*, 24/1 (1991), 3–24.

59. These studies include Joseph Fewsmith, *Dilemmas of Reform in China: Political Conflict
and Economic Debate* (Armonk, NY: M. E. Sharpe, 1994), ch. 1; David Zweig, 'Opposition
to Change in Rural China: The System of Responsibility and People's Communes', *Asian
Survey*, 23/7 (1983), 879–900; id., 'Context and Content in Policy Implementation'; and Dali
L. Yang, *Calamity and Reform in China: State, Rural Society, and Institutional Change Since
the Great Leap Famine* (Stanford: Stanford University Press, 1996), ch. 6.

60. For earlier efforts to comprehend patterns and norms of reaction on the part of grass-
roots-level cadres, see Richard J. Latham, 'The Implications of Rural Reforms for Grass-
Roots Cadres', in Perry and Wong (eds.), *The Political Economy of Reform in Post-Mao
China*, 157–73; and John P. Burns, 'Local Cadre Accommodation to the "Responsibility
Reform" in Rural China', *Pacific Affairs*, 58/4 (1985–6), 607–25.

61. For a characterization of the decollectivization reform as having a low resource-related
stake, see Susan L. Shirk, *The Political Logic of Economic Reform in China* (Berkeley and
Los Angeles: University of California Press, 1993), 41.

62. For detailed discussions of the measures of administrative decentralization pertinent to
the period of decollectivization, see Chapter 2.

63. Fewsmith (*Dilemmas of Reform in China*) provides an excellent discussion of the complex
policy dynamics in the centre and Anhui over the decollectivization reform but mentions
very little about other localities. While Yang (*Calamity and Reform in China*) discusses
other provinces mostly anecdotally (pp. 152–3) and about Heilongjiang a bit longer
(pp. 174–6), his main analysis also rests on Anhui (pp. 149–52, 154–72).

64. From the mid-1980s, a wide array of measures—most notably, the policies of 'putting prefecture-level cities in charge of counties' (*shi guan xian*), fourteen 'coastal open cities'
(*yanhai kaifang chengshi*) and 'central economic cities' (*jihua danlie chengshi*)—were
adopted to provide sub-provincial levels of government with an expanded scope of policy
discretion, contributing significantly to the rise of conflicts between the provinces and sub-
provincial units. As for the period of decollectivization (1979–83), however, sub-provincial
levels of government had not yet been formally granted a meaningful boundary of policy
discretion.

65. Case selection requires a minimum level of contextual familiarity a priori. When the
number of potential cases is too large, however, selecting representative as well as

comparable cases in line with theoretical reasoning is inevitably difficult, if not impossible. For the numbers cited, see Diao Tianding (ed.), *Zhongguo difang guojia jigou gaiyao* (Overview of Local Government Organizations in China) (Beijing: Falu chubanshe, 1989), 152.

66. For a useful guide in documentary research, see Michel Oksenberg, 'Politics Takes Command: An Essay on the Study of Post-1949 China', in Roderick MacFarquhar and John K. Fairbank (eds.), *The Cambridge History of China* (Cambridge: Cambridge University Press, 1987), xiv. 543–90; and Jae Ho Chung, 'Study of Provincial Politics and Development in the Post-Mao Reform Era: Issues, Perspectives, and Sources', in Peter Cheung, Jae Ho Chung, and Zhimin Lin (eds.), *Provincial Strategies of Economic Reform in Post-Mao China: Leadership, Politics and Implementation* (Armonk, NY: M. E. Sharpe, 1998), 442–56.

67. Many provinces have published one or two volumes devoted to the process of agricultural decollectivization with detailed chronologies and compilations of local policy documents. Examples include *Sichuansheng nongye hezuo jingji shiliao* (Historical Materials on Sichuan's Co-operative Agricultural Economy) (Chengdu: Sichuan kexue jishu chubanshe, 1989); *Heilongjiang Nongye hezuoshi* (History of Agricultural Co-operativization in Heilongjiang) (Beijing: Zhonggong dangshi ziliao chubanshe, 1990); *Hubei nongcun jingji, 1949–1989* (Rural Economy in Hubei, 1949–1989) (Beijing: Zhongguo tongji chubanshe, 1990); Shandong Provincial Party Committee, *Shandongsheng nongye hezuohua shiliaoji* (Historical Materials on Shandong's Agricultural Co-operativization) (Jinan: Shandong renmin chubanshe, 1990), two volumes; and Historical Archives Commission of the Anhui Provincial Political Consultative Conference (ed.), *Nongcun gaige de xingqi* (The Rise of Rural Reform) (Beijing: Zhongguo wenshi chubanshe, 1993). Also, the 'contemporary China' (*dangdai zhongguo*) series have to date been published on all province-level units and they all have sections on decollectivization, although the depth of each provincial volume's coverage differs rather significantly.

68. Obviously, it cannot be argued that this set of data is free of the problems of reliability and political bias generally associated with Chinese government statistics. For the omnipresent problems in government statistics, see A. P. Tant, 'The Politics of Official Statistics', *Government and Opposition*, 30/2 (1995), 254–66. More detailed justifications for the data set are found in Chapter 3.

69. In executing the fieldwork in China, the following references were particularly helpful: Ann Thurston and Burton Pasternak (eds.), *The Social Sciences and Fieldwork in China: Views from the Field* (Boulder, Colo.: Westview, 1983) and Stephen Devereux and John Hoddinott (eds.), *Fieldwork in Developing Countries* (Boulder, Colo.: Lynne Rienner, 1993).

70. At the central level, interviewees included those with positions as high as ministers and vice-ministers; and the bureaucratic ranks of the local-level interviewees varied significantly from a commune cadre to a governor. A total of 42 interviews were conducted with 32 people (some interviewed on multiple occasions) in Beijing, Anhui (Hefei), Shandong (Jinan and Qingdao), and Heilongjiang (Harbin). For a list of interviewees and their positions, though their names withheld, see Appendix.

71. Charles C. Ragin, *The Comparative Method: Moving Beyond Qualitative and Quantitative Strategies* (Berkeley and Los Angeles: University of California Press, 1987), 70.

72. See Robert K. Yin, 'Studying the Implementation of Public Programs', in Walter Williams *et al.*, *Studying Implementation: Methodological and Administrative Issues* (Chatham: Chatham House, 1982), 50, 55. Despite the obvious advantages, multiple-case research has been very rare in the field of contemporary China studies. See Chung, 'Studies of Central–Provincial Relations in the People's Republic of China', 494–7.

73. The first question is tackled by univariate analyses of the provincial pace data. And the second is answered by multivariate analyses by regressing provincial variables on the provincial pace of decollectivization. In assessing the degree of change in provincial discretion in longitudinal terms, a comparison will be made with the provincial implementation data regarding the collectivization and communization policies compiled by Frederick C. Teiwes, 'Provincial Politics in China: Themes and Variations', in John M. H. Lindbeck (ed.), *China: Management of A Revolutionary Society* (Seattle: University of Washington Press, 1971), 116–89.

74. The cases of Anhui and Heilongjiang are designed to illustrate the operational effects of administrative decentralization in promoting local innovation and deviation, respectively, while the Shandong case is intended to show the resilience of bureaucratic careerism. For the rationales of comparative case studies, see Robert K. Yin, *Case Study Research: Design and Methods* (Beverly Hills: Sage Publications, 1994), 2nd edn., 44–51.

2

Central–Provincial Policy Relations in China: Decentralization Experiences, Bureaucratic Norms, and Post-Mao Changes

This chapter, providing an overview of central–provincial policy relations in the People's Republic of China, consists of four sections. The first critically assesses the decentralization experiences of the Maoist period and argues that neither the devolution of fiscal authority nor the organizational breakdown during the Great Leap Forward and the Cultural Revolution expanded the scope of provincial policy discretion due mainly to the self-policing power of ideological norms. The second section supplies a list of four analytical dimensions—statutory precision, oversight, systemic norms, and modes of inducement—on the basis of which the administrative environments of the Maoist and reform eras are compared in the third and fourth sections, respectively. The fourth section also delineates the crucial changes pertinent to the period of decollectivization, particularly concerning the reformist leadership's efforts to transform the systemic norms of local policy implementation.

CENTRAL–PROVINCIAL POLICY DYNAMICS IN MAOIST CHINA: AN OVERVIEW

When we match the sheer size of China's land and population with the highly centralized unitary system on which it has insisted for so long, it is not hard to realize that such a 'misfit' is quite rare in other parts of the world. Not surprisingly, the macro-historical question of why China never adopted a federal structure even nominally has been asked over and again.[1] Whatever the answers may be, China's consistent refusal to adopt a federal arrangement reflects its deep-rooted concerns for what such a change might possibly bring about.[2] Such concerns have been directed toward the age-old problems of provincialism and localism. As Owen Lattimore once put it, '[O]ld China was a decentralized country in which every province had a life of its own . . . independent of the national life.'[3] Since central authority was largely incapable of penetrating into the units below the county level in traditional China, de facto local autonomy was occasionally combined with regionalism to facilitate rebellions against the imperial court, often resulting in the collapse of the ruling dynasty. Such bitter memories never escaped the rulers of China, who devised various measures to reduce the gap between what was to be controlled and what was indeed controlled.[4]

While the founding of the People's Republic led to the eradication of warlords and local bandits, regionalism deeply rooted in China's political and economic structures had yet to be struggled against. Since one crucial reason for the prevalence of regionalism was regarded as physical in the sense that rugged terrain and primitive transport and communication reinforced territorial and cultural fragmentation, the communist leadership built many roads and railways to connect various remote regions.[5] More importantly, the scheme of six 'great administrative regions' (*da xingzhengqu*) was implemented to incorporate numerous sub-national localities into the new communist state. The great administrative regions were abolished in 1954, with their role of linking the centre with localities taken over by the provinces. At the same time, highly centralized planning and fiscal bureaucracies were established to oversee local administration and Communist Party branches were set up throughout the territorial hierarchies, penetrating for the first time the sub-county levels which had hitherto remained the realm of society rather than that of the state.[6]

In the midst of all these changes toward territorial integration and administrative centralization, the 'Yan'an tradition'—epitomized by the adherence to the principle of 'implement according to local conditions' (*yindi zhiyi*)—began to be challenged.[7] Although the Yan'an tradition found its way into the post-1949 period, the faithful adherence to it was rather short-lived. Once the ultimate goal of revolution was accomplished, local preferences had to give way to national priorities. With the entire national territory to rule, as opposed to a few provinces in the 'liberated bases', the goal of the regime also changed accordingly from dispersed survival to centralized development. After territorial integration was completed through the 'great administrative regions', Beijing increasingly resorted to centralized and ideological control in its management of the provinces, stifling local initiatives and incentives.[8]

Particularly since 1957 after the traumatic anti-rightist purges against numerous intellectuals and cadres who had voiced local concerns, the principle of *yindi zhiyi* became largely an empty slogan. During the successive radical phases of the Great Leap Forward (1958–9), the Socialist Education Campaign (1962–5), and the Cultural Revolution (1966–76), all of which involved purges of dissenters, local incentives were dictated solely from above and local variation became nearly extinct. With the institutionalization of tight centralist norms, standardized implementation (*yidao qie*) became widespread, and swift total compliance was regarded as a key expression of ideological purity and loyalty to Mao Zedong as well as the safest option for local implementors.[9]

What merits our attention is that, despite such a 'totalitarian dictatorship' by Beijing, we hardly know of outright central–provincial conflicts in the Maoist era. It seems that generally provinces were highly compliant with the centre, very often without due regard for local interests. Due to rigid ideological norms and harsh political punishments against provincial foot-dragging, 'compliance-in-advance'—manifested either by pioneering at Beijing's initiatives or by early bandwagoning—was the predominant pattern of policy implementation. The argument that Mao's China lacked outright central–provincial conflicts does not suggest that there was no provincial variation or intergovernmental friction at all, which would be a gross oversimplification. Rather, it is only suggested here that, except for the period of 1955–7 when provinces were permitted (and even encouraged) to exercise their discretionary power in interest articulation and policy implementation, provincial discontent does not seem to have produced outright confrontations with Beijing.[10] Given such structural and normative constraints, even if some provinces had indeed sought to resist the centre, the act must have taken a very tacit form of implementation slippage on relatively unimportant issues for which Beijing had little incentives to monitor local behaviour closely. Then, again, under the system of rigid ideological control and rampant purges, few provincial leaders would have had sufficient motivations to risk their political fate for local policy interests.

Centralization alone, of course, cannot tell the whole story of the Maoist era. In fact, Maoist China was replete with cycles of centralization and decentralization, although, overall, the former was usually the final outcome while the latter was largely a failed effort. Why was this the case? Two issues are pertinent. First, does decentralization of resource allocation (e.g. fiscal decentralization) necessarily expand the scope of local discretion in policy implementation across the board? It seems that resources are context- and issue-specific and, therefore, expanded local discretion in one policy area may not necessarily mean increased local autonomy in others.[11] Second, if the decentralization measures adopted were administrative in nature, would they necessarily expand the scope of local discretion? It does not appear that the stipulations of the centre *ipso facto* produce increased local autonomy. The main reason is that local implementors continue to have strong senses of uncertainty about their careers, future policy directions, and central intentions. Therefore, centralist norms may still dominate the *modus operandi*, eventually bringing in the centralizing paradox.

The above arguments can be further elaborated by examining the nature of the decentralization experiences during the Great Leap and the Cultural Revolution periods commonly associated with the extensive devolution of resource-allocating authority. First, with regard to the Great Leap, did the fiscal decentralization have identifiable effects on changing the norms of local policy implementation? The answer must be a negative since the fiscal experiment was halted within a year and its impact on expanding the scope of local discretion was minimal, if any.[12] The ultimate importance of administrative decentralization is underscored when we consider some exemplary cases in which the *yindi zhiyi* principle was grossly violated during the Great Leap period.

The first case concerns communization. Within only one month after the Beidaihe decision in August 1958 that ratified the nationwide implementation of the controversial scheme of communization, fifteen provinces claimed that all of their peasant households had already been incorporated into the people's communes, with the performance of seven other provinces ranging from 92 to 99 per cent. The outcome was an extreme average compliance rate of 93.3 per cent for twenty-five province-level units (except for the three municipalities and Tibet), reflecting a total, swift, and standardized pattern of local implementation.[13] *Pro forma* compliance was obviously pervasive and many provinces must have inflated their performance statistics to please Beijing. The prevalence of such *pro forma* compliance itself points to the very failure of decentralization.

The second case concerns the policy of 'walking on two legs', by which hitherto agriculture-oriented provinces were to invest more in industrial production and previously industry-geared ones would pay more attention to agricultural development. This policy not only contradicted the principle of comparative advantage, but it also grossly constricted the scope of local discretion. An analyst highlights the lack of local discretion during the Great Leap on the basis of his research on Liaoning:

[M]any analysts conclude that the decentralization measures of 1957–58 led to more provincial autonomy. However, if the decision-making powers of the provinces were expanded, one would expect that they would exploit them to suit their own perceived needs and well-being. However, the Great Leap Forward principle of 'simultaneous development' of agriculture and industry meant that industrial provinces like Liaoning were obliged to promote agriculture. . . . Furthermore, Liaoning was hamstrung by an increasingly interventionistic center—the decentralization in 1958 seemed more apparent than real.[14]

The third case concerns the 'deep-ploughing' policy of 1958–9. The central leadership under Mao, then fascinated by mechanized farming but well aware of the general unavailability of machinery, came up with an ambitious nationwide scheme of popularizing deep-ploughing with cable-drawn ploughs irrespective of topographical and cropping variations among different regions. As for the eventual failure of this highly standardized policy, an analyst explains as follows: '[P]articular innovations may or may not have been sensible but even the best innovation cannot be implemented everywhere. . . . [T]he erroneous popularization of inappropriate tools probably weakened the program significantly . . . by unnecessarily associating the legitimacy of the leadership and the theory of farm tool reform with a mistake.'[15]

'Mass irrigation campaigns', 'grain production wars', and the 'iron and steel movement' were no exceptions in that once the Centre (usually Mao) sent out a signal, a few model units (*yangban*) were selected, increasingly higher targets disseminated, target overfulfilment reported from below, and the task completed swiftly in a highly standardized manner. In the case of the 'iron and steel movement', several hundred thousand backyard iron-casting furnaces were built within less than a year employing 60 million people away from their farmwork. In the case of the 'mass irrigation campaigns', too, to take the reported accomplishments at face value, a total of 353 million *mu* of land (i.e. about 30 per cent more than the area of land irrigated since 1949) was irrigated within only five months from October 1957. Here, again, total, swift and standardized implementation was the norm.[16]

On the basis of the above discussions, the following observations may be offered. First, the execution of the Great Leap policies was overly standardized without taking varied local conditions into account, thereby sacrificing the benefits of comparative advantage, local discretion, and adaptive implementation. Second, despite the absurd misfit between the content and context of these policies, the nationwide pattern of implementation was such that provincial compliance was both extremely fast and highly standardized. Most provinces complied in advance by pioneering and the rest jumped on the bandwagon soon after. Thus, provincial deviation became a rarity and uniform compliance was the norm. Third, we may therefore conclude that the measures of fiscal decentralization during the Great Leap did not in any way expand the scope of provincial discretion in policy implementation.[17]

Another pre-reform period commonly associated with decentralization is that of the Cultural Revolution. Concerning the early years of the Cultural Revolution decade (i.e. 1966–9), it is widely accepted that the provinces gained some room for discretion since much of the central administration was disabled by radical purges and successive campaigns. It should be noted, however, that the dissolution of the formal administrative structure was not identical to the total absence of overhead control. Mao and the Cultural Revolution Small Group (*wenge xiaozu*) built *ad hoc* informal networks of control and supervision, which the provinces could hardly ignore.[18] Besides, between late 1970 and mid-1971, provincial party committees were re-established to limit the powers of the revolutionary committees.[19] Most importantly, even in the middle of organizational breakdown and administrative disruption, the self-policing ideological norms continued to operate to demand conformity and detect deviations. Abundant factions and rivalries induced many to become more than willing and ready to take advantage of the ever-changing ideological criteria to advance their careers by bringing down their opponents.[20]

The wilful neglect of *yindi zhiyi* during the Cultural Revolution decade is best exemplified by the centre's imposition of 'single models' for nation-wide implementation, which included the Dazhai Brigade for agricultural production, the Daqing oilfield for industrial management, and the 'eight model works' for theatrical performances. Despite the nonsense that only one model was supplied for agricultural development or industrial man-agement to be emulated by the entire country, these policies nevertheless seem to have obtained their status as guiding principles as well as concrete objects of learning for over a decade. The extent to which these models were actually emulated on a nationwide scale remains unknown. While very few studies have been done on provincial policy implementation of this period, recent Chinese materials suggest that the overall level of provincial com-pliance with these model policies was much higher than the outside observers have previously assumed.[21]

The gross violation of *yindi zhiyi* and neglect of local variation were also manifested by the nationwide application of standardized policy in a variety of issue areas. The policy of 'taking grain as the key link' (*yiliang weigang*), for instance, was imposed indiscriminately on all localities during the Cul-tural Revolution decade, ignoring regional meteorological and topographi-cal variations. Furthermore, as a manifest outcome of Beijing's decade-long emphasis on local autarchy and 'all-round development,' provincial per capita agricultural and industrial outputs became increasingly highly cor-related (from −0.16 in 1957 to 0.75 in 1980), further dwindling the base for interprovincial trade.[22]

Let us now examine the later phase of the Cultural Revolution decade (1971–6), which is also quite commonly associated with decentralization. During this period, central–provincial revenue sharing was in principle based upon a 'fiscal contract' system (*shouzhi baogan*) in 1971–3 and a 'fixed-ratio retention' system (*guding bili liucheng*) in 1973–5. Despite the policy stipulations, some cast doubt on their operational effects. For instance, a Chinese analyst suggests that the two systems of fiscal contract and fixed-ratio retention were implemented only nominally and this five-year period was in fact one of 'total centralization' (*tongshou tongzhi*).[23] A detailed study of Jiangsu's fiscal relations with Beijing during this under-researched period concurs that 'if decentralization had meant a weaken-ing of central control, we might expect provincial remittances to have decreased, [but] remittances to the center increased [and] decentralization did not result in smaller revenue transfers from the province to the center.'[24] While the evidence still remains sketchy, it seems that the scope of fiscal decentralization was highly limited and the centre was much less con-strained in extracting financial resources from the provinces than we used to take for granted.

A crucial question remains to be answered: how was central control effec-tively sustained during this period associated with bureaucratic paralysis? Despite the deleterious damages inflicted on formal government structures during the earlier phase of the Cultural Revolution, Beijing's capacity to impose its priorities remained fairly strong, mainly because its ideological control mechanism was highly independent of bureaucratic institutional bases. Whipping up an ideologically motivated 'policy wind' to force a controversial policy onto the agendas of the provinces was by no means rare. Furthermore, patron–client relations were another important non-institutional instrument central leaders extensively utilized in their efforts to rein in the provinces.[25] Victor C. Falkenheim's observation sheds light on this highly politicized period:

[I]n order to argue that provincial independence has grown in the years since the Cultural Revolution, one must demonstrate both that the Cultural Revolution significantly impaired the old systems of central control and that no new mechanisms of control had taken their place. Even more important, the identification of trends toward growing localism should be based . . . on observed behavioral changes.[26]

The foregoing discussions of the Great Leap and Cultural Revolution periods suggest that neither fiscal decentralization nor institutional paralysis facilitated any significant expansion of provincial discretion. It becomes more apparent if we choose to take the benefits of hindsight by comparing them with the reformist era. On the basis of these discussion, we may derive three key implications. First, fiscal decentralization alone cannot make the centre sincerely committed to the cause of decentralization. That is, without administrative decentralization, the impatient centre may quickly revert back to centralized control. Second, without weakening the centre's ideological control mechanism—i.e. unless decentralized norms became widely accepted—local discretion and variation would continue to be deemed ideologically problematic and politically unsafe. Third, despite that *pro forma* compliance and inflated reporting were prevalent due to Beijing's limited monitoring capability, the centre was still able to enforce its preferences with regard to the national priority policies.[27]

DIMENSIONS OF ADMINISTRATIVE DECENTRALIZATION: A PRE-COMPARISON CHECKLIST

Having discussed the limitations of fiscal decentralization in expanding the scope of local policy discretion in pre-reform China, a close examination of administrative decentralization is due before we set out to compare the Maoist and reformist eras. The pre-comparison checklist consists of four dimensions of administrative decentralization: statutory precision, oversight, systemic norms, and modes of inducement. First, statutory precision refers to the degree to which the centre's policy instructions define the specifics of how the policy ought to be implemented. The centrality of statutory precision lies in that it delineates the permissible boundary of local adaptive implementation. Statutory precision becomes critical particularly when the level of uncertainty rises. When the proposed policy departs from the status quo and involves a large number of targets, central policy-makers may not have sufficient information to account for varied local conditions. Policy-makers then usually opt for an easy way out by enhancing the level of statutory precision through standardization. While it makes the task of monitoring easier, standardization may grossly violate local variations.[28]

Second, in order to match the intentions and outcomes of policy, central policy-makers need a sufficient capacity for administrative oversight. Oversight refers to the function in which the central policy-makers collect pertinent local information and monitor local policy performance. An intricate system of data collection, documentation, reporting, inspection, auditing, and feedback is a prerequisite for effective oversight.[29] When administrative oversight is regularized in timing, tight in enforcement, and complete in scope, *ceteris paribus*, local implementing agencies may find little room for manœuvring, cheating, or other deviations. When the centre's oversight is infrequent, lax, and limited, local implementors are tempted to put different thrusts into the policy, if not to sabotage its implementation.

Third, systemic norms are rarely treated in the implementation literature based largely on the experiences of federal, developed and democratic countries where norms against local deviation are generally lenient. In non-democratic systems, violence and ideology tend to 'manufacture' local compliance.[30] Robert Axelrod identifies two dimensions of norm: boldness and vengefulness. Applied to central–local dynamics, boldness denotes the size of incentives for local implementors to deviate, while vengefulness refers to the magnitude of punitive action by the centre against local deviation. According to Axelrod, when vengefulness is high, boldness tends to decrease.[31] That is, when systemic norms are such that local deviations are severely persecuted, incentives for implementation biases are minimized. Systemic norms could operate toward an opposite direction as well. Local implementors may choose to implement a proposed policy with expectations of specific rewards—such as promotion and prioritized resource allocation. Especially when the centre does not possess adequate capabilities of oversight, *pro forma* compliance in the form of quantitatively outperforming other localities could often be rewarded.[32]

Equally important, particularly in systems like China, is the horizontal operation of systemic norms that are self-policing. This is highly analogous to what Axelrod calls a 'metanorm' which provides a strong incentive for an individual to be vengeful simply to escape punishment for not punishing an observed deviation. When everybody else is complying, a non-complier is extremely vulnerable to easy detection. Such a high possibility of getting caught and huge costs associated with deviation are combined to provide the disincentives for deviation.[33]

The institutionalization of systemic norms may provide the central government with unsurpassed degrees of penetration into local implementors and society since ideological control mechanisms are both convenient and encompassing. They are convenient because, once activated, they are self-policing and therefore involve relatively low maintenance costs. They are also encompassing since the centre commands a large pool of potential agents more than willing to detect deviation on the centre's behalf either to advance their own careers or simply to express their ideological conformity.[34]

Fourth, the mode of inducement refers to instruments the centre employs to guide the route of local implementation. Coercion demands unilateral concessions by local implementors with the threat and use of violence. Administrative decentralization generally reduces the incentives for the centre to apply coercion and instead induces it to engage in bargaining and negotiations. Bargaining and negotiations presuppose side payments designed to induce local compliance by way of accommodating some of their crucial endogenous interests.[35] Pertinent to the discussion of side payments is the willingness of the centre. That is, since coercive instruments are largely 'non-depletable' (although their marginal utility may decline over time), central policy-makers usually prefer coercion to time-consuming processes of bargaining especially when their image as the ultimate regulator is critical.[36]

ADMINISTRATIVE ENVIRONMENTS OF MAOIST CHINA: AN ASSESSMENT

Statutory Precision

Quite contrary to the highly centralized nature of the policy process, many of the central directives of the Maoist period were general, vague and undetailed. According to a study of the formal document system of this period, central directives usually took the less binding formats of 'regulation' (*guiding*), 'instruction' (*zhishi*), 'circular' (*tongzhi*), 'opinion' (*yijian*), 'draft' (*caoan*), and 'notification' (*tongbao*), and avoided more binding designations such as 'order' (*mingling*) and 'decision' (*jueding*). The underlying rationale was, at least in theory, that non-binding policy directives would allow more room for local adaptation and flexible implementation.[37]

Low levels of statutory specification and non-binding designations of central directives belie what actually transpired in the implementation process. When the provincial authorities received ambiguous directives, they somehow had to figure out concrete ways to implement them. Indispensable sources of reference were the commentaries and feature articles in newspapers, most notably *Renmin ribao* (*People's Daily*), which usually delineated official positions on and assessments of a few advanced model

units. Since the core purpose of giving publicity to these units was specifically to call on other localities and units to emulate (or criticize) them,
provincial leaders rarely failed to get the message. This way, the ambiguity
of central directives was dispelled and concrete instructions were supplied.[38]
Other widely consulted sources of information were on-site instructions.
When top central leaders were on inspection tours, they often delivered
speeches at meetings with provincial leaders over a variety of policy issues,
and these speeches then became specific instructions on how to go about
implementing them.[39]

In Maoist China, the advanced model unit for nationwide emulation was
frequently a single one—such as Dazhai for agricultural production, Xiyang
for agricultural machinery production, and Daqing for industrial management—so that provincial authorities did not have a wide range of alternatives to choose from: they almost always had to adopt the only single model
irrespective of its suitability. Furthermore, provincial implementors very
often had to follow all of the specific features of the model unit to the letter
lest they be singled out for pursuing 'localism'. In sum, the initial ambiguity of Beijing's directives posed few problems as the centre's specific preferences and demands became progressively clear to the extent which
provincial officials were left with no other options but the one dictated from
above.

Oversight

Concerning the centre's capacity to monitor and guide local policy performance during Mao's rule, two contrasting views exist. One contends that
Beijing's administrative oversight was drastically constricted by successive
efforts toward decentralization. The other argues the contrary that, despite
the measures of decentralization, the centre remained highly effective
in dictating its preferences in any policy it prioritized.[40] According to the
latter view, despite the series of decentralization and the organizational
breakdowns during the Cultural Revolution, Beijing remained capable
of mitigating interprovincial disparities. By implication, Beijing possessed
relatively effective systems of monitoring regional inequalities and collect-
ing local information. Given that Beijing's key oversight mechanisms—such
as the State Statistical Bureau and the Ministry of Supervision—had been
largely incapacitated after the Great Leap and particularly during the
Cultural Revolution, what kind of alternative monitoring systems did
Beijing depend on?[41]

The Chinese central government utilized a wide range of methods for
administrative oversight. First, an intricate document system was maintained to ensure that all local governments constantly reported to the
central authorities concerning their policy performance. Second, since
central leaders (particularly Mao) did not wish to rely exclusively on local

government reports, they took trips to localities themselves using different formats including 'to the countryside' (*xiaxiang*), 'squatting at a point' (*dundian*), routine inspection (*diaocha*), and investigation (*jiancha*). Third, another widely adopted method was to dispatch central work teams to localities.[42] Fourth, both ordinary people and officials of all ranks were encouraged to write letters to central and local government units, individual leaders, and media to voice their concerns and file their complaints.[43] Fifth, the official propaganda apparatus was also fully harnessed to provide central leaders with pertinent information on local policy performance. For instance, the New China News Agency constantly informed central policy-makers of progress and problems associated with local implementation of central policy through its 'internal reference' (*neibu cankao*) materials published twice daily.[44]

These systems of oversight were by no means free from ideological fervour and 'policy winds'. As the Great Leap fiasco well illustrates, the 'ratchet problems'—overriding concerns with quantitative performance and output-based growth resulting in ever-increasing targets—were generated despite these oversight measures.[45] Nevertheless, such systems of oversight were duplicated along the administrative hierarchy to prevent loopholes in the middle. A case study on the mass-irrigation campaign during 1957–8 well illustrates the dynamics of administrative oversight:

Under pressure from above, the county officials were concerned lest foot-dragging basic-level cadres cause the county to fall short of the targets which it was expected to meet. . . . As the campaign got underway, the leading party officials spread throughout the countryside to supervise in person. . . . In some cases, when the county undertook a large project, the county committee moved its office temporarily to the construction site.[46]

Under the circumstances where administrative oversight was *ad hoc* but very tight, local implementors were granted very little room for discretion. Of course, this does not refute the fact that there were local variations, deviations, and feigned compliance. It is only suggested here that, at least with regard to the national priority policies to which the centre demonstrated a strong commitment, the provincial authorities usually had no other choice but to comply. Severe difficulties in communications and transportation must have constrained Beijing's close monitoring, yet they do not seem to have inhibited effective central control to the extent that local deviations in crucial policy issues went unnoticed or unpunished.[47]

Systemic Norms

Maoist China's systemic norms against local deviation were rigid beyond casual imagination. As the earlier discussions of the failed decentralization during the Great Leap and the Cultural Revolution periods have suggested,

Beijing's intermittent calls for provincial discretion and adaptive implementation fell on deaf ears. Through organizational learning, provincial officials knew from the past experiences of frequent policy oscillations and subsequent purges that deviations were not to go unpunished.[48] The internalization and sharing of such norms dictated that provincial officials implement central policy to the letter out of the fear that even a slight deviation would invite central retaliation. When it came down to the issue of survival, compliance was no longer an option.

An excerpt from a study of local policy implementation during the early 1970s captures the essence of the shared norms that deviant behaviour could be a matter of life and death for local implementors:

[H]earing that the new policy had been implemented in neighboring locations, [local officials] might reconsider their hostility toward it. As the policy spread, a non-conforming official could become an obvious target. And as the wind intensified, support or opposition in this highly politicized environment could become a question of political stand, confronting bureaucrats with the possibility that resistance could become a political error.[49]

An editorial in *People's Daily* also provides persuasive accounts of the fears that prevented local officials from engaging in local adaptive implementation:

Under the circumstances where people are constantly told that they must not revise any central document and must follow them in everything they do, how can they solve new problems and difficulties which arise from the new conditions, and whose solutions are not provided by the documents? . . . [The most important problem is that] they dare not speak of irrational orders, inflated production statistics, and policies unsuitable for local conditions. . . . [The core reason lies in] nothing but fears. The fear of being labelled as a 'capitulationist'; the fear of being dismissed from one's post; the fear of being expelled from the party; the fear of being divorced by one's wife; the fear of serving a prison term; and the fear of being beheaded.[50]

When systemic norms bred constant fears on the part of provincial officials, faithful representation of local interests became impossible since few provincial cadres would value them more than their own careers. Thus, the survival imperative further reinforced bureaucratic careerism irrespective of local endogenous interests they were supposed to serve. Furthermore, the vertical norm control against local discretion was constantly supplemented by the horizontal operation of self-policing metanorms. As ideological conformity became the ultimate criterion of career advancement, everyone sought to avoid punishment for not punishing deviant acts. As the result, everyone strove to detect someone else's deviation so that their own allegiance became known and their careers got promoted at someone else's expense. When betrayal and informing were rewarded, there was little room left for interpretive discretion and adaptive implementation which entailed too high risks for anyone to bear.[51]

Modes of Inducement

Under the circumstances where the centre's demands were highly standardized, local adaptation met with punitive actions, and ideological standards were employed to mould conformity, the salience of policy to localities was hardly a factor in the equation. Since local interests were easily and arbitrarily suppressed, coercion constituted the most widely adopted means of conflict resolution. That is, the systemic norms dictated that the process of implementation be largely unilateral, replete with Beijing's arbitrary imposition regardless of local conditions. Of course, this is not to suggest that there were no politics at all. In certain issue areas closely related to the allocation of fiscal and material resources, central–provincial bargaining and negotiations did occur, sometimes very intensely. Yet, such activities seem to have taken place mostly in the policy-making phase rather than during implementation. While the centre may have solicited local opinions in its search for policy alternatives, once the decision was made into a policy, provinces had little room for bargaining, particularly when Beijing was strongly committed to the given policy.[52]

POST-MAO CHANGES: THE DECOLLECTIVIZATION CONTEXT OF 1977–83

The post-Mao reform differs significantly from the Maoist equivalents in that administrative decentralization preceded the devolution of substantive decision-making authority in the allocation of fiscal and material resources. This contrast may perhaps reflect the post-Mao reformist leadership's painful recognition that economic reforms were bound to fail without first transforming the rules and norms of local policy implementation.[53] Post-Mao changes in the administrative environment were more drastic in nature and more extensive in scope than this section indicates since many radical measures were adopted in the post-decollectivization period that falls outside the purview of this book. In this section, the discussion is limited to the early reform period of 1977–83 in line with the study's focus on decollectivization.[54]

Transforming Systemic Norms

Only with fundamental changes in the perceptions of local implementors concerning the permissible boundaries of their discretion, can the problems of bureaucratic careerism be mitigated. The most distinctive aspect of post-Mao reforms concerned the new leadership's efforts to redress the pernicious effects of excessive ideological control over human relations in general and economic management in particular. These efforts were directed mainly toward the 'emancipation of mind' (*sixiang jiefang*). It was a painstaking decision since the post-Mao leadership had to carry out this arduous task as completely as possible yet without critically damaging the legitimacy of the regime dependent heavily on ideological control by the centre, the Communist Party, and Mao Zedong Thought.

During 1977–82, official news media were literally flooded with numerous attacks on 'ultra-leftism'. These attacks were conveniently launched against the disgraced 'Gang of Four' but they were in fact disguised criticisms of the Maoist era and Mao in particular. They initially took the subtle form of theoretical debates through which ultra-leftist policies were severely criticized for their excessive idealism and urgent needs for empiricism were emphasized.[55] Theoretical debates soon gave way to the calls for 'independent thinking' based on objective facts not on empty ideological tenets. An article in *People's Daily* persuasively links 'independent thinking' with central–local relations:

Many cadres should dare to seek truth from facts and solve problems in light of reality. . . . Some believe that it is forbidden to say or do anything that has not been mentioned by the central leadership or in central documents. Furthermore, they hold that central documents, once issued, can never be revised even if they no longer suit the present situation. . . . If one really wants to implement a policy, he must comprehend it in light of the actual situation of his own unit. It is the lower level's responsibility to provide correct information and pertinent opinions when the central document is at variance with local conditions.[56]

As a more concrete manifestation of the leadership's determination to shake the ideological yoke off local cadres, large-scale pardons were granted to many of those who had been stigmatized as rightists and other 'bad elements' and severely persecuted during the successive campaigns and purges since 1957. The pardoned included a large group of former provincial and local cadres who had dared to speak out against the policies that they had considered unsuitable for their localities.[57] These measures, along with the leadership's strenuous efforts to weed out 'leftists' and beneficiaries of the Cultural Revolution, must have contributed to the mitigation of doubts held by many concerning the determination of the central leadership.

The reformist leadership's efforts to transform systemic norms were soon translated into its strong emphasis on the *yindi zhiyi* principle as the following excerpt well epitomizes:

[T]o uphold the principle of seeking truth from facts . . . we must combine the spirit of the central directives with the actual conditions of our localities . . . and rectify any tendency for policy standardization by 'whipping up a gust of ideological wind'. . . . Our country is vast and populous and has varied conditions. Since different localities have their own distinct conditions . . . we must not allow the same pattern everywhere.[58]

Beijing's stress on *yindi zhiyi* meant that local discretion in interpreting and implementing central policy should be permitted to account for varied local conditions and that the past malpractice of imposing 'blanket policies' (*yidao qie* or *yiguo zhu*) should be avoided. Subsequently, the idea of 'a single model for the whole country' came under severe criticisms, eventually to be abolished.[59]

The reformist leadership also employed a variety of measures to minimize ideological influence over local policy implementation. First, many central and provincial policy documents over and again stressed the stability of reformist policy. Particularly concerning the decollectivization reform, frequent reminders were issued that, unlike the past, the new rural policy would not change in tandem with abrupt ideological shifts at the centre. Since the new leadership was keenly aware of the prevalent local fears of policy change, guarantees were made to ensure that the local perceptions about the rule of 'safer being left than right' (*ningzuo huyou*) were groundless. Beijing also sought to prohibit rushed implementation rooted in another popular belief that it was 'safer being faster than slower' (*ningkuai human*).[60]

Second, in order to rationalize the processes of policy-making and implementation, the centre called for the redress of the widespread practice of reporting inflated statistics. The prevalence of fraudulent reporting and its deleterious ratchet effects forced the new leadership to recognize that underachievement was not necessarily an act of non-compliance and, therefore, should not automatically be stigmatized. In order to halt the malpractice of distorting local performance statistics, the State Planning Commission, the Ministry of Agriculture, and the State Statistical Bureau issued a joint circular in October 1980, which supplied five multiple indices for grain production and four for animal husbandry, replacing the hitherto single index of 'per mu grain output' and the 'number of livestock in possession'.[61]

Third, the reformist leadership made a pledge to reduce the government's use of overly ambitious and militant slogans as a key instrument of policy implementation. A derivative of these efforts was in part the disappearance, or at least a considerable reduction, of direct quotations from Mao Zedong Thought in the formulation and implementation of policy. Related were strenuous efforts to criticize the widespread use of 'hackneyed slogans' for the imposition of standardized policy.[62] Fourth, measures were also taken to promote the comparative advantages of different regions. In 1978–80, a series of regional planning conferences were convened to identify regional economic conditions and developmental priorities on the basis of which central policy was to be formulated. Furthermore, multiple models were promoted to reflect regional variations.[63]

Fifth, in order to expand provincial initiatives and enhance local adaptability in implementation, the reformist leadership might have assumed that the appointment of provincial leaders well tuned to local conditions was desirable. Since the personnel decisions for provincial first party secretaries (PFPSs) were handled exclusively by the Central Organization Department with the *nomenklatura* power, the increased share of PFPSs assigned to their native provinces and neighbouring ones seems to reflect Beijing's intention to expand local policy discretion. While the share of PFPSs assigned to their native provinces was only 5 per cent in 1969–71 and 21 per cent for 1949–79, that for 1983 rose to 26.6 per cent. With the inclusion of PFPSs assigned to the neighbouring provinces, the figure rose from an average of 41.3 per cent for 1949–78 to 53.3 per cent in 1983.[64]

Post-Mao Changes in Oversight: The Decollectivization Phase

Measuring the changes that occurred in the frequency and intensity of oversight by the centre during the post-Mao era is a daunting task, not only because it is impossible to obtain all the relevant information (e.g. the total number and nature of inspection trips by leading central officials and the frequency of work-team dispatches), but also because administrative oversight was frequently conducted in various unofficial and informal ways in addition to official media reports and investigative journalism. Given the rapid pace at which the centre's reliance on telecommunications and statistical data was increasing, we may probably argue that Beijing's overall capacity for administrative oversight has significantly improved in the post-Mao era.[65]

If we limit our discussion to the period of decollectivization, however, the same assessment may not apply. First of all, many key institutions of administrative oversight were established and restored after or toward the end of the decollectivization reform: the Ministry of Supervision (*jianchabu*) was restored in 1987 and the General Auditing Administration (*shenjishu*) established in 1983.[66] Second, the State Statistical Bureau (SSB) had been significantly weakened during the Cultural Revolution period when its status had been downgraded to a bureau under the State Planning Commission with a 97 per cent personnel reduction at the central headquarters. As of 1981, for instance, the SSB's central staff size was only 230, way below the 1965 level. Furthermore, it was not until 1984 (i.e. after the completion of decollectivization) that statistical employees at the county level or above were included in the central *nomenklatura* with their operating expenses funded centrally. Even then, their salaries were mostly financed locally, leaving them vulnerable to capture by the respective local governments.[67] Third, it was only in 1983 that the legislation of the 'statistics law' (*tongjifa*) was enacted. And it was not until 1987 that Beijing forced the province-level governments to draft legislation against statistical manipulations.[68]

While Beijing's oversight capacity had not improved significantly during the decollectivization period, both institutionalized and *ad hoc* mechanisms were established to help inform the centre of the reform's progress. More specifically, according to a knowledgeable interviewee in Beijing, at least four channels of oversight were widely utilized. First, the central leaders received progress reports from provincial leaders at least twice a year—at the annual rural work conference convened in winter and at the discussion meeting held in spring. Second, through the agricultural work system (*nongye xitong*), 'summary reports' (*jianbao*) were sent upward regularly and very frequently. Third, the centre occasionally dispatched work-teams to check on local performance. Finally, and perhaps most importantly, in 1980 the Central Rural Policy Research Office (*zhongyang nongcun zhengce yanjiushi*) established 'information points' (*xinxidian*) in over seventy counties around the country to monitor the progress of decollectivization.[69]

Statutory Precision in the Decollectivization Case

Under administrative decentralization, statutory precision may be reduced in two ways. First, the central government unit may formulate policy directives in such a way that only general guidelines are stipulated, leaving most of the specifics of implementation—such as the time-table, designated outputs, scope of application, and resource involvement—to be determined by local implementors. Second, statutory precision may also be reduced by the provision of multiple alternatives from which local implementors choose to match their varied conditions. The household responsibility policy was an encompassing policy targeted at all province-level units. In terms of the scope of change proposed, the policy challenged the long-cherished system of collective production. More importantly, it was an agricultural policy that required a considerable amount of bottom-heavy information on varied local conditions. In order to avoid the malpractice of standardization, therefore, the central leadership had to find ways of reducing the level of statutory precision.

The level of statutory precision in the case of the household responsibility policy was reduced in two ways. First, the total number of central documents pertaining to the decollectivization reform was relatively smaller than that of similarly radical policies of the pre-reform period. There were a total of six central party documents known to have been issued specifically on the household responsibility policy for the period of 1979–83.[70] That is, there was roughly one central party document related to decollectivization per year. Compared to the Maoist period during which more than three central party documents were issued for a policy in a single year, the figure may represent a significantly reduced level of statutory precision.[71] Furthermore, out of these six central party documents, with the notable exception of the September 1979 directive which had a more

TABLE 2.1. *Number of alternatives manifested in provincial documents*

Heilongjiang	Liaoning	Shandong	Jiangsu	Hubei	Guangdong	Shaanxi
5	4	5	6	6	2	5

Sources: (1) Heilongjiang Provincial Party Document No. 55 of 1981; (2) Liaoning Provincial Party Document No. 52 of 1981; (3) Shandong Provincial Party Document No. 23 of 1982; (4) Jiangsu Agricultural Department Document No. 5 of 1982; (5) Hubei Provincial Party Document No. 27 of 1982; (6) Guangdong Provincial Party Document No. 42 of 1982; and (7) Shaanxi Provincial Party Document No. 51 of 1981. See *Nongcun jingji zhengce huibian 1981–1983* (Collection of Rural Policy Documents in 1981–1983: Internal Publication) (Beijing: Nongcun duwu chubanshe, 1984) i. 159–60, 223–5, 267, 364–5, 425, 465, and 606–10.

binding designation of 'decision' (*jueding*), the rest were all 'notices' (*tongzhi*).

Another way of reducing statutory precision was to supply multiple alternatives from which provinces might choose. In the case of the September 1980 document, five different responsibility systems were offered, and the January 1982 document provided a total of seven alternatives. Since there is always a possibility that the centre's policy stipulations might not have been transmitted to the sub-national levels of administration, it is necessary to examine whether the provincial directives indeed adopted multiple alternatives in line with the 'spirit' of the central documents. As Table 2.1 illustrates, the number of alternatives adopted by seven provinces, as manifested in their provincial documents, was not only large but also varied significantly among themselves.[72]

The foregoing discussions have described mainly the input side of administrative decentralization by focusing on the measures that the central government had stipulated and employed to promote provincial adaptive implementation. In order to assess the output side, the degree to which such measures actually expanded the scope of provincial discretion should be examined. The operational effects of administrative decentralization can be discerned at two different levels. First, at the system level, the nationwide aggregate pattern of implementation may be observed. More specifically, we can measure the extent of variation among the provinces in their pace of decollectivization. If the measures of post-Mao administrative decentralization had been successful, not only would high levels of interprovincial variation in the pace of decollectivization be identified, but certain associations would also be established between the provincial conditions (i.e. endogenous interests) and the interprovincial variation found.[73] Empirical tests of these issues are presented in Chapter 3.

By reducing statutory precision and relaxing systemic norms, administrative decentralization might have widened a window of opportunity for some provinces, whose non-average implementation behaviour might not have been detected by system-level aggregate analyses. The triple-mix typology is to be utilized in order to examine the relative weight of provincial endogenous interests, patron–client relationships, and local leadership in inducing the provinces to opt for pioneering, bandwagoning, or resisting. Since aggregate outcomes often shroud the complex dynamics of human agency and strategic decision-making at the individual province level, three provincial case studies are employed to explicate the rationales, processes, and outcomes of each of the three patterns of provincial policy implementation. They constitute Chapters 4 to 6.

NOTES

1. While the former Soviet Union had maintained the constitutional stipulations of a federal administration, its *modus operandi* was more like that of a centralized unitary system. See John Yin, 'Soviet Federalism Re-Identified', in C. Lloyd Brown-John (ed.), *Centralizing and Decentralizing Trends in Federal States* (Lanham, Md.: University Press of America, 1988), 347–56. For an ominous observation about the relationship between the size of the Soviet Union and levels of territorial-economic 'compartmentalization', see B. S. Khorev, 'Economic Decentralization and Regionalism', *Soviet Geography*, 31/7 (1990), 509–16.

2. For efforts to explore this macro-historical question, see Arthur Waldron, 'Warlordism Versus Federalism: The Revival of A Debate', *China Quarterly*, 121 (1990), 116–28; Karl Bünger, 'Concluding Remarks on Two Aspects of the Chinese Unitary State as Compared with the European State System', in Stuart R. Schram (ed.), *Foundations and Limits of State Power in China* (London: University of London Press, 1987), 313–23; and Prasenjit Duara, 'Provincial Narratives of the Nation: Centralism and Federalism in Republican China', in Harumi Befu (ed.), *Cultural Nationalism in East Asia* (Berkeley: Institute of East Asian Studies, 1993), 9–35. For more contemporary perspectives, see Jin Ji, *Banglianzhi: Zhongguo de zuijia chulu* (Confederation: The Best Way Out For China) (Hong Kong: Baixing Publishing Co., 1992); and Yan Jiaqi, *Lianbang zhongguo gouxiang* (Thoughts On a Federal China) (Hong Kong: Ming Pao Publisher, 1992).

3. *The Making of Modern China* (New York: W. W. Norton, 1944), 186.

4. Principal measures included: (1) the 'rule of avoidance' by which no officials were assigned to rule their native provinces; (2) the 'rule of short-term stay' by which local officials served only for fixed terms; (3) the 'rule of separation', by which no governors were allowed to hold military positions concurrently; (4) the 'rule of dual control', by which provinces were ruled by both governors and viceroys, who were required to check on each other on behalf of the imperial court; (5) the direct appointment of regional finance commissioners by the imperial court to supervise the collection of tax revenues by provinces; and (6) stationing Tartar garrisons at strategic points on the way to Beijing to defend the Manchu court. See Wei-chin Mu, *Provincial–Central Government Relations and the Problem of National Unity in Modern China* (Ann Arbor: University Microfilms, 1965), 31, 56–7, 59, 62. For the importance of local power in toppling the centre in both traditional and modern China, see Frederick Wakeman, Jr., *The Fall of Imperial China* (New York: Free Press, 1975), chs. 10–11 and James E. Sheridan, *China in Disintegration: The Republican Era in Chinese History, 1912–1949* (New York: Free Press, 1975), ch. 6.

5. Alan P. Liu, *Communication and National Integration in Communist China* (Berkeley: University of California Press, 1971), 12–16.

6. The *locus classicus* on the 'great administrative regions' is Dorothy J. Solinger, *Regional Government and Political Integration in Southwest China, 1949–1954* (Berkeley: University of California Press, 1977). The abolition of the great administrative regions reduced

the number of local units under direct central control from 28 provinces, 15 municipalities (*zhixiashi*), 8 districts (*qu*), and one area (*difang*—Tibet), to 21 provinces, 3 municipalities, and 5 province-level autonomous regions. See Cheng Xingchao, *Zhongguo difang zhengfu* (Chinese Local Governments) (Xianggang: Zhonghua shuju, 1987), 236–42. For the process of state formation in this period, see Frederick C. Teiwes, 'Establishment and Consolidation of the New Regime', in Roderick MacFarquhar and John K. Fairbank (eds.), *The Cambridge History of China*, xiv. *The People's Republic of China*, pt. 1, *The Emergence of Revolutionary China 1949–1965* (Cambridge: Cambridge University Press, 1987), 51–143.

7. The Yan'an experience encompassed various bottom-up dynamics such as land reform campaigns, the mass line, and anti-bureaucratism movements. As to policy implementation, *yindi zhiyi* calling for flexible local adaptation was perhaps the most crucial component. More specifically, the Yan'an experience not only distinguished between the 'consolidated bases' and 'unliberated areas' in its formulation and execution of policy, but it also relaxed ideological commitments whenever the need arose, contributing in a major way to the Communist victory over the Nationalists. On the Yan'an system in general, see Mark Selden, *The Yenan Way in Revolutionary China* (Cambridge, Mass.: Harvard University Press, 1971). For the Yan'an system's flexibility, see Carl E. Dorris, 'Peasant Mobilization in North China and the Origin of Yenan Communism', *China Quarterly*, 68 (1976), 697–720; Elizabeth Perry, *Rebels and Revolutionaries in North China, 1845–1945* (Stanford: Stanford University Press, 1980), 225–39; and Ralph Thaxton, *China Turned Rightside Up: Revolutionary Legitimacy in the Peasant World* (New Haven: Yale University Press, 1983), 185–90.

8. For the process in which Beijing gradually gained control over local affairs during the land reform, see Ezra F. Vogel, *Canton under Communism: Programs and Politics in A Provincial Capital, 1949–1968* (Cambridge, Mass.: Harvard University Press, 1969), ch. 3. For later periods, see Chalmers Johnson, 'Chinese Communist Leadership and Mass Response: The Yenan Period and the Socialist Education Campaign', in Ping-ti Ho and Tang Tsou (eds.), *China in Crisis* (Chicago: University of Chicago Press, 1968), i. 397–437; and Lowell Dittmer, 'Political Development: Leadership, Politics, and Ideology', in Joyce E. Kallgren (ed.), *The People's Republic After Thirty Years: An Overview* (Berkeley: Center for Chinese Studies, 1979), 27–43.

9. As for the deleterious effects of the anti-rightist campaign, David Bachman notes: '[D]uring and after this campaign, no one dared to contradict the views coming down from above for fear of being sentenced to labor reform.' See *Bureaucracy, Economy, and Leadership in China: The Institutional Origins of the Great Leap Forward* (Cambridge: Cambridge University Press, 1991), 5. Also see William A. Joseph, 'A Tragedy of Good Intentions: Post-Mao Views of the Great Leap Forward', *Modern China*, 12/4 (1986), 427–8. And for the predominance of ideological and political criteria in China's policy process in the Maoist era, see Carl Riskin, 'Neither Plan Nor Market: Mao's Political Economy', in William A. Joseph, Christine P. W. Wong, and David Zweig (eds.), *New Perspectives on the Cultural Revolution* (Cambridge, Mass.: Harvard University Press, 1991), 138–9.

10. For the period of 1955–7, see Frederick C. Teiwes, *Politics and Purges in China: Rectification and the Decline of Party Norms, 1950–1965* (White Plains, NY: M. E. Sharpe, 1979), 349–66. The validity of the commonly conceived linkage between the purges of provincial leaders and their 'alleged' resistance to the centre is dubious as the purges were not so much the result of their conscious actions of non-compliance as the results of the intricate high politics in Beijing. See Peter R. Moody, Jr., 'Policy and Power: The Career of T'ao Chu, 1956–66', *China Quarterly*, 54 (1973), 267–93; and David S. G. Goodman, 'Li Jingquan and the South-West Region, 1958–66: The Life and 'Crimes' of a Local Emperor', *China Quarterly*, 81 (1981), 66–96.

11. See Jae Ho Chung, 'Studies of Central–Provincial Relations in the People's Republic of China: A Mid-Term Appraisal', *China Quarterly*, 142 (1995), 491–2, 504–6.

12. The Great Leap system of 'sharing specific revenues' (*fenlei fencheng*) designated categories of provincial fixed incomes and fixed central–provincial budgetary-sharing ratios for five years. Other key measures included the delegation of 88 per cent of centrally owned enterprises and of decision-making authority for basic construction investment, as well as the transfer of 20 per cent of the profits from the remaining centrally owned

enterprises to the provinces. After the Great Leap fiasco, however, Beijing recentralized fiscal control by adopting the system of 'sharing overall revenues' (*zonge fencheng*), with the budgetary-sharing ratios to be determined annually. Furthermore, many state enterprises were reassigned to the central government and basic construction investment was again to be controlled solely by Beijing. See *Dangdai zhongguo caizheng* (Contemporary China's Finance) (Beijing: Zhongguo shehuikexue chubanshe, 1988), i. 159–60, 172–3, 205, 210; and Song Xinzhong, *Zhongguo caizheng tizhi gaige yanjiu* (Study of China's Fiscal Reform) (Beijing: Zhongguo caizheng jingji chubanshe, 1992), 53–4.

13. The data are adapted from Frederick C. Teiwes, 'Provincial Politics: Themes and Variations', in John M. H. Lindbeck (ed.), *China: Management of A Revolutionary Society* (Seattle: University of Washington Press, 1971), 172.
14. Alfred L. Chan, 'The Campaign for Agricultural Development in the Great Leap Forward: A Study of Policy-Making and Implementation in Liaoning', *China Quarterly*, 129 (1992), 54–5.
15. Benedict A. Stavis, *The Politics of Agricultural Mechanization in China* (Ithaca, NY: Cornell University Press, 1978), 121.
16. Carl Riskin, *China's Political Economy: The Quest for Development since 1949* (New York: Oxford University Press, 1987), 125–6; Chu Han, *Sannian ziran huihai changbian jishi* (Records of Natural Calamities of the Three Years of 1959–61) (Chengdu: Sichuan renmin chubanshe, 1996), 105–42; and Li Rui, *Dayuejin qinliji* (Personal Recollections of the Great Leap Forward) (Shanghai: Shanghai yuandong chubanshe, 1996), 119–28.
17. For the same conclusion drawn on the basis of research on Henan, see Jean-Luc Domenach, *The Origins of the Great Leap Forward: The Case of One Chinese Province* (Boulder, Colo.: Westview, 1995), 157–60.
18. See, for instance, David Zweig, 'Strategies of Policy Implementation: Policy 'Winds' and Brigade Accounting in Rural China', *World Politics*, 37/2 (1985), 267–93.
19. David S. G. Goodman, 'The Provincial Revolutionary Committee in the People's Republic of China, 1967–1979: An Obituary', *China Quarterly*, 85 (1982), 49, 54, 70.
20. For these self-policing norms at work, see Keith Forster, *Rebellion and Factionalism in A Chinese Province: Zhejiang 1966–1976* (Armonk, NY: M. E. Sharpe, 1990); and Anita Chan, Richard Madsen and Jonathan Unger, *Chen Village: The Recent History of A Peasant Community in Mao's China* (Berkeley and Los Angeles: University of California Press, 1984). For the prevalence of ideological insanity during this period, see Wang Shaoguang, *Lixing yu fengkuang: wenhua dageming zhongde qunzhong* (Rationality and Insanity: The Masses during the Cultural Revolution) (Hong Kong: Oxford University Press, 1993).
21. See Tang Tsou, Marc Blecher, and Mitch Meisner, 'National Agricultural Policy: The Dazhai Model and Local Change in the Post-Mao Era', in Mark Selden and Victor Lippit (eds.), *The Transition to Socialism in China* (Armonk, NY: M. E. Sharpe, 1982), 269–72; and Sun Qitai and Xiong Zhiyong, *Dazhai hongqi de shengqi yu duoluo* (The Rise and Fall of Dazhai's Red Banner) (Huixian: Henan renmin chubanshe, 1990), 258–68.
22. For the lack of local discretion in cropping decisions, see Marc Blecher and Wang Shaoguang, 'The Political Economy of Cropping in Maoist and Dengist China: Hebei Province and Shulu County, 1949–90', *China Quarterly*, 137 (1994), 73–80. And for the correlation coefficients, see Thomas Lyons, *Economic Integration and Planning in Communist China* (New York: Columbia University Press, 1987), 174.
23. See Song, *Zhongguo caizheng tizhi gaige yanjiu*, 48, 51.
24. Penelope B. Prime, 'Central–Provincial Investment and Finance: The Cultural Revolution and Its Legacy in Jiangsu Province', in Joseph, Wong, and Zweig (eds.), *New Perspectives on the Cultural Revolution*, 212.
25. See Zweig, 'Strategies of Policy Implementation', 267–93, and Dorothy J. Solinger, 'Politics in Yunnan Province in the Decade of Disorder: Elite Factional Strategies and Central–Local Relations, 1967–1980', *China Quarterly*, 92 (1982), 646–8.
26. 'Continuing Central Predominance', *Problems of Communism*, 21/4 (1972), 82–3. Some dissenting views do exist, however, on the extent of local autonomy during this period. See Parris C. Chang, 'Peking and the Provinces: Decentralization of Power', *Problems of Communism*, 21/4 (1972), 67–74; and Lynn T. White, III, 'Local Autonomy in China during the Cultural Revolution: The Theoretical Uses of an Atypical Case', *American Political Science Review*, 70/4 (1976), 479–91.

27. Variation, *pro forma* compliance, and deviation all existed, producing variable levels of conformity in different sectors for different periods. For instance, variation characterized the provincial policies toward the size of private plots since 1962 as they gradually entered the realm of the 'grey economy' which the centre was not highly motivated to regulate. As a result, different ceilings were set for the area of the collective land allotted for private plots in different provinces. See William L. Parish and Martin K. Whyte, *Village and Family in Contemporary China* (Chicago: University of Chicago Press, 1978), 34–5, 118–19; and Norma Diamond, 'Taitou Revisited: State Policies and Social Change', in William L. Parish (ed.), *Chinese Rural Development: The Great Transformation* (Armonk, NY: M. E. Sharpe, 1985), 259. The point is, once Beijing committed itself to a priority policy, there was very little room left for local implementors to manœuvre or bargain for in Maoist China. See David S. G. Goodman, 'Political Perspectives', in David S. G. Goodman (ed.), *China's Regional Development* (London: Routledge, 1989), 22–6.

28. For statutory precision, see Frank Thompson, 'Policy Implementation and Overhead Control', in George C. Edwards, III (ed.), *Public Policy Implementation* (Greenwich, Conn.: JAI Press, 1984), 5. For standardization, see Robert D. Thomas, 'Implementing Federal Programs at the Local Level', *Political Science Quarterly*, 94/3 (1979), 423–4.

29. For the importance of administrative oversight, see Joel D. Aberbach, *Keeping a Watchful Eye: The Politics of Congressional Oversight* (Washington: The Brookings Institution, 1990).

30. For a comparison between bureaucratic-authoritarian and liberal-democratic regimes in terms of implementation norms, see Oscar Oszlak, 'Public Policies and Political Regimes in Latin America', *International Social Science Journal*, 108 (1986), 219–35. Also see R. Kenneth Godwin, 'Policy Formation and Implementation in Less Industrialized Countries: A Comparative Analysis of Institutional Effects', *Western Political Quarterly*, 45/2 (1992), 423–4.

31. 'An Evolutionary Approach to Norms', *American Political Science Review*, 80/4 (1986), 1098–1100.

32. See, for instance, David A. Dyker, 'Decentralization and the Command Principle—Some Lessons from Soviet Experiences', *Journal of Comparative Economics*, 5/2 (1981), 121–48.

33. See 'An Evolutionary Approach to Norms', 1101–2. Also see Paul Claval, 'Center–Periphery and Space: Models of Political Geography', in Jean Gottmann (ed.), *Centre and Periphery: Spatial Variation in Politics* (Beverly Hills: Sage, 1980), 66–7.

34. See John Echeverri-Gent, 'Between Autonomy and Capture: Embedding Government Agencies in Their Societal Environment', *Policy Studies Journal*, 20/3 (1992), 354–5.

35. Michael Howlett calls these 'effectors'. See 'Policy Instruments, Policy Styles, and Policy Implementation: National Approaches to Theories of Instrument Choice', *Policy Studies Journal*, 19/2 (1991), 9.

36. See Howlett, 'Policy Instruments, Policy Styles, and Policy Implementation', 11; and Robert A. Baron, 'Conflict in Organizations', in Kevin R. Murphy and Frank E. Saal (eds.), *Psychology in Organizations: Integrating Science and Practice* (Hillsdales, NJ: Lawrence Erlbaum Associates, 1990), 209–10.

37. See Kenneth Lieberthal, *Central Documents and Politburo Politics in China* (Ann Arbor: Center for Chinese Studies, 1978), 11–15.

38. See Michel Oksenberg, 'Aspects of Local Government and Politics in China: 1955–58', *Journal of Development Studies*, 4/1 (1967), 37–8; and Wu Guoguang, 'Command Communication: The Politics of Editorial Formulation in the *People's Daily*', *China Quarterly*, 137 (1994), 195–6.

39. On this point, see Michel Oksenberg, 'Methods of Communication within the Chinese Bureaucracy', *China Quarterly*, 57 (1974), 11.

40. Contrast, for instance, Audrey Donnithorne, 'China's Cellular Economy: Some Economic Trends since the Cultural Revolution', *China Quarterly*, 52 (1972), 605–19 with Nicholas R. Lardy, 'Centralization and Decentralization in China's Fiscal Management', *China Quarterly*, 61 (1975), 25–60; and subsequent exchanges between Donnithorne and Lardy, 'Centralization and Decentralization in China's Fiscal Management: Comment', and 'Reply', ibid. 66 (1976), 328–54.

41. For detailed discussions of the State Statistical Bureau, see Yasheng Huang, 'The Statistical Agency in China's Bureaucratic System: A Comparison with the Former Soviet Union',

Communist and Post-Communist Studies, 29/1 (1996), 59–75. For the abolition of the Ministry of Supervision in 1959, see Zhou Jizhong, *Zhongguo xingzheng jiancha* (Administrative Supervision in China) (Nanchang: Jiangxi renmin chubanshe, 1989), 598–608. And for the collapse of the statistical system during the Cultural Revolution period, see Li Huicun, *Zhongguo tongjishi* (History of Statistics in China) (Beijing: Zhongguo tongji chubanshe, 1993), 365–73.

42. Oksenberg, 'Methods of Communication within the Chinese Bureaucracy', 21–2.

43. See Diao Jiecheng, *Renmin xinfang shilue* (History of Popular Letter-Writing) (Beijing: Beijing jingji xueyuan chubanshe, 1996).

44. See Michael Schoenhals, 'Elite Information in China', *Problems of Communism*, 34/5 (1985), 66.

45. For the ratchet problems, see Dyker, 'Decentralization and the Command Principle', 121–48.

46. Oksenberg, 'Aspects of Local Government and Politics in China', 37–8.

47. 'Commitment' is the key word here since, given the size of the territory under its control and the constant shortage of operational funds, Beijing had to concentrate its resources on closely monitoring one or two priority policies at one time. It is possible, therefore, that many loopholes were created for local deviations regarding non-priority polices.

48. For organizational learning, see Brian Levitt and James G. March, 'Organizational Learning', *Annual Review of Sociology* (Palo Alto, Calif.: Annual Review Press, 1988), 319–40. Memories of previous campaigns, such as the anti-rightist campaign, played a key role in constraining the choices of local officials. See Joseph, 'A Tragedy of Good Intentions', 427–8.

49. Zweig, 'Strategies of Policy Implementation', 275.

50. *Renmin ribao* (*People's Daily*), 7 Dec. 1978.

51. For such metanorms in operation, see Solinger, 'Politics in Yunnan Province in the Decade of Disorder'; and Anne F. Thurston, *Enemies of the People: The Ordeal of the Intellectuals in China's Great Cultural Revolution* (Cambridge, Mass.: Harvard University Press, 1987); and Hongda Harry Wu, *Laogai: The Chinese Gulag* (Boulder, Colo.: Westview, 1992), 25–6, 31–2.

52. See Zhao Suisheng, 'China's Central–Local Relationship: A Historical Perspective', in Jia Hao and Lin Zhimin (eds.), *Changing Central–Local Relations in China: Reform and State Capacity* (Boulder, Colo.: Westview, 1994), 19–34.

53. Such recognition is implicitly, and often explicitly, manifested in *Guanyu jianguo yilai dang de ruogan lishi wenti de jueyi* (Resolutions on Some Historical Problems of the Party Since 1949) (Beijing: Renmin chubanshe, 1985), *passim*. More specifically, in his personal recollections of the Maoist era, Bo Yibo pointed out the deleterious symptoms of the 'right-aversive disease' (*kongyouzheng*), referring to the widely shared norms that cadres sought to avoid anything that could at any time be perceived and labelled as a 'rightist' act regardless of its practical utility. See *Ruogan zhongda juece yu shijian de huigu* (Recollections of Some Crucial Decisions and Events) (Beijing: Zhonggong zhongyang dangxiao chubanshe, 1993), ii. 778.

54. In all resource-related issue areas except for agriculture, meaningful measures of decentralization were implemented after or toward the end of the decollectivization reform. As for the planning system, the State Planning Commission document issued in January 1983 signalled the beginning of serious changes. In the area of investment control, the devolution of authority was stipulated in the State Council documents nos. 123 and 138 of 1984. In taxation, the 'profit-turned-tax' (*ligaishui*) reform was initiated in April 1983. In budgetary sharing, while some experiments were conducted from 1980 onwards with the systems of 'sharing specific revenues' and 'fixed-sum remittances', the major system remained the same as before until 1988. See, respectively, Gui Shiyong, *Zhongguo jihua tizhi gaige* (Reforming the Planning System in China) (Beijing: Zhongguo caizheng jingji chubanshe, 1994), 2–3; Yao Zhenyan, *Zhongguo touzi tizhi gaige* (Reforming the Investment System in China) (Beijing: Zhongguo caizheng jingji chubanshe, 1994), 4–9; Zhang Zhongcheng, *Zhongguo shuishou zhidu gaige* (Reforming the Tax System in China) (Beijing: Zhongguo caizheng jingji chubanshe, 1994), 6–12; and Song Xinzhong, *Zhongguo caizheng tizhi gaige yanjiu*, 52–4.

55. See, for instance, Xinhua Domestic Service, 2 Mar. 1977 in *Foreign Broadcast Information*

Service: Daily Report—China (hereafter *FBIS*), 7 Mar. 1977, E17–21; *Renmin ribao*, 23 Jan. 23 and 17 July 1978, and 3 July 1979; *Zhengming* (*Contend*), Mar. 1979, 4 in *FBIS*, 2 Mar. 1979, N2–3; and *Guangming ribao* (*Guangming Daily*), 9 Aug. 1979 in *FBIS*, 16 Aug. 1979, L8–9.

56. See the issue of 7 Dec. 1978.

57. See *Renmin ribao*, 17 Nov. 1978. For this process of 'verdict-reversing' (*pingfan*), see Hong Yung Lee, *From Revolutionary Cadres to Bureaucratic Technocrats* (Berkeley and Los Angeles: University of California Press, 1991), chs. 7–8. In the case of Shandong, previous verdicts on 2,458 cases were reversed between October 1976 and November 1978. Between 1977 and 1986, 81 per cent of the verdicts on 68,000 cases involving persecuted local cadres were reversed, and 91 per cent of those on 76,000 cases involving basic-level cadres were reversed. See Research Office of the Shandong Provincial Party Committee, *Shandong sishinian* (Shandong in the Last Forty Years) (Jinan: Shandong renmin chubanshe, 1989), 133–41.

58. *Renmin ribao*, 3 July 1979. Also see ibid. 15 Oct. 1979 and 20 July 1980.

59. For the process in which the Dazhai model was severely criticized and abolished, see Tsou, Blecher, and Meisner, 'National Agricultural Policy', 286–95. For the downgrading of the Dazhai model of mechanization, see Jae Ho Chung, 'The Politics of Agricultural Mechanization in the Post-Mao Era, 1977–87', *China Quarterly*, 134 (1993), 273–7.

60. See 'How Change and No Change in Policy Should be Understood', *Hongqi* (*Red Flag*), Feb. 1981, 24–6 in *FBIS*, 11 Mar. 1981, L21–5; Beijing Xinhua Domestic Service, 9 July 1980 in *FBIS*, 15 July 1980, T3–6; Guizhou Provincial Service, 20 Nov. 1981 in *FBIS*, 25 Nov. 1981, Q1–2; and *Renmin ribao*, 4 Aug. 1981.

61. See *Renmin ribao*, 16 Nov. 1977; Beijing Xinhua Domestic Service, 24 Oct. 1980 in *FBIS*, 27 Oct. 1980, L4–5.

62. *Renmin ribao*, 23 Dec. 1977; *Dongxiang* (*Trend*), 16 July 1979, 27–9 in *FBIS*, 20 July 1979, U1–2; and *Zhejiang ribao* (*Zhejiang Daily*), 30 Sept. 1980 in *FBIS*, 21 Oct. 1980, O5–6. Also see Michael Schoenhals, *Doing Things with Words in Chinese Politics: Five Studies* (Berkeley: Institute of East Asian Studies, 1992), 20, 44; and Zhang Wenhe, *Kouhao yu zhongguo* (Slogans and China) (Beijing: Zhonggong dangshi chubanshe, 1998).

63. For the proceedings of agricultural planning conferences, see *Nongye buju yu nongye quhua* (Agricultural Production Composition and Regional Planning) (Beijing: Kexue chubanshe, 1982).

64. In retrospect, this was only the beginning of a long-term trend. By 1988, 44 per cent of all provincial party secretaries and governors in China were natives. See Xiaowei Zang, 'Provincial Elite in Post-Mao China', *Asian Survey*, 31/6 (1991), 516. For a similar trend at the sub-provincial level, see Cheng Li and David Bachman, 'Localism, Elitism, and Immobilism: Elite Formation and Social Change in Post-Mao China', *World Politics*, 42/1 (1989), 71, 80–1.

65. See, for instance, Nina Halpern, 'Information Flows and Policy Coordination in the Chinese Bureaucracy', in Kenneth G. Lieberthal and David M. Lampton (eds.), *Bureaucracy, Politics and Decision-Making in Post-Mao China* (Berkeley and Los Angeles: University of California Press, 1992), 147.

66. See Yasheng Huang, 'Administrative Monitoring in China', *China Quarterly*, 143 (1995), 836–7.

67. Li, *Zhongguo tongjishi*, 373–80; and Yasheng Huang, *Inflation and Investment Controls in China: The Political Economy of Central–Local Relations During the Reform Era* (Cambridge: Cambridge University Press, 1996), 104–5.

68. State Statistical Bureau, *Zhongguo tongji gongzuo nianjian 1993* (China Statistical Work Yearbook 1993) (Beijing: Zhongguo tongji chubanshe, 1993), i. 51–4, iii. 13–14.

69. Interviews in Beijing in 1994.

70. Since all of these documents will receive close attention in the next chapter, only a list is provided here. They are: (1) 'the Party Centre's Notice Regarding the Summary of the Discussion Meeting on the Problems of Rural Work' issued on 3 Apr. 1979; (2) 'the Party Centre's Decision Concerning Certain Problems in Accelerating the Development of Agriculture' issued in Sept. 1979; (3) Central Document No. 75 of 1980 on 'Some Problems on Further Improving Agricultural Production Responsibility Systems' issued on 27 Sept. 1980; (4) Central Document No. 13 of 1981; (5) 'A Summary of the National Rural

Work Conference' issued in Jan. 1982; and (6) 'the Party Centre's Notice Regarding Some Problems of the Current Rural Economic Policy' issued in Jan. 1983.

71. There were three in 1957 on the mass irrigation campaign, three in 1958 on the communization, three in 1964 on the socialist education campaign, and five in 1966 on the Great Proletarian Cultural Revolution. See Oksenberg, 'Methods of Communication within the Chinese Bureaucracy', 14.

72. Undoubtedly, provinces attached their priorities to different alternatives as later chapters will elaborate in detail. Important at this juncture, however, is to establish that provinces indeed had multiple alternatives for the implementation of decollectivization.

73. There are generally three kinds of measurement for local discretion: (1) that of fiscal autonomy indicated by patterns of budgetary sharing or the extent of local dependence on central subsidies; (2) that of personnel control indicated by shares of centrally appointed officials in the local administration; and (3) that of local variation in implementation. It is argued here that, while the former two measures concern the input dimension of decentralization, the local-variation measurement gets closer to the manifested outcome of decentralization. It has its own problems: since no ready-made indicators are available, researchers must improvise them for the particular policy concerned. Such methodological difficulties explain why the fiscal indicators were so widely utilized in most of the studies on decentralization. See Chung, 'Studies of Central–Provincial Relations in the People's Republic of China', 492, 499–500.

3

Central Control and Provincial Discretion during Decollectivization: System-Level Analyses

One of the most astounding changes that occurred in the Chinese countryside in the post-Mao era was decollectivization—the dissolution of collective forms of agricultural production. Despite the colossal nature of the changes involved, which can be justifiably characterized as a 'great reversal',[1] it seems that we are just beginning to comprehend the highly complex process of this far-reaching transformation. While some studies are available on the processes of policy-making at the top (i.e. the central party and government level) and of policy implementation at the very bottom (i.e. the commune-township and production brigade-village levels), few have examined the role of the intervening levels and, most importantly, the provinces.[2]

This study utilizes an intergovernmental perspective with which the operational effects of post-Mao administrative decentralization on provincial discretion in the implementation of the household responsibility reform are investigated. The household responsibility reform refers to a set of policy measures that brought about fundamental changes in the incentive structure and the size of the primary unit of agricultural production in 1978–84.[3] While there were a variety of responsibility systems based upon the production brigade, the production team, the work group, the individual labourer, or the household, this study concentrates on the last form as it was the system that the overwhelming majority of peasants in China eventually settled with.[4] More specifically, two types of household-based responsibility systems are the focus of this study: *baochan daohu* and *baogan daohu*.

Baochan daohu, translated as 'household production quotas', is a system of contract between the production team and the individual household, under which peasant households are responsible only for the production of the assigned quota and entitled to bonuses if the quota is over-fulfilled, and decisions pertaining to cropping, investment, and management are still made by the collective (that is, the production team). Payments are also centrally distributed by the collective according to the work-points system. Under *baogan daohu*, translated as the system of 'household contract with fixed levies', each household as the sole managing and accounting unit is allocated 'contract land' for its own use although its ownership remains with the collective. Almost all production and investment decisions are made by the households. Distribution is not based upon the work-points system: excluding the delivery quotas and agricultural taxes to the state and investment and welfare funds to the collective, all the rest is retained by the households for their free disposal.[5]

This chapter, examining the system-level effects of post-Mao administrative decentralization on the implementation of the household responsibility reform, consists of five sections. The first section traces the centre's evolving positions on the reform of household farming. The second presents a large set of implementation data on twenty-six provinces in terms of their pace of decollectivization during 1979–83. The third section measures the extent of interprovincial variation in the pace and pattern of implementing the decollectivization reform. The fourth examines to what extent the interprovincial variation identified was induced by different provincial conditions and interests. The final section offers concluding observations regarding the effects of post-Mao administrative decentralization on provincial discretion in implementation.

THE EVOLVING POSITION OF THE CENTRE ON DECOLLECTIVIZATION

The position of the central leadership—that is the Party Centre—varied considerably over time and over different systems of responsibility. Not only was the Party Centre itself divided as it was seriously plagued with power struggles, but also some responsibility systems were initiated at the grass-roots level often without central approval.[6] Spontaneous local initiatives were manifested not only with the relatively moderate (in terms of the extent to which the particular system departed from the Maoist norms of collective production and remuneration) system of 'production quotas to the work group' (*baochan daozu*) but also with the more radical systems of *baochan daohu* and *baogan daohu*.[7]

Given the significant inputs from spontaneous local innovation and experimentation, the central leadership had constantly to follow up, review, and regulate the developments to ensure that local spontaneity would remain well within the politically and ideologically acceptable boundary at a given time. In fact, the centre's official position on the household responsibility systems evolved over time from 'prohibition' (*buxu*) and 'conditional permission' (*chuwai*) to 'allowance' (*yunxu*), and eventually to 'popularization' (*tuiguang*).[8] An excellent study is available for this entire evolutionary process in which various responsibility systems ranging from 'task rates' (*dinge baogong*) to 'comprehensive contracts' (*dabaogan*) were introduced, opposed, permitted, endorsed, and popularized at the central stage of policy-making.[9] It is, therefore, only necessary for us to focus on the evolution of the centre's position on two household-based responsibility systems in particular.

The initial position of the Party Centre on *baochan daohu* was that of strong opposition. One important document passed at the Third Plenum of the Eleventh Central Committee held in November 1978—'Regulations on the Management of the Rural People's Commune' (*Nongcun renmin gongshe gongzuo tiaoli*)—clearly stipulated that *baochan daohu* was not permitted to be implemented.[10] According to the 'Party Centre's Notice Regarding the Summary of the Discussion Meeting on the Problems of Rural Work' (*Zhonggong zhongyang pizhuan guojia nongwei dangzu baosong de guanyu nongcun gongzuo wenti zuotanhui jiyao de tongzhi*) issued on 3 April 1979, 'except for the special cases that have been approved by the county party committee, no one is to be allowed to implement *baochan daohu*'.[11] The 'Party Centre's Decision Concerning Certain Problems in Accelerating the Development of Agriculture' (*Zhonggong zhongyang guanyu jiakuai nongye fazhan ruogan wenti de jueding*)—originally drafted at the Third Plenum, subsequently revised, and officially endorsed at the Fourth Plenum of September 1979—relaxed its across-the-board opposition to *baochan daohu* by delineating three functional and geographical categories for which exceptions could be made. These categories were: (1) those engaged in special sideline occupations (*teshu fuye*) more suitable for household management; (2) areas that were peripheral, distant, and mountainous (*bianyuanshanqu*); and (3) single households that lived in isolation due to transportation difficulties (*jiaotong bubian de danjia duhu*).[12]

By September 1980, the centre's position on *baochan daohu* became more permissive. According to a 'notice' (*tongzhi*) issued by the Party Centre, 'in addition to those peripheral, distant, and mountainous areas (which had already been permitted to implement *baochan daohu* by the Fourth Plenum decision), "poor and backward areas" (*pinkun luohou diqu*) and "production units heavily dependent on state subsidies" (*sankaodui*) could also adopt *baochan daohu* and even *baogan daohu*.'[13] This document merits our attention in two respects: (1) economic factors (poverty and backwardness) were newly added to the geographical and functional considerations; and (2) *baogan daohu* was also allowed for the first time, though only conditionally. By August 1981, the centre's position on *baochan daohu* and *baogan daohu* became much more liberalized. According to a survey mission composed of seventeen teams (involving more than 140 people including ministers and vice-ministers of the agriculture-related bureaucracy or *nongye xitong*) sent to fifteen provinces, '*baochan daohu* and *baogan daohu* are not only methods of relieving poverty but also ways of enhancing productivity; and neither has changed the production relations of the collective economy.'[14]

The formal co-optation of *baochan daohu* and *baogan daohu* as officially endorsed forms of responsibility systems was made in Central Document No. 1 of 1982 (hereafter CD [82] No. 1) which stipulated that 'both *baochan daohu* and *baogan daohu* are the production responsibility systems of the socialist economy.'[15] Subsequently, *baochan daohu* and *baogan daohu*, or *shuangbao* as they were called collectively, became the key policy to follow although *baogan daohu* was generally more popular than *baochan daohu* due to the wider decisional latitude the former granted to the peasant households.[16]

While the foregoing chronological overview may generate an impression that the entire process of decollectivization was well regulated and controlled by the centre, that was not the case for the first half of the period concerned (i.e. 1979–81). A couple of provinces had consistently been going ahead of the official policy prescription in implementing the household responsibility reform. As of July 1980, that was even before the dissemination of CD [80] No. 75 of September 1980 that permitted poor and backward areas to implement the household responsibility systems, Guizhou and Anhui already had 50 and 30 per cent, respectively, of their production teams implementing *baochan daohu*.[17] As of June 1981, that was half a year before the issuance of CD [82] No. 1, Guizhou, Gansu, Anhui, and Ningxia had 95, 72, 69, and 52 per cent, respectively, of their production teams under household farming.[18] These provinces constituted pace-setters in the sense that their provincial leadership did not prohibit province-wide experimentation and diffusion of local innovations related to household farming by taking advantage of such vague designations as 'distant, mountainous, poor, and backward regions' as well as their political linkages with Beijing.[19]

The local experimentation with and the popularization of household farming in these 'pioneer' provinces prior to the centre's approval can be partly attributed to the slow policy responses from the Party Centre. Important to note is that the centre's slow responses may well have reflected its new approach to policy implementation. That is, the cautious approach was a calculated choice on the part of the 'reformist' centre without the prestige of Mao to solicit provincial initiatives in popularizing the policy whose potential impact (and costs), in both ideological and economic terms, could be enormous. On the other hand, more importantly for our concern, this cautious approach also represented its commitment to the principle of *yindi zhiyi* ('implement according to local conditions').[20]

As early as April 1979—well before its conditional permission of *baochan daohu*—the Party Centre warned against a standardized policy by stressing the need to maintain various forms of responsibility systems suitable for different regions. Strict observation of the *yindi zhiyi* principle and avoidance of standardization were consistent themes of the central directives during 1979–80.[21] CD [80] No. 75, for instance, was very clear on the importance of taking into account the varied conditions of different regions:

Our land is vast with a backward economy and unbalanced development. Besides, agricultural production, unlike industrial production, is highly contingent upon various constraints of natural conditions. In accordance with actual needs and varied situations, different responsibility systems must be allowed for different areas, communes, brigades, and even production teams.[22]

Accordingly, the document recommended three responsibility systems for three different categories of regions: (1) a brigade-based system of 'specialized production contract' (*zhuanye chengbao*) for regions such as Jiangsu, Zhejiang, three north-east provinces, and suburban districts of Beijing, Shanghai, and Tianjin where the level of mechanization was high and diversified production was well developed; (2) *baochan daohu* and *baogan daohu* for 'peripheral, distant, mountainous, poor, and backward areas'; and (3) team or work-group based systems for most other areas.[23]

The emphasis on *yindi zhiyi* continued to dominate the process of decollectivization during 1981 and the commitment was officially reaffirmed in CD [82] No. 1.[24] Up until the second half of 1982, therefore, the pace of decollectivization varied greatly among different provinces, indicating the absence of a centrally imposed push. In December 1981, for instance, Guizhou had 98.2 per cent of its teams implementing *baogan daohu*, while the comparable figure for Jilin was only 10 per cent for *baochan daohu* and *baogan daohu* combined. By June 1982, Anhui had 92 per cent of its teams under *baogan daohu*, while Heilongjiang had only 8.7 per cent.[25]

The permission for provincial variations and the avoidance of political push ended quite abruptly in mid-1982, however. As early as April 1982, the Administrative Office of the Party Centre (*zhongyang bangongting*) issued a notice that severely criticized the provinces whose pace of adopting the household responsibility systems was deemed too sluggish.[26] In the summer of 1982, such top leaders as Hu Yaobang and Zhao Ziyang made inspection trips to several sluggish provinces where they severely criticized the provincial leadership.[27] Key newspapers like *People's Daily*, too, carried articles that stressed the effectiveness of household farming and created increased pressure on the sluggish provinces by publishing the performance figures on fast-implementing regions.[28] In October 1982, the Chinese Research Centre for Rural Development (*Zhongguo nongcun fazhan yanjiu zhongxin*), which had constituted the locomotive of rural reforms under the directorship of Du Runsheng, offered harsh criticisms of the sluggish provinces and called for the continued relaxation of regulations against the spread of the household responsibility systems.[29]

Most importantly, on 5 November 1982, Wan Li (then, vice-premier in charge of agriculture) delivered a keynote speech at the National Agricultural Secretaries Conference and the Work Conference on Rural Ideology and Politics, which was published in late December. Considering the more than one-and-a-half month lapse between the speech and its publication, the content of the speech might have been considered controversial. And the published speech indeed contained some surprising recommendations in favour of the swift popularization of *baogan daohu*:

Comparatively speaking, the responsibility system reform has not been successful in all corners of our countryside. In fact, there exists certain passivity [*xiaoji xianxiang*] in many areas, and in some areas such passivity is of a very bad sort. . . . Of many different responsibility systems, *baogan daohu* is the one the masses like the most. . . . [Yet] the implementation of *baogan daohu* has not been very smooth due to obstruction in the forms of misunderstanding and misconception on the part of some leading cadres . . . [who] were afraid of *baochan daozu* and *baochan daohu* [and] would be far more afraid of *baogan daohu*. . . . Since there still are some people who resist this system of responsibility, we have to help them to correctly understand the situation by educating and advising them. [emphasis added][30]

Wan Li's speech stipulated two things. First, *baogan daohu* was the policy considered to be most popular among the peasants and, therefore, was to be the focus of swift popularization. Second, there existed serious opposition to the system of household farming and it was surely to be corrected.[31] The impact of Wan's speech was both quick and enormous.[32] With a few exceptional 'resisters' (most notably, Heilongjiang, Liaoning, Jilin, Zhejiang, and Xinjiang), almost all other provinces had more than 90 per cent of their production teams under the household responsibility systems—mainly *baogan daohu*—by the end of 1982. An emphasis on speed was absent in Wan's speech, yet the overall pace of decollectivization accelerated considerably within less than two months, which was quite reminiscent of the Maoist era. Hebei, with 73 per cent of production teams under *baogan daohu* in November, had to reach 96 per cent by December. Hubei, with 50 per cent of its teams under *baogan daohu* in October, accomplished 94 per cent by December.[33]

In addition to the numerous media reports in support of household farming, the dissemination of CD [83] No. 1 passed at a Politburo meeting generated more direct and heavier pressure on the few remaining sluggish provinces.[34] Consequently, by February and March 1983, 'resisters' like Jilin and Liaoning had 94.5 and 92 per cent, respectively, of their teams under *baogan daohu*. Even the most fierce resister, Heilongjiang, had 73 per cent of its teams under *baogan daohu* by February 1983.[35] In December 1983, the Party Centre proudly boasted of the predominance of household-based farming in the five areas with advanced levels of economic development and agricultural mechanization: Jilin (95%), Suzhou region in Jiangsu (93%), Yantai region in Shandong (90%), Heilongjiang (85.4%), and suburban Shanghai (73%). And the national figure, too, reached 98.3 per cent for *baogan daohu* in December 1983.[36]

Why did the central leadership in general and Wan Li in particular have to intervene at the later stage to speed up the pace of decollectivization, which had previously been left for the provinces to determine as they saw fit? What accounts for such a drastic transformation of the context of imple-mentation?[37] More importantly for this study, how did the provinces react to Beijing's imposition? Which provinces quickly complied and which provinces continued to resist even after Wan Li's speech? How are the provincial variations in responding to the centre related to different condi-tions of the provinces? In order to answer these questions, it is necessary first to investigate the pace of decollectivization for as many provinces as possible.

ASSESSING THE DATA ON PROVINCIAL IMPLEMENTATION OF DECOLLECTIVIZATION

Quite a number of studies have to date been conducted on the process in which the decollectivization reform had been decided and implemented.[38] As discussed in Chapter 1, there are crucial differences between these studies concerning the extent of state intervention and local variation. Some stress the role of peasant power in dissolving the collectives, others under-score the imposition by the central state, and still others focus on the role of local governments and cadres as the key intervening variables.[39] Another source of debate concerns the reasons for regional and local variation. Most studies attribute them to different economic conditions of the provinces and lower administrative units implying that provinces were then granted a sig-nificant level of discretion to implement the controversial reform in accor-dance with varied local conditions. These studies differ, however, on the factors responsible for the variations. Some take wealth—or the lack of it—as the most important variable, others argue for cropping patterns, and still others focus on the level of mechanization, collective sidelines, land/labour ratios, the average size of production teams and so on.[40] Yet few take up the political variables to account for regional variations.

Why do these studies present different and even contradicting pictures of the decollectivization processes? There may have been some biases intrinsic to the ways the research for some of these studies was conducted. First, several studies are based on field trips made in January–July and October 1981.[41] These time-points, as discussed earlier in this chapter, come before the dissemination of CD [82] No. 1 in which Beijing's firm commit-ment to the popularization of household farming was first manifested. Therefore, it was natural for these studies to believe the local patterns of decollectivization to have varied rather significantly. On the other hand, some studies are based on interviews conducted in mid-1983 with those who had recently returned to their homes probably during the Lunar New Year Festival of early February.[42] This time-point is precisely when the Party Centre was pushing the provinces for a faster popularization of the house-hold responsibility systems. It was thus quite natural for those interviewees to relay their impression that the process was administratively imposed from the top down.

Second, many of these studies based on field work, field trips, and émigré interviews take either communes or brigades as their primary units of analysis.[43] These units are perhaps too small in size and located too low in the administrative hierarchy to provide meaningful generalizations as to the province- or nationwide process of the decollectivization reform. Furthermore, they often have only three to five case units in a single province, thereby causing the problem of 'more variables than cases'. Additionally, despite the presentation of many variables assumed to have caused regional variations, with the notable exceptions of Lin and Yang, all other studies have fallen short of establishing persuasive linkages between these variables and the provincial and local pace of decollectivization. Kelliher, on the basis of (very brief) case studies of Anhui and Hubei, provides a more persuasive picture of the national trend than Zhou who argues for an all-China peasant-power thesis, although the former, too, suffers from the problem of excluding key provinces in north and north–east China which played a crucial role in shaping the overall process of decollectivization.[44]

Third, a few studies that utilized the provincial level of analysis are based on surveys of media reports and on statistical analyses of the data from statistical yearbooks.[45] Since many of the source materials utilized by these studies were published during the very period of decollectivization, a significant portion of local implementation data might have reliability problems. Chinese official data are generally notorious for their low reliability due to the pervasive practice of amalgamating political considerations with the reporting of performance statistics. The data on the provincial pace of decollectivization was probably no exception in this regard. In the case of Hubei, for instance, its provincial newspaper pointed to 94 per cent as the province's rate of adopting *baogan daohu* in December 1982, while a later publication indicates a far lower figure of 75 per cent for the same time-point.

The foregoing discussion points to the direction this study is heading. First, as a post-facto analysis of the decollectivization reform, this study covers the entire period of 1978–84 and seeks to take the benefits of hindsight. Second, in order to capture a nationwide pattern of decollectivization, this study takes the provinces to be the principal level of analysis.[46] Third, this study utilizes a large set of newly available data on the provincial pace of decollectivization, much of which contradicts the data published during the decollectivization reform. Fourth, statistical methods are employed to measure the scope of interprovincial variation and to establish the relationships between key independent variables and the provincial pace of decollectivization as the dependent variable. Fifth, multiple case studies are adopted to show in detail both varied patterns of provincial implementation and political variables that are difficult to quantify.

Documentary research has produced a large set of data from all of China's twenty-six provinces.[47] Formerly, the central and provincial media were the only major sources of information on the provincial pace of decollectivization and, more often than not, they provided partial, fragmented, and often distorted information. More recently, however, various central and provincial publications—both issue- and region-specific—were made available.[48] While not all provinces have the same temporal data points, a large enough number of provinces have comparable data points so that they can be systematically compared. The implementation data for the twenty-six provinces for the period of 1979–83 are shown in Table 3.1.

MEASURING INTERPROVINCIAL VARIATIONS IN THE PACE OF DECOLLECTIVIZATION

As discussed in Chapter 2, various measures of post-Mao administrative decentralization were geared to the promotion of local initiatives and discretion by avoiding the political imposition of standardized policy. Ideally, administrative decentralization is likely to reduce the incentive of the centre to suppress local interests, while it is likely to expand room for provincial discretion in implementation. If we use the size of interprovincial variation as the proxy for the scope of provincial discretion, the hypothesis is stated as follows: had the post-Mao decentralization measures been effective, we would expect a relatively high level of variation in the provincial pace of decollectivization.

Table 3.2 is a retabulation of the provincial implementation data presented in Table 3.1, focusing on the two time-points of June 1981 and December 1982.[49] From these implementation data, we derive an estimate of interprovincial variation for each time-point. In measuring the average extent to which provinces varied among themselves in adopting the household responsibility reform, the value of the coefficient of variation—standard deviation divided by the mean—is used.[50] Table 3.3 presents the mean performance, the standard deviation, and the coefficient of variation for seventeen provinces on which the implementation data are available for both time-points.[51]

As for June 1981, both the standard deviation and coefficient of variation indicate that the size of interprovincial variation was very large. After a one-and-a-half year lapse, however, during which the Party Centre had become strongly committed to the swift nationwide popularization of household farming, the mean performance more than doubled from 38 per cent in June 1981 to 81 per cent in December 1982. As a result of Beijing's strong push for its swift popularization during 1982, the size of interprovincial variation expressed in the value of the coefficient of variation dropped by a half. That is, once the centre asserted itself, the level of

TABLE 3.1. *The provincial pace of decollectivization, 1979–1983 (% of a province's production teams under household farming)*

	1979	1980	1981	1982	1983
Nationwide		1: 1.02[abc] 12: 14.4[c] 5.0 (g)[c]	6: 28.2[c] 11.3 (g)[c] 7: 32.0[b] 10: 45.1[c] 38.0 (g)[c] 12: 50.0[c]	6: 71.9[a] 67.0 (g)[a] 12: 78.2[c]	1: 78.7[g] 8: 93.0[c] 12: 98.3 (g)[a]
Anhui	12: 10.0 (c)[bcX]	3: 25.0 (c)[a] 7: 30.0 (c)[a] 10: 43.0 (c)[b] 12: 66.9[B] 21.1 (g)[B]	6: 69.3[c] 12: 84.6[X]	2: 90.0 (g)[h] 6: 97.0[X] 91.7 (g)[B] 12: 98.9[bh] 95.0 (g)[bh]	
Fujian			6: 33.1[c]	6: 80+[j] 12: 91.0 (g)[i]	
Gansu		8: 38.8[C] 12: 60.0[D]	6: 72.2[c] 8: 80.0[D] 45.0 (g)[D]	6: 92.4[A] 12: 99.0 (g)[s]	
Guangdong		5: 25.0 (c)[Y]	6: 41.8[c]	12: 91.8 (g)[s]	
Guangxi		6: 7.1 (g)[L]	6: 35.7[Lc] 12: 62.4[Z]	6: 93.0 (g)[s] 12: 96.3 (g)[sZ]	
Guizhou		3: 17.0 (c)[a] 7: 50.0 (c)[a] 12: 61.8 (g)[K]	4: 86.8(g)[F] 6: 95.0[c] 12: 98.2 (g)[K]	12: 99.7 (g)[s]	
Hebei		9: 1.0 (g)[P]	1: 7.0 (g)[l] 7: 36.4[P] 29.0 (g)[P] 10: 50+[c] 12: 65.0 (g)[l]	7: 67.0 (g)[P] 11: 73.3(g)[l] 12: 96.0 (g)[cP]	
Heilongjiang			9: 0.7[x]	5: 8.7 (g)[m] 12: 12.0[x]	2: 73.0 (g)[m] 3: 85.0[E] 10: 87.1[x] 12: 90+ (g)[t]
Henan			6: 33.2[c]	12: 93.1 (g)[M]	
Hubei			12: 30.0 (g)[y]	4: 39.1 (g)[F] 10: 50.0 (g)[o] 12: 94.0 (g)[o] 75.3 (g)[y]	12: 99.2 (g)[y]
Hunan		4: 1.5[l] 0.6 (g)[l]	4: 11.2[l] 12: 95.0[l]	12: 98.1[v] 93.0 (g)[F]	
Jiangsu			12: 21.7[F] 12.0 (g)[F]	7: 61.9[N]	7: 98.6[N]
Jiangxi				6: 80+[j] 12: 94.1[S]	
Jilin		12: 1.0[f]	9: 4.0[R] 12: 10.0[f]	6: 28.0 (g)[R] 10: 29.0 (g)[m] 12: 30.0 (g)[fR]	2: 94.5 (g)[nF] 12: 95.5 (g)[R]

TABLE 3.1. *(cont.)*

	1979	1980	1981	1982	1983
Liaoning			6: 6.4^F	10: 31.0 (g)^m 12: 38.7^r 31.8 (g)^r	3: 92.0 (g)^m 12: 90.9^r 87.9 (g)^r
Neimenggu		12: 40.0 (c)^2	6: 40.1^c	6: 80+^{j} 12: 97.1^s 90.0 (g)^s	
Ningxia		8: 1.4 (c)^U	6: 51.6^U	6: 90+^{j}	
Qinghai				6: 68.8^R 65.6 (g)^R 12: 92.0 (g)^s	
Shaanxi				6: 30.0 (g)^T 10: 90.0^p 86.6 (g)^p 12: 90.0 (g)^T	12: 99.2^T
Shandong	12: 2.4^G (g = 0)	6: 7.1 (c)^L 12: 27.6 (c)^G (g = 0)	6: 38.2^e 12: 55.9^G 47.5(g)^G	3: 62.9^L 5: 69.3^G 62.7 (g)^G 12: 96.8^H 82.8 (g)^s	3: 96.8 (g)^L 1.2 (c)^L
Shanxi		12: 9.5 (g)^q	6: 58.4^q 12: 79.3^W 24.1 (g)^F	12: 81.7^z	1: 95.0 (g)^q
Sichuan		8: 9.1^w 0.16 (g)^w	12: 62.3^w 43.7 (g)^w	11: 98.0^{kw} 89.2 (g)^{kw}	3: 99.3^{kw}
Xinjiang		10: 23.8^u 17.5 (g)^u	6: 33.3^c 12: 42.2^l 19.4 (g)^l	12: 82.5 (g)^l	12: 94.6^u
Xizang			6: 39.2^c	6: 82.0 (g)^V 12: 90.0^s	
Yunnan		12: 22.7^J 13.3 (g)^J	5: 35.5^{cJ}	6: 84.2(g)^F 12: 91.7 (g)^J	3: 97.4 (g)^J
Zhejiang				12: 90.0^O	

Notes: Figures to the left of the colon refer to the month of the respective year and those to the right denote the percentages of each province's production teams under the household responsibility systems; (c) and (g) refer to *baochan daohu* and *baogan daohu*, respectively. Superscripts refer to the sources and some have multiple sources.

Sources:
[a] Guo Shutian, *Zhongguo nongcun gaige yu fazhan shinian* (Beijing: Nongye chubanshe, 1990), 7–10.
[b] Lu Xueyi, *Lianchan chengbao zerenzhi yanjiu* (Shanghai: Shanghai renmin chubanshe, 1986), 80.
[c] Zhongguo shehuikexueyuan nongcun fazhan yanjiusuo (ed.), *Nongye shengchan zerenzhi lunwenji* (Beijing: Renmin chubanshe, 1986), 87–8, 329, 471.
[d] 'Quanguo nongye shengchan zerenzhi wenti taolunhui jiyao', *Nongye jingji wenti*, 2 (1982), 3.
[e] Interview in Jinan in 1992.
[f] *Renmin ribao*, 22 Jan. and 1 Aug. 1983.
[g] Xinhua News Agency, 8 Feb. 1983, in *Heilongjiang ribao*, 10 Feb. 1983.

(cont.)

Notes to Table 3.1. (*cont.*)

[h] *Anhui ribao*, 23 Feb. 1982 and 7 Jan. 1983.

[i] *Fujian ribao*, 27 Jan. 1983.

[j] Zhang Guangyou, 'Guanyu shuangbao zerenzhi fazhan qushi de tantao', *Nongye jingji wenti*, 7 (1982), 24.

[k] Lo Chuhua, 'Nongye shengchan zerenzhi fazhanxingshi he shixianzhong tichu de jige wenti', *Nongye jingji wenti*, 3 (1983), 3.

[l] *Hebei ribao*, 10 Dec. 1982.

[m] *Nongmin bao*, 22 Mar. 1983, cited in Zweig, 'Context and Content in Policy Implementation', 273.

[n] *Jilin ribao*, 19 Feb. 1983.

[o] *Hubei ribao*, 29 Oct. and 26 Dec. 1982.

[p] *Shaanxi ribao*, 5 Nov. 1982.

[q] *Shanxi ribao*, 20 June 1981 and 13 Feb. 1983.

[r] *Liaoning jingji tongji nianjian 1984* (Shenyang: Liaoning renmin chubanshe, 1984), III-63.

[s] *Zhongguo nongye nianjian 1983* (Beijing: Nongye chubanshe, 1984), 172, 183, 185, 189, 190, 195, 197.

[t] *Heilongjiang ribao*, 1 Apr. 1984.

[u] *Xinjiang ribao*, 22 Nov. 1980 and 28 Mar. 1984.

[v] *Hunansheng tongjinianjian 1982* (Changsha: Hunan renmin chubanshe, 1984), 52.

[w] *Sichuansheng nongye hezuo jingji shiliao* (Chengdu: Sichuan kexue jishu chubanshe, 1989), 702.

[x] *Heilongjiang Nongye hezuoshi* (Beijing: Zhonggong dangshi ziliao chubanshe, 1990), 492, 530–1, 555, 560.

[y] *Hubei nongcun jingji, 1949–1989* (Beijing: Zhongguo tongji chubanshe, 1990), 108.

[z] *Shanxi Sishinian* (Beijing: Zhongguo tongji chubanshe, 1989), II-104.

[A] *Gansu sishinian* (Lanzhou: Zhongguo tongji chubanshe, 1989), 52.

[B] Historical Archives Commission of the Anhui Provincial Political Consultative Conference (ed.), *Nongcun gaige de xingqi* (Beijing: Zhongguo wenshi chubanshe, 1993), 9–10.

[C] Lu Xueyi, *Dangdai zhongguo nongcun yu dangdai zhongguo nongmin* (Beijing: Zhishi chubanshe, 1991), 45.

[D] Hartford, 'Socialist Agriculture Is Dead', 40.

[E] Zhou Qiren (ed.), *Nongcun biange yu zhongguo fazhan 1978–89* (Hong Kong: Oxford University Press, 1994), 64.

[F] *Nongcun jingji zhengce huibian 1981–1983* (Beijing: Nongcun duwu chubanshe, i. 1984), 158, 203, 265, 425, 565.

[G] Shandong Provincial Party Committee, *Shandongsheng nongye hezuohua shiliaoji* (Jinan: Shandong renmin chubanshe, 1990), ii. 732.

[H] Research Office of the Shandong Provincial Party Committee, *Shandong Sishinian* (Jinan: Shandong renmin chubanshe, 1989), 150.

[I] *Dangdai zhongguo de Hunan* (Beijing: Zhongguo shehuikexue chubanshe, 1990), i. 201–3.

[J] *Dangdai zhongguo de Yunnan* (Beijing: Dangdai zhongguo chubanshe, 1991), i. 213–15.

[K] *Dangdai zhongguo de Guizhou* (Beijing: Zhongguo shehuikexue chubanshe, 1989), i. 118, 132.

[L] *Dangdai zhongguo de Shandong* (Beijing: Zhongguo shehuikexue chubanshe, 1989), i. 290–4, 302.

[M] *Dangdai zhongguo de Henan* (Beijing: Zhongguo shehuikexue chubanshe, 1990), i. 180.

[N] *Dangdai zhongguo de Jiangsu* (Beijing: Zhongguo shehuikexue chubanshe, 1989), i. 148.

[O] *Dangdai zhongguo de Zhejiang* (Beijing: Zhongguo shehuikexue chubanshe, 1989), i. 132.

[P] *Dangdai zhongguo de Hebei* (Beijing: Zhongguo shehuikexue chubanshe, 1990), i. 578.

[Q] *Dangdai zhongguo de Qinghai* (Beijing: Dangdai zhongguo chubanshe, 1991), i. 130.

[R] *Dangdai zhongguo de Jilin* (Beijing: Dangdai zhongguo chubanshe, 1991), i. 182–4.

[S] *Dangdai zhongguo de Jiangxi* (Beijing: Dangdai zhongguo chubanshe, 1991), i. 96.

[T] *Dangdai zhongguo de Shaanxi* (Beijing: Dangdai zhongguo chubanshe, 1991), i. 164–5.

[U] *Dangdai zhongguo de Ningxia* (Beijing: Zhongguo shehuikexue chubanshe, 1990), i. 204–5.

[V] *Dangdai zhongguo de Xizang* (Beijing: Dangdai zhongguo chubanshe, 1991), ii. 8.

[W] *Dangdai zhongguo de Shanxi* (Beijing: Dangdai zhongguo chubanshe, 1991), i. 185–6.

[X] *Dangdai zhongguo de Anhui* (Beijing: Dangdai zhongguo chubanshe, 1991), i. 186, 188, 189.

[Y] *Dangdai zhongguo de Guangdong* (Beijing: Dangdai zhongguo chubanshe, 1991), i. 158.

[Z] *Dangdai zhongguo de Guangxi* (Beijing: Dangdai zhongguo chubanshe, 1992), i. 164.

[1] *Dangdai zhongguo de Xinjiang* (Beijing: Dangdai zhongguo chubanshe, 1991), 185–6.

[2] *Dangdai zhongguo de Neimenggu* (Beijing: Dangdai zhongguo chubanshe, 1992), 147.

TABLE 3.2. *Data on provincial decollectivization at two time-points*

	June 1981 (*baochan daohu* and *baogan daohu*)	December 1982 (*baogan daohu* only)
Anhui	69.3	95.0
Fujian	33.1	91.0
Gansu	72.2	99.0
Guangdong	41.8	91.8
Guangxi	35.7	96.3
Guizhou	95.0	99.7
Hebei	36.4	96.0
Heilongjiang	0.7[b]	12.0
Henan	33.2	93.1
Hubei	—	75.3
Hunan	11.2[a]	93.0
Jiangsu	—	—
Jiangxi	—	94.1
Jilin	4.0[b]	30.0
Liaoning	6.4	31.8
Neimenggu	40.1	90.0
Ningxia	51.6	—
Qinghai	—	92.0
Shaanxi	—	90.0
Shandong	38.2	82.8
Shanxi	58.4	95.0[c]
Sichuan	—	89.2
Xinjiang	33.3	82.5
Xizang	39.2	—
Yunnan	35.5	91.7
Zhejiang	—	—

[a] This figure is for April.
[b] This figure is for September.
[c] This figure is for January 1983.

TABLE 3.3. *Provincial variations in the pace of decollectivization*

N = 26	June 1981	December 1982
	n = 17	n = 17
Mean performance (%)	37.9	80.6
Standard deviation	25.2	27.4
Coefficient of variation	.67	.34

provincial compliance doubled, effectively sabotaging the norms of *yindi zhiyi* based on expanded local discretion.

What merits our attention is the standard deviation value for December 1982. Despite the sharp increase in the mean performance, the standard deviation for December 1982 increased by 2.2 over that of June 1981. This was mainly because, while twelve out of the seventeen provinces had 90 per cent or more of their production teams under household farming, three of the remaining provinces—Heilongjiang, Jilin, and Liaoning—were resisting the province-wide implementation of household farming. That is, while Beijing was generally successful in inducing a majority of the provinces to speed up the adoption of household farming during 1982, a few recalcitrant provinces continued to delay its popularization. This finding is crucial since some provinces dared to take advantage of their discretion granted under the decentralization framework stressing *yindi zhiyi*.[52]

We may conduct a small but interesting experiment here by contrasting the decollectivization data with two other sets of provincial implementation data from the pre-reform era.[53] One set concerns the provincial implementation of agricultural co-operativization during 1954–6 by which peasant households were organized into 'advanced producers' co-operatives' (*gaoji shengchan hezuoshe*; hereafter APCs). The other set contains the provincial implementation data on the communization during 1958 by which peasant households (an average of 2,000 per commune) were incorporated into the much larger unit of the 'people's communes' (*renmin gongshe*). These two data sets are given in Table 3.4.

A short note is due on these two pre-reform periods which, despite the short temporal gap of two to three years, were under drastically different norms of policy implementation. The co-operativization movement (i.e. initially for a basic transition to lower-stage producers' co-operatives) was first decided by the Politburo in October 1954, only to be met by the State Council's call for a halt in March 1955. Yet, a series of subsequent meetings and decisions, including the second session of the First National People's Congress in July and the January 1956 Politburo meeting, steered the movement in the direction of accelerated nationwide popularization.[54] Nevertheless, by the summer of 1956 for which provincial implementation data are available, provinces had a period of almost two years for its implementation. In stark contrast, while the idea of communization was first proposed by Mao at the Nanning Conference in January 1958 and positively received at the Chengdu Conference in March 1958, its nationwide popularization was officially stipulated at the Beidaihe Conference in August 1958. Within only one month after the Beidaihe decision, as the September 1958 data in Table 3.4 indicate, almost all provinces displayed an extreme level of swift and standardized compliance.[55]

Table 3.5 presents the mean performance, standard deviation, and coefficient of variation for the provincial pace of co-operativization and

TABLE 3.4. *Data on provincial co-operativization and communization (% of each province's households under the respective system)*

	Implementation of co-operativization by Summer 1956	Implementation of communization by September 1958
Anhui	80.7	100.0
Fujian	62.2	95.1
Gansu	34.5	100.0
Guangdong	44.1	100.0
Guangxi	98.2	100.0
Guizhou	51.6	94.5
Hebei	99.4	100.0
Heilongjiang	98.7	100.0
Henan	97.2	100.0
Hubei	69.0	96.1
Hunan	13.8	100.0
Jiangsu	78.9	99.4
Jiangxi	62.2	92.0
Jilin	95.7	100.0
Liaoning	91.8	100.0
Neimenggu	77.5	98.6
Ningxia	—	67.3
Qinghai	92.0	100.0
Shaanxi	65.2	100.0
Shandong	67.2	100.0
Shanxi	97.9	100.0
Sichuan	7.4	99.1
Xinjiang	42.1	59.3
Xizang	—	—
Yunnan	27.9	31.0
Zhejiang	60.0	100.0

Source: Teiwes, 'Provincial Politics', 168, 172.

TABLE 3.5. *Extent of provincial variation in the pre-reform periods*

	Co-operativization	Communization
N = 26	n = 24	n = 25
Mean performance (%)	67.3	93.3
Standard deviation	27.9	16.5
Coefficient of variation	.41	.18

communization. Table 3.5 offers a couple of interesting points regarding the norms of policy implementation during these two pre-reform periods. First, the co-operativization movement entailed a far slower pace of compliance and a much higher level of interprovincial variation than communization. The 1955–6 period is conventionally viewed as one of national integration, political penetration, and functional centralization, while 1958 is largely associated with the 'highly decentralized' Great Leap. How could it be that the size of interprovincial variation was far smaller during the supposedly more decentralized period? The answer reverts back to the point that the decentralization efforts during the Great Leap were mainly fiscal and largely devoid of the administrative dimension, especially pertaining to local policy implementation.[56] More importantly, such 'guided' efforts for decentralization were closely linked with the politics at the Centre which was in turn steered by excessive ideological fervour. Notable outcomes illustrated in Tables 3.4 and 3.5 are thus self-explanatory: (1) an extremely high mean compliance rate of 93.3 per cent within just one month of the formal policy decision; (2) fifteen provinces that reached 100 per cent; and (3) a very low level (0.18) of interprovincial variation.

Second, compared with that of communization, the implementation of co-operativization was much more gradual and involved a higher level of interprovincial variation. It seems that as of 1956 the centre had not yet completely departed from the norms of *yindi zhiyi*.[57] By 1958, however, having gone through the fearful and painful experiences of the anti-Rightist purges, the norms of implementation had been fundamentally transformed so that exercising discretion came to be regarded as pursuing 'departmentalism' and delayed implementation as anti-centre and anti-Mao acts.[58] The implementation of communization thus reflected the operational effects of the dominant systemic norms that had become so excessively ideologized as to make decentralization efforts into empty slogans.

Third, compared to the mid-1950s, Beijing's capacity for administrative monitoring must have significantly improved by the early 1980s, generally reducing the local incentive for deviation. Given that, the interprovincial variation value of 0.67 for the household responsibility reform in June 1981 points to a significant departure from the Maoist pattern of rushed and standardized implementation. For the same reason, even the interprovincial variation value of 0.34 for December 1982 may be interpreted as being at least as equally high as that (0.41) of the co-operativization movement.

Finally, pro forma compliance poses an intricate problem in comparing the implementation dynamics of communization and decollectivization. Pro forma compliance refers to the situation where central policy is carried out only on documents so that the central government is provided with inflated performance statistics. Such distortions were epidemic during the Maoist era and the communization period in particular. The provincial implementation of decollectivization was by no means free of such malpractices.[59] Yet, if the degree of feigned compliance was similar for both periods, the larger size of interprovincial variation for decollectivization testifies to some positive effects of the post-Mao administrative decentralization on the scope of provincial discretion. If the degree of distortion was not similar, that is smaller for the decollectivization reform, it then implies that, under the decentralized context stressing *yindi zhiyi*, provinces had less incentives to inflate their performance statistics. Both scenarios point to an expanded scope of provincial discretion during the post-Mao rural reform relative to the Great Leap period.

ACCOUNTING FOR THE INTERPROVINCIAL VARIATIONS

In order for the interprovincial variations identified to represent the magnitude of discretion actually exercised by the provinces, certain differences in the provincial conditions must be associated with the variations in the provincial pace of decollectivization. That is to say, the stronger the association between the interprovincial variations in the pace of decollectivization and the differences in provincial conditions, the more confidently we can preclude a rival hypothesis that the provinces adopted household farming merely out of a passive compliance to Beijing's pressure without due regard for local conditions.

Independent Variables: Rural Economic Conditions of Provinces

We consider the following five variables related to provincial rural economic conditions: peasant living standards, levels of dependence on collective-run enterprises, levels of mechanization, cropping patterns, and the average size of production teams in each province.[60]

Peasant Living Standards

As noted earlier, Beijing's position on the household responsibility systems took an evolutionary path in that the controversial reform was permitted initially as a means of relieving poverty (i.e. only for poor areas) and later as a way of enhancing productivity (i.e. suitable for nationwide popularization). Central directives, most notably CD [80] No. 75 and CD [82] No. 1, thus recommended that provincial discretion be fully utilized in determining the pace of decollectivization in accordance with the province's 'level of economic development' (*jingji fazhan shuiping*).[61] If the process had indeed been an ideal one in which differing provincial rural economic conditions were taken into consideration, the nationwide process would have reflected a gradual diffusion of household farming from poor (i.e. more receptive to innovation) to affluent provinces (i.e. with less incentives for change). Operationally speaking, the stronger the negative relationship between the provincial pace of decollectivization and the levels of economic development, the more confidently we can argue that the *yindi zhiyi* principle was well observed.

One important question remains: what is meant by 'levels of economic development'? Official documents and interviews suggest that they referred to peasant living standards. What kind of indicators would then best capture this variable? Per capita gross national product (GNP) in agriculture and per capita national income in agriculture were not adopted due to their measurement problems.[62] Instead, 'per capita income distributed within the commune' (*gongshe nei renjun fenpei shouru*) is chosen as the key indicator.[63] Two additional proxies are also chosen and they are per capita national income and per capita grain consumption by province.[64]

Dependence on Collective Sideline Endeavours

Several studies have suggested that collective sideline endeavours such as brigade-run enterprises might have played a crucial role in determining the pace of decollectivization.[65] The underlying rationale is that the more heavily the peasants of a locality depended upon collective sidelines for their income, the more likely they maintained 'collective spirit' in production and, consequently, they would be more inclined to resist household-based responsibility systems. If a province had exercised its discretion fully, we would then find a strong negative relationship between the provincial pace of decollectivization and the level of its dependence on collective sidelines. The share of 'industrial output value of brigade-run enterprises' (*duibangongye zongchanzhi*) in 'gross value of agricultural output' (*nongye zongchanzhi*) is taken as the indicator for this variable.[66]

Levels of Mechanization

The level of mechanization is another variable assumed to have affected the provincial pace of decollectivization. The underlying rationale is that, given the predominantly collective- and large machinery-based scheme of mechanization in pre-reform China, the provinces dependent heavily upon machine-used work would be less inclined to support household farming that would require a much reduced scale of institutional framework and large new investments for the purchase of smaller machinery.[67] Operationally speaking, if provinces had been able to exercise discretion, we would find a strong negative relationship between the level of mechanization and the pace of decollectivization. This study utilizes the share of mechanized land in total sown area as the key indicator for this variable.[68]

Cropping Patterns

Some studies focus on cropping patterns as a key determinant of the pace of decollectivization. There are two competing perspectives, however. One contends that localities dependent upon crops that required intensive capital (i.e. fertilizer and water-pumps) and labour (i.e. transplantation) inputs—most notably rice—were more likely to resist the household responsibility systems.[69] The other perspective argues to the contrary: rice cultivation was associated with a faster diffusion of household farming.[70] If we could establish a strong relationship regardless of its direction, we may infer that provinces did exercise some degrees of discretion on the basis of differing cropping patterns. As the indicator of the cropping variable, this study takes the relative share of rice and wheat cultivation by province in terms of their sown area.[71]

Average Size of the Production Team

The average size of the production team of a given province is another variable assumed to have affected the pace of decollectivization. The rationale behind the selection of this variable is that the larger the average size of the production team, the more difficult and cumbersome was it to monitor the individual team member's performance, leading to the problems of free-riding and team-shirking. Consequently, the incentives to work were reduced, and the resultant low productivity would make the peasants more receptive to a better institutional mechanism to monitor each other's work, i.e. household farming. Operationally speaking, those provinces with a large average size of production teams would be more likely to implement decollectivization at a faster pace.[72] The average size of the production team is calculated by dividing the total commune population (*gongshe renkou*) of each province by the total number of its production teams.[73]

Regression Analysis: Effects of Provincial Conditions on the Pace of Decollectivization

In order to discern the extent to which differing rural economic conditions were reflected in the provincial variations in the pace of decollectivization, the aforementioned five variables were regressed on the dependent variable of the provincial pace of decollectivization for the two time-points of June 1981 and December 1982. For these two time-points, implementation data are available for nineteen and twenty-one provinces, respectively. A brief note is due on the regressor for the variable of peasant living standards. Having run multiple regressions by alternating each of the three regressors, all are found to have a negative association with the pace of decollectivization. Eventually, per capita income distributed within the

TABLE 3.6. *Impact on the pace of decollectivization in June 1981*

	Coefficients	Standard errors	t-ratios
Per capita income	−0.426	0.173	−2.467*
Cropping pattern	−0.005	0.003	−1.882
Collective sideline	−0.312	0.814	−0.383
Mechanization	0.068	0.366	0.187
Team size	−0.230	0.105	−2.195*

Notes: Number of cases: 19, R^2: 0.60.

* $p < 0.05$; ** $p < 0.01$, two-tailed tests.

TABLE 3.7. *Impact on the pace of decollectivization in December 1982*

	Coefficients	Standard errors	t-ratios
Per capita income	−0.463	0.153	−3.025**
Cropping pattern	−0.001	0.002	−0.459
Collective sideline	0.924	0.681	1.357
Mechanization	0.242	0.303	0.799
Team size	−0.351	0.089	−3.937**

Notes: Number of cases: 21, R^2: 0.74.

* $p < 0.05$; ** $p < 0.01$, two-tailed tests.

commune was chosen since it seems to possess more power to forecast than the other two proxies (compare the coefficients provided in the note).[74] The correlation matrix of the five variables also suggests that the proxy of per capita income distributed within the commune is less plagued by the multicollinearity problem than the other two.[75] Furthermore as mentioned earlier, the commune-distributed per capita income was the criterion that was actually used by many provincial and local officials.

Tables 3.6 and 3.7 present the regression outcomes. For both June 1981 and December 1982, the variable of peasant living standards is significantly associated in a negative direction with the provincial pace of decollectivization. This suggests that the poorer provinces were generally more receptive to the innovation, while the better-off provinces were more reluctant to accept the radically reduced scale of agricultural production. The significant negative association, however, has different implications for the two time-points. That for June 1981 suggests that poor provinces more receptive to changes implemented decollectivization faster, which was also in line with the Centre's guideline (e.g. CD [80] No. 75). Even the slower pace of the better-off provinces then did not contradict Beijing's position.

On the other hand, the significant negative association for December 1982 denotes that, while the nationwide pace of decollectivization picked up dramatically due to Beijing's push in late 1982, better-off provinces remained much slower than the poor ones in adopting *baogan daohu*.

The variable of cropping patterns was not significantly associated with the pace of decollectivization. Two explanations can be offered. While the cultivation of wheat, generally demanding less capital and labour inputs than rice production, was widely assumed to have been more receptive to household farming, such an assumption may have had a missing link. In China, not only for topographical reasons, but also due to its compatibility with large machinery, wheat production was highly mechanized and, therefore, went along with larger units of production. Demographic factors may also have intervened, however: even if wheat production was generally associated with high levels of mechanization, variations in the size of surplus labour may have affected the relationship among cropping patterns, mechanization, and the propensity to adopt household farming.[76] Rice production, on the other hand, because of the complicated routines of work involved (e.g. transplanting), was assumed to have been less susceptible to mechanization and more compatible with household farming. Yet, the complexities involved in the allocation of rice paddies and irrigation rights might have negatively constrained the swift reactivation of the household-based production of rice. The combination of these factors may have cancelled out the effects of cropping patterns on the provincial pace of decollectivization.

The variable of dependence on collective-run enterprises showed no significant association with the provincial pace of decollectivization. The best guess is that the division of labour in the countryside was perhaps far better delineated than most observers would simply take for granted. In other words, despite the adoption of a much reduced size of production and accounting unit in farming, its effects (both perceived and actual) on collective sideline endeavours might have been minimal. It is also possible that the overall importance of brigade-run enterprises in the total agricultural output value was too small—only a national average of 9.5 per cent (for the pool of twenty-five provinces)—to constitute a crucial deterrent to the popularization of household farming.[77]

The mechanization variable also had no significant association with the provincial pace of decollectivization. Given the theoretical reasoning that the household responsibility systems and especially *baogan daohu* would render the collective- and large machinery-based scheme of mechanization largely useless, and the empirical findings that provinces like Heilongjiang vehemently resisted decollectivization just on this ground (see Chapter 6), this result was surprising.[78] One plausible explanation would be that many provinces were simply maintaining their mechanization levels in feigned compliance and, therefore, were both willing and ready to abort them at any time.[79] Alternatively, as the Shandong case clearly illustrates in Chapter 5, the opting for bandwagoning in some provinces was not deterred by specific economic interests or conditions related to mechanization.

The most interesting variable is that of the average team size, which was significantly associated with the provincial pace of decollectivization for both June 1981 and December 1982. What merits our attention is the negative direction of the association. We would normally expect that the larger the average size of the production team, the more difficult it was to monitor the individual's work and, therefore, the more incentive to adopt household farming. Yet, the negative association for the variable suggests that the provinces with smaller teams were faster in decollectivization. Two explanations may be offered. First, larger teams may generally have taken a longer time to reach a consensus among the team members regarding whether to adopt the controversial system and, if so, how to divide land and other collective properties such as draught animals and farm tools. If this complex team-level process was repeated and accumulated to the provincial level, it seems reasonable for the provinces with larger teams to have decollectivized at a slower pace.

Second, provinces with larger teams also had higher levels of mechanization (correlation coefficient of 0.58). Perhaps, the average size of the production team evolved over time to accommodate different conditions of agricultural production in the provinces.[80] Both the impact and significance of the association increased for December 1982 compared with June 1981. Given that Beijing strongly pushed for the swift popularization of *baogan daohu* in 1982, provinces with larger teams heavily dependent upon mechanization might have put up more fierce resistance to the reform.[81] This may imply that the process of decollectivization was not solely shaped by the rational peasants opting for an incentive- and profit-maximizing scheme. Rather, the overall control of the 'movement' may have come from elsewhere, perhaps from the higher local authorities (i.e. provincial and prefecture units) which wished to protect heavy capital investments already committed to collective-based schemes of rural production and construction.[82]

VOLATILE EFFECTS OF DECENTRALIZATION AND VARIED PATTERNS OF IMPLEMENTATION

Implementation requires a complex process of co-ordinating central priorities with local preferences. In the Maoist era, as best illustrated by the Great Leap Forward and its communization drive discussed earlier, such a co-ordination process was totally absent and, instead, ideologically motivated bureaucratic commandism was in full operation. During the post-Mao decollectivization, Beijing was quite faithful to the principle of 'implement according to local conditions' and many provinces exercised their discretion to produce a high level of interprovincial variation up until its last phase. Once the Centre's strong preference for household farming and *baogan daohu* in particular was manifested in 1982, however, many provinces quickly popularized the policy, leaving a handful of recalcitrant provinces with crucial endogenous interests in maintaining the collective system. Overall, the decollectivization process reflected a situation where the norms of administrative decentralization were still highly volatile since, in the face of Beijing's pressure, most provinces were quick to revert to the familiar behaviour of fast and uniform compliance.

In sum, the central leadership once again revealed its limited patience with local discretion and varied patterns of implementation. While some provinces took advantage of the newly granted discretion by way of innovation and resistance, many still clung to the Maoist norm of bandwagoning. This conclusion is based on the system-level aggregate analyses. The power of human agency—perceptions and tactics of the provincial leadership, intra-provincial policy dynamics, and intergovernmental incentive relations for compliance and resistance—is very often shrouded in the numbers game of statistical analyses.[83] And this is where the need for case studies comes in. The next three chapters deal with detailed analyses of Anhui as a representative of the 'pioneer' provinces (Chapter 4), Shandong representing the 'bandwagoners' (Chapter 5), and Heilongjiang as the ultimate 'resister' (Chapter 6).

NOTES

1. The quoted phrase is adapted from William Hinton, *The Great Reversals: The Privatization of China, 1978–1989* (New York: Monthly Review Press, 1990).
2. Given the political and administrative importance of the provinces in China's policy process, such a lack of provincial-level studies leaves a significant part of the question unexplored and unanswered.
3. The household responsibility reform was an encompassing governance policy as it was directed at all province-level units and involved few direct exchanges of resources between the centre and the provinces. Yet, it was also a radical policy that introduced a fundamentally different institutional framework of agricultural production. A crucial implication is that, despite the necessity of tight central control and strict provincial compliance dictated by the encompassing and governance attributes of the policy, its radical nature (i.e. lack of local information and prior experiences) necessitated an expanded scope of local discretion in implementation.
4. By 1986, more than 99.6 per cent of peasants and over 70 per cent of employees in state farms in China were under the system of household farming. See Wang Yuzhao, *Dabaogan yu daqushi* (Comprehensive Contracts and the Great Trend) (Beijing: Guangming ribao chubanshe, 1987), 37.
5. For details of these two systems, see Xu Jingyong, *Zhongguo nongye jingji lilun yu shijian* (Theory and Practice in China's Agricultural Economy) (Fuzhou: Fujian renmin chubanshe, 1986), 41–2.
6. For discussions of the political situations at the centre during 1978–82, see Richard Baum, *Burying Mao: Politics in the Age of Deng Xiaoping* (Princeton: Princeton University Press, 1994), chs. 3–5.

7. For the prevalence of local innovations, see *Renmin ribao*, 15 Mar. 1979. Detailed discussions of the genesis of local innovations related to household farming are provided in Chapter 4.
8. For the evolution of 'formalized expressions' (*tifa*) concerning decollectivization, see Guo Shutian, *Zhongguo nongcun gaige yu fazhan shinian* (Ten Years' Development of China's Rural Reform) (Beijing: Nongye chubanshe, 1990), 8.
9. See David Zweig, 'Context and Content in Policy Implementation: Household Contracts and Decollectivization, 1977–83', in David Lampton (ed.), *Policy Implementation in Post-Mao China* (Berkeley and Los Angeles: University of California Press, 1987), 255–83.
10. See the text in *Nongcun jingji zhengce huibian 1978–1981* (Collection of Rural Policy Documents for 1978–1981) (internal publication) (Beijing: Nongcun duwu chubanshe, 1982), 18–44. The part cited is on p. 32.
11. See the text in Xiang Xiyang and Shen Chong (eds.), *Shinianlai lilun zhengce shijian: ziliao xuanbian* (Theory, Policy, and Implementation in the Last Ten Years: A Compilation of Select Materials; hereafter *Ziliao xuanbian*) (Beijing: Qiushi chubanshe, 1988), ii. 123.
12. See the text in *Zhongguo nongye nianjian 1980* (Agricultural Yearbook of China 1980; hereafter *ZGNYNJ*) (Beijing: Nongye chubanshe, 1981), 56–62.
13. See 'Zhongyang guanyu jinyibu jiaqiang he wanshan nongye shengchan zerenzhi de jige wenti de tongzhi' (A Notice from the Party Centre Regarding Some Problems on Further Improving Agricultural Production Responsibility Systems, Central Document no. 75 issued on 27 Sept. 1980), *Ziliao xuanbian*, ii. 36.
14. *Renmin ribao*, 4 Aug. 1981.
15. 'Quanguo nongcun gongzuo huiyi jiyao' (A Summary of the National Rural Work Conference), *Ziliao xuanbian*, ii. 40.
16. See, for instance, *Renmin ribao*, 22 Aug. and 16 Sept. 1982. For the incentive structure of *baogan daohu*, see Frederick W. Crook, 'The *Baogan Daohu* Incentive System: Translation and Analysis of a Model Contract', *China Quarterly*, 102 (1985), 298–303.
17. Guo Shutian, *Zhongguo nongcun gaige yu fazhan shinian*, 8. By August 1980, Gansu had 39 per cent of its teams under the two household responsibility systems. See Lu Xueyi, *Dangdai zhongguo nongcun yu dangdai zhongguo nongmin* (Contemporary China's Countryside and Its Peasants) (Beijing: Zhishi chubanshe, 1991), 45.
18. Chen Jiaji, 'Lun baogan daohu' (On the System of Household Contract with Fixed Levies), Zhongguo shehui kexueyuan nongcun fazhan yanjiusuo (ed.), *Nongye shengchan zerenzhi lunwenji* (A Collection of Essays on Agricultural Production Responsibility Systems) (Beijing: Renmin chubanshe, 1986), 87–8. The figure for Ningxia is from *Dangdai zhongguo de Ningxia* (Contemporary China's Ningxia) (Beijing: Zhongguo shehui kexue chubanshe, 1990), i. 205.
19. For details on provincial 'pioneers' and their political linkages with Beijing, see Chapter 4.
20. For the entanglements among ideological debates, power struggles, and policy conflicts during this period and the cautious approach taken by the 'Reformist' leadership, see Jae Ho Chung, 'The Politics of Agricultural Mechanization in the Post-Mao Era, 1977–87', *China Quarterly*, 134 (1993), 265, 273–7, 289–90.
21. See 'Zhonggong zhongyang pizhuan guojia nongwei dangzu baosong de "guanyu nongcun gongzuo wenti zuotanhui jiyao" de tongzhi' (3 Apr. 1979), *Ziliao xuanbian*, ii. 122. Also see the editorial entitled 'Yindi zhiyi jianli jianquan shengchan zerenzhi' (Establish and Improve the Production Responsibility Systems According to Local Conditions), *Renmin ribao*, 2 Apr. 1980.
22. 'A Notice from the Party Centre Regarding Some Problems on Further Improving Agricultural Production Responsibility Systems,' *Ziliao xuanbian*, ii. 35.
23. Ibid. 35–6. This recommendation was nevertheless criticized for proposing 'three cuts of a knife' (instead of 'one cut of a knife'). See *Renmin ribao*, 4 Aug. 1981.
24. Despite its emphasis on *yindi zhiyi*, the central leadership's core intention of drafting the first number one central document on rural reform—CD [82] No. 1—lay in providing a complete official endorsement for household responsibility systems, thus accelerating the nationwide popularization of decollectivization. For the detailed background to the making of CD [82] No. 1, see Wu Xiang, 'Kaichuang xinjumian de wuge yihao wenjian'

(The Five Path-Breaking Number-One Central Documents), *Zhongguo renli ziyuan kaifa* (Human Resource Development in China), 3 (1994), 33.

25. For Guizhou, see *Dangdai zhongguo de Guizhou* (Contemporary China's Guizhou) (Beijing: Zhongguo shehui kexue chubanshe, 1989), 132; for Jilin, *Renmin ribao*, 22 Jan. 1983; for Heilongjiang (this figure is for May), see *Heilongjiang nongye hezuoshi* (History of Agricultural Co-operativization in Heilongjiang) (Beijing: Zhonggong dangshi ziliao chubanshe, 1990), 530; and for Anhui, see Historical Archives Commission of the Anhui Provincial Political Consultative Conference (ed.), *Nongcun gaige de xingqi* (The Rise of Rural Reform) (Beijing: Zhongguo wenshi chubanshe, 1993), 9–10.

26. This notice was entitled 'Wanshan nongye shengchan zerenzhi zhongde jige renshi wenti de tongzhi' (A Notice on Some Problems in Improving the Agricultural Production Responsibility Systems) and was published in *Renmin ribao*, 27 Apr. 1982.

27. Zhao visited Liaoning in July and Hu visited Heilongjiang in August. Information based on interviews in Beijing and Harbin in 1992. Given that their visits were not reported in provincial newspapers, these trips may have been of a secret and unofficial nature designed specifically to push for decollectivization in these provinces.

28. See, for instance, *Renmin ribao*, 29 July 1982.

29. Ibid. 20 Oct. 1982.

30. Ibid. 23 Dec. 1982.

31. Several interviewees confirmed that Wan Li's speech was indeed a serious warning and many provincial leaders, too, perceived it as such. Interviews in Beijing and Jinan in 1992. For a media report that attributed the sluggish pace of decollectivization in Liaoning to the 'leftist ideas' held by the provincial leadership, see ibid. 11 Nov. 1982.

32. Since the speech was delivered at the two national conferences held in early November which were attended by provincial representatives, provinces had at least one-and-a-half months to speed up their pace of decollectivization. Therefore, the time lapse between the speech and its publication is rather irrelevant.

33. See *Hebei ribao* (*Hebei Daily*), 10 Dec. 1982 and *Dangdai zhongguo de Hebei* (Contemporary China's Hebei) (Beijing: Zhongguo shehui kexue chubanshe, 1990), 578. For Hubei, see *Hubei ribao*, 29 Oct. and 26 Dec. 1982. While the 26 Dec. issue of *Hubei ribao* provides the figure of 94 per cent for Dec. 1982, it seems to have been inflated as the later publication gives a more modest figure of 75.3 per cent. For the latter figure, see *Hubei nongcun jingji, 1949–1989* (Hubei Rural Economy, 1949–1989) (Beijing: Zhongguo tongji chubanshe, 1990), 108.

34. For newspaper reports in support of *baogan daohu*, see *Renmin ribao*, 22 and 23 Jan. and 7 Mar. 1983. For CD [83] No. 1, see 'Dangqian nongcun jingji zhengce de ruogan wenti' (Some Problems of the Current Rural Economic Policy), *Ziliao xuanbian*, ii. 52–65. Among the five number one central documents on rural policy, CD [83] No. 1 is the only one passed by the Politburo (the remaining four were passed by the Central Secretariat). This information is from an interview in Beijing in 1994.

35. See *Nongmin bao*, 22 Mar. 1983, cited in Zweig, 'Context and Content in Policy Implementation', 273 and *Jilin ribao*, 19 Feb. 1983.

36. For figures on these five regions, see *Zhongguo nongminbao* (*China Peasant Daily*), 1 Dec. 1983. For the national figure, see Guo Shutian, *Zhongguo nongcun gaige yu fazhan shinian*, 10. Heilongjiang remained the slowest as it continued to put up a fight against Beijing (see Chapter 6 for more details).

37. The reasons for the Centre's sudden push for uniformity in 1982 are not entirely clear. Although the evidence is extremely sketchy, three possibilities may be suggested. First, having been accustomed to the control-oriented system of governance for so long, the Chinese central leadership had very little patience and understanding of local autonomy. Thus, faced with provincial foot-dragging and resistance, the central leadership immediately resorted to administrative imposition to ensure full local compliance. Second, the new reformist leadership had to prove that its programmes were working and it had to do it fast (perhaps to show some positive results at the Twelfth Party Congress in the autumn of 1982). This view is suggested in Jonathan Unger, 'The Decollectivization of the Chinese Countryside: A Survey of Twenty-Eight Villages', *Pacific Affairs*, 58/4 (1985–6), 591. Third, one retired senior official suggested that there had been crucial issue linkages between decollectivization and other policy issues—e.g. permitting individual ownership of key

production materials, designating specialized households, allowing hired labour, and so on—which could only be implemented after the completion of the household responsibility reform. This last point is indebted to an interview in Beijing in 1994.

38. These studies include Kate Xiao Zhou, *How the Farmers Changed China: Power of the People* (Boulder, Colo.: Westview, 1996), chs. 1 and 3; Dali L. Yang, *Calamity and Reform in China: State, Rural Society, and Institutional Change Since the Great Leap Famine* (Stanford: Stanford University Press, 1996), ch. 6; Joseph Fewsmith, *Dilemmas of Reform in China: Political Conflict and Economic Debate* (Armonk, NY: M. E. Sharpe, 1994), 19–55; Daniel Kelliher, *Peasant Power in China: The Era of Rural Reform 1979–1989* (New Haven: Yale University Press, 1992), ch. 3; Helen F. Siu, *Agents and Victims in South China: Accomplices in Rural Revolution* (New Haven and London: Yale University Press, 1989), ch. 12; Justin Yifu Lin, 'The Household Responsibility System Reform in China: A Peasant's Institutional Choice', *American Journal of Agricultural Economics*, 69/2 (1987), 410–15; David Zweig, 'Context and Content in Policy Implementation'; id., 'Peasants, Ideology, and New Incentive Systems: Jiangsu Province, 1978–1981', in William L. Parish (ed.), *Chinese Rural Development: The Great Transformation* (Armonk, NY: M. E. Sharpe, 1985), 141–63; id., 'Opposition to Change in Rural China: The System of Responsibility and People's Communes', *Asian Survey*, 23/7 (1983), 879–900; Unger, 'The Decollectivization of the Chinese Countryside'; Kathleen Hartford, 'Socialist Agriculture Is Dead: Long Live Socialist Agriculture! Organizational Transformation in Rural China', in Elizabeth J. Perry and Christine Wong (eds.), *The Political Economy of Reform in Post-Mao China* (Cambridge, Mass.: The Council on East Asian Studies, Harvard University Press, 1985), 31–61; Andrew Watson, 'New Structures in the Organization of Chinese Agriculture: A Variable Model', *Pacific Affairs*, 57/4 (1984), 621–45; Graham E. Johnson, 'The Production Responsibility System in Chinese Agriculture: Some Examples from Guangdong', *Pacific Affairs*, 55/3 (1982), 430–51; Greg O'Leary and Andrew Watson, 'The Production Responsibility System and the Future of Collective Farming', *Australian Journal of Chinese Affairs*, 8 (1982), 1–34.

39. Zhou, Kelliher, Lin, Watson, and O'Leary and Watson belong to the first category; the second category includes Hartford, Siu, and Unger; and Fewsmith, Yang, and Zweig (1987, 1985, and 1983) belong to the third.

40. Detailed discussions are provided in a later section on indicators.

41. These are Zweig (1985), Johnson, and O'Leary and Watson.

42. See Unger, 'The Decollectivization of the Chinese Countryside', 585; and Hartford, 'Socialist Agriculture Is Dead', 283.

43. These studies include Johnson, O'Leary and Watson, Zweig (1985), Unger, and Siu.

44. Kelliher seems to have relied too heavily on the Anhui case as well as on official descriptions of the process. Fewsmith, for instance, characterizes Kelliher's version as a 'romantic rendition'. See his *Dilemmas of Reform in China*, 19. For a persuasive critique of Zhou, see David Zweig, 'Rural People, the Politicians, and Power', *China Journal*, 38 (1997), 153–68.

45. Zweig (1983 and 1987) represents the former, and Lin the latter (using the *China Agricultural Yearbook, 1983*). Yang belongs to a category of his own in that he sought to link the impact of the Great Leap Famine with provincial reform propensity. One point of contention, however, concerns his indicator for the dependent variable—brigade accounting rates (BAR). BAR could be a proxy for the provincial pace of decollectivization, but it certainly is no substitute for the direct data on how fast (or slow) household responsibility systems were adopted by the provinces.

46. For a fuller justification on this issue, refer to Chapter 1.

47. Hainan was not yet a province during the period concerned. And this study excludes three provincial-level municipalities (Beijing, Tianjin, and Shanghai) as they are quite incomparable in many respects (especially regarding agriculture) with the provinces.

48. Among the fifty-four sources used, twelve are official media reports. In terms of the data points, the share of official media reports amounts to only 17 per cent (27/163).

49. As of June 1981, the decollectivization reform entailed both *baochan daohu* and *baogan daohu* to similar degrees as *baogan daohu* constituted 40 per cent of the household-based responsibility systems adopted nationwide. By June 1982, *baogan daohu* became predominant as its share rose to 93 per cent of the household responsibility systems adopted

nationwide. This is why the combined figures are used for the first time-point and *baogan daohu* figures for the second in Table 3.2. When different sources cite conflicting figures for the same time-point, the figures given by later publications were selected.

50. Standard deviation is not scale-invariant (i.e. it is not mean-independent). Therefore, coefficient of variation is perhaps a better proxy than standard deviation because the former takes into account the effects of the changes in the mean, particularly when dealing with the data in percentage terms.

51. These seventeen provinces, distributed fairly evenly among the six large geographical regions, are: Anhui, Fujian, Gansu, Guangdong, Guangxi, Guizhou, Hebei, Heilongjiang, Henan, Hunan, Jilin, Liaoning, Neimenggu, Shandong, Shanxi, Xinjiang, and Yunnan.

52. The magnitude of discretion a provinces wishes to utilize and the number of provinces which become willing to exercise discretion are associated with the relative salience of a policy to the respective province(s). That is, the more salient the given policy is to the province(s), the more likely is it to utilize discretion to pursue its own priorities.

53. See Frederick Teiwes, 'Provincial Politics: Themes and Variations', in John Lindbeck (ed.), *China: Management of A Revolutionary Society* (Seattle: University of Washington Press, 1971), 168, 172. Unfortunately, we do not have similar sets of provincial implementation data from the 1960s or 1970s.

54. For the chronology of the co-operativization movement, see Frederick C. Teiwes and Warren Sun (eds.), *The Politics of Agricultural Cooperativization in China: Mao, Deng Zihui, and the 'High Tide' of 1955* (Armonk, NY: M. E. Sharpe, 1993), 33–50.

55. See Roderick MacFarquhar, *The Origins of the Cultural Revolution*, ii. *The Great Leap Forward, 1958–60* (New York: Columbia University Press, 1983), 77–90. For a vivid recollection of the communization movement by a high-level official, see Bo Yibo, *Ruogan zhongda juece yu shijian de huigu* (Recollections of Key Decisions and Events in the Past) (Beijing: Zhonggong zhongyang dangxiao chubanshe, 1993), ii. 727–50.

56. The lack of provincial discretion in policy implementation during this period is well documented in Alfred Chan, 'The Campaign for Agricultural Development in the Great Leap Forward: A Study of Policy-Making and Implementation in Liaoning', *China Quarterly*, 129 (1992), 52–71; and Jean-Luc Domenach, *The Origins of the Great Leap Forward: The Case of One Chinese Province* (Boulder, Colo.: Westview, 1995), 157–9.

57. This is not to deny that there were some localities that responded to Beijing in an overzealous fashion. Yet, compared to the Great Leap period, their responses seemed quite contained. For overzealous responses during the co-operativization, see Teiwes and Sun, *The Politics of Agricultural Cooperativization in China*, 19–20.

58. For the impact of the anti-Rightist campaign on the norms of local policy implementation, see William A. Joseph, 'A Tragedy of Good Intentions: Post-Mao Views of the Great Leap Forward', *Modern China*, 12/4 (1986), 427–8; and David Bachman, *Bureaucracy, Economy, and Leadership in China: The Institutional Origins of the Great Leap Forward* (Cambridge: Cambridge University Press, 1991), 5.

59. For Beijing's capacity for monitoring local behaviour and pro forma compliance in the post-Mao era, see Jae Ho Chung, 'Central-Provincial Relations', in Lo Chi Kin, Suzanne Pepper, and Tsui Kai Yuen (eds.), *China Review 1995* (Hong Kong: Chinese University Press, 1995), 3.18–21.

60. Needless to say, non-economic variables such as central–provincial patron–client dynamics and intra-provincial politics must have also operated to affect the size of the interprovincial variation. Yet, the general unavailability of pertinent information, proxies, and indicators that cover a sufficiently large number of provinces makes the operationalization of these non-economic variables extremely difficult, if not impossible. Further, the shorter time frame (1981–2) concerned precludes the utilization of such proxies as cadre tenures and appointments used in Yasheng Huang, *Inflation and Investment Controls in China: The Political Economy of Central–Local Relations during the Reform Era* (Cambridge: Cambridge University Press, 1996), ch. 8. Thus, only rural economic variables are considered here while political factors receive their due attention in detailed case studies of three provinces in the subsequent chapters.

61. See the text of these documents published in Xiang Xiyang and Shen Chong (eds.), *Ziliao xuanbian*, ii. 35–6, 41.

62. Per capita GNP in agriculture is perhaps the ideal indicator as it captures the most

comprehensive dimensions of rural economic standards. Yet, it has a measurement problem: it is very difficult to derive per capita share due to the unavailability of the data that break down the agricultural population into different services, especially for these early years of the reform. Per capita national income in agriculture has a similar measurement problem and, furthermore, it does not include data on the production of services. For difficulties associated with the use of agricultural and non-agricultural population data in China, see Chan Kam Wing and Tsui Kai Yuen, *'Agricultural' and 'Non-Agricultural' Population Statistics of the People's Republic of China: Definitions, Findings and Comparisons* (Hong Kong: University of Hong Kong, 1992).

63. Per capita income distributed within the commune is the most commonly used indicator: it was adopted by Chinese official histories of decollectivization as well as by many of the studies reviewed earlier (Zweig, 1985; and O'Leary and Watson). This indicator has its own problem of not including the incomes from private plots and individual sidelines. Yet, this indicator has an important merit. Unlike the former two indicators, these statistics were most widely available in China so that provincial and local officials actually utilized them in determining their respective levels of rural economic conditions. Author's interviews with provincial officials in Beijing, Jinan, and Harbin supported such a view. Provincial data on this dimension are available only for 1981. The data are adapted from *Zhongguo tongji nianjian 1981* (Statistical Yearbook of China, 1981) (Beijing: tongji chubanshe, 1982), 198.

64. The data on the former proxy are the average of 1980 and 1981 and adapted from State Statistical Bureau, *Guomin shouru tongji ziliao huibian 1949–1985* (Compendia of National Income Statistics) (Beijing: Zhongguo tongji chubanshe, 1987), 120–422. The data on the latter proxy are for 1979 calculated on the basis of the agricultural population (*nongye renkou*) and adapted from *Zhongguo nongye nianjian 1980* (Agricultural Yearbook of China, 1980) (Beijing: Nongye chubanshe, 1981), 132.

65. See Zweig, 'Peasants, Ideology, and New Incentive Systems', 146, 149; id., 'Opposition to Change in Rural China', 889; and O'Leary and Watson, 'The Production Responsibility System and the Future of Collective Farming', 11–13.

66. The data on this, averaged for 1979–81, are adapted from *Zhongguo nongye nianjian 1980*, 130; *Zhongguo nongye nianjian 1981*, 18–19; and *Zhongguo tongji nianjian 1981*, 137.

67. For the collective- and large machinery-based scheme of mechanization in the pre-reform era, see Benedict Stavis, *The Politics of Agricultural Mechanization in China* (Ithaca, NY: Cornell University Press, 1978) and On Kit Tam, *China's Agricultural Modernization: The Socialist Mechanization Scheme* (London: Croom Helm, 1985). For studies that place importance on the mechanization variable, see Zweig, 'Peasants, Ideology, and New Incentive Systems', 152–3; Lin, 'The Household Responsibility Reform in China', 410–15; and Unger, 'The Decollectivization of the Chinese Countryside', 588.

68. There are three possible indicators of mechanization: (1) ratio of total number of large and medium-sized machines to that of small machines; (2) ratio of total horsepower of large and medium-sized machines to that of small machines; and (3) share of mechanized land in total sown area. The former two indicators are plagued with two critical problems. One is related to the fact that a significant number of agricultural machines in China was then left unused in many localities due to the problems of *ad hoc* distribution irrespective of local conditions, and difficulties associated with the lack of parts and implements. The other concerns the degree to which small machines, especially small and hand-tractors, was used for short-haul transportation instead of farming. See Bai Renpu and Liu Tianfu, 'Lun nongye jixie de heli toufang wenti' (On the Issue of Rationally Distributing Agricultural Machinery) and Xia Zhenkun, 'Shilun nongye jixiehua de jingji fenxi' (An Economic Analysis of Agricultural Mechanization), *Nongye jishu jingjixue wenxuan* (Selected Essays in Agricultural Technology and Economics) (Beijing: Nongye chubanshe, 1981), 80 and 100–1; and *Dangdai zhongguo de nongye jixie gongye* (Agricultural Machinery Industry in Contemporary China) (Beijing: Zhongguo shehuikexue chubanshe, 1988), 275. The data used for this variable, averaged for 1979 and 1981, are adapted from *Zhongguo nongye nianjian 1980*, 143; and *Zhongguo tongji nianjian 1981*, 183

69. Zweig, 'Peasants, Ideology, and New Incentive Systems', 145, 160; Johnson, 'The Production Responsibility System in Chinese Agriculture', 443–4; and Siu, *Agents and Victims in South China*, 279–80.

70. Kelliher, *Peasant Power in China*, pp. x, 31.
71. The data used for this variable, averaged for 1979–81, were calculated on the basis of the information provided in *Zhongguo nongye nianjian 1980*, 103, 105; *Zhongguo nongye nianjian 1981*, 23–6; and *Zhongguo nongye nianjian 1982*, 35–6.
72. Lin, 'The Household Responsibility Reform in China', 411–12, 415.
73. The data used for this variable, averaged for 1979 and 1980, are adapted from *Zhongguo nongye nianjian 1980*, 6; and *Zhongguo nongye nianjian 1981*, 10.
74. Regression coeffecients of the three regressors

	June 1981	Dec. 1982
Per capita commune income	−0.426*	−0.463**
Per capita national income	−0.089	−0.144**
Per capita grain consumption	−0.064*	−0.078**

   * $p < 0.05$, ** $p < 0.01$, two-tailed test.

75. Both per capita national income and per capita grain consumption had the multi-collinearity problem with the mechanization variable.
76. An exclusive concern with the increase in the share of non-agricultural rural employment may be misleading because the absolute number of people engaged in farming increased at a fast pace by 32 million in 1978–84. See Jeffrey R. Taylor, 'Rural Employment Trends and the Legacy of Surplus Labor, 1978–86', *China Quarterly*, 116 (1988), 745–6, 754–5.
77. In a personal correspondence, David Zweig pointed out the significance of Jiangsu on this matter, a province which this study was forced to exclude due to the unavailability of key implementation data. Several interviewees in China also commented that Jiangsu's slow adaptation (especially in the Sunan region) may have been strongly influenced by its heavy dependence on commune- and brigade-run enterprises, accounting for 23.6 per cent of the total provincial agricultural output value in Jiangsu, producing 27 per cent of the total industrial output value of the Suxichang region (Suzhou, Wuxi, and Changzhou), and employing 22 per cent of rural labour force in the Suzhou city region in 1980. See Wan Jieqiu, *Zhengfu tuidong yu jingji fazhan: Sunan moshi de lilun sikao* (State-led Economic Development: Theoretical Views on the Sunan Model) (Shanghai: Fudan University Press, 1993), 71; and Zhou Haile (ed.), *Suxichang fazhan baogao* (Report on the Development of Suzhou-Wuxi-Changzhou Region) (Beijing: Renmin ribao chubanshe, 1994), 154.
78. The bivariate regression of mechanization on the pace of decollectivization showed a strong negative association for both time-points—0.638 for June 1981 and −0.702 for December 1982 at the 95 per cent significance level.
79. See Chung, 'The Politics of Agricultural Mechanization in the Post-Mao Era', 281.
80. For instance, the average number of people in a production team in Anhui and Guizhou, two fastest implementors, was 110 and 126, and their mechanization level was 24 and 1.8 per cent, respectively. On the other hand, the corresponding figures for Liaoning and Heilongjiang, two slowest implementors, were 241 and 313 for the team size, and 49 and 68 per cent for mechanization.
81. In June 1981, the nationwide share of *baochan daohu* was 16.9 per cent while that of *baogan daohu* was 11.3 per cent. By December 1982, the share of *baogan daohu* rose to more than 67 per cent while that of *baochan daohu* dropped to less than 10 per cent (see Table 3.1). *Baogan daohu*, under which investment decisions for machinery service were made by the individual households, had a very significant impact. Since the contract land allocated to the individual household was much smaller than that formerly allotted to the collective, machinery service offered by the collective was largely incompatible with household farming. For a detailed analysis on this point, see Chung, 'The Politics of Agricultural Mechanization in the Post-Mao Era', 277–80.
82. See Zweig, 'Peasants, Ideology, and New Incentive Systems', 152–3; id., 'Opposition to Change in Rural China', 891; and Unger, 'The Decollectivization of the Chinese Countryside', 588.
83. While there were several studies on the perceptions and actions by the cadres at the grass-

roots level, no comparable study has been produced at the provincial level. For exemplary studies on village-level cadres, see Richard J. Latham, 'The Implications of Rural Reforms for Grass-Roots Cadres', in Perry and Wong (eds.), *The Political Economy of Reform in Post-Mao China*, 151–73; and John P. Burns, 'Local Cadre Accommodation to the "Responsibility System" in Rural China', *Pacific Affairs*, 58/4 (1985–6), 607–25.

4

The Politics of 'Pioneering' in Anhui: Local Innovation, Provincial Support, and Central Auspices

An unresolved debate over the process of decollectivization concerns the role played by the state in general and by the central government in particular. One influential perspective characterizes the central government of the period concerned as a 'passive state' conducting benign neglect toward local innovations and deviations. This perspective attributes such passivity to the circumstances in which the central government was then placed. Facing a systemic crisis of shortage, falling productivity, lingering dangers of food riots, and plummeting regime legitimacy, the central government had no other choice but gradually to relax its control over the egalitarian collective system of production and work-point distribution. Yet, the centre did not have a well thought-out package of alternative policies to remedy the situation. Such a gap between the need for a new policy and the absence of an alternative was filled by local innovations of household farming which the central government gradually co-opted as a national policy. This perspective thus depicts a highly decentralized bottom-up process of policy-making and implementation, in which the reversal of collectivization was based upon peasants' voluntary choices. It also contends that peasants pushed radical changes at such a fast pace that state policy had continually to chase after what they had already accomplished and, therefore, the central government in fact lost control over much of the process from the beginning.[1]

A competing perspective offers a different view with regard to the role of the state during decollectivization. According to this perspective, while there may have been key occasions of local innovation and Beijing's co-optation of it, it was still the central government and the intervening levels of bureaucratic administration which had over time set the tone for the overall reform, defined the boundary of permissible practices, and provided the particular types of responsibility systems to be popularized. In other words, higher authorities were not all that passive but rather actively pursued certain preferences of their own, thus significantly affecting the course and outcomes of the reform. This top-down perspective thus stresses the regulatory role of the central government and local administration in constraining the range of choices available to the peasants.[2]

The presence of the debate in itself points to the complex patterns of local implementation of decollectivization. It seems that the two perspectives are not necessarily mutually exclusive and they are perhaps two sides of the same coin in that both local innovation and state control were crucial dimensions of the process, which interacted with each other in a highly complicated manner over time. It may be that the peasant-power perspective fits better for the earlier period of 1978–81 when state policy constantly fell behind the spread of local innovation in some provinces which took advantage of their newly acquired discretion in implementation. For the later period of 1982–4, however, the central-imposition perspective provides a better explanation as to why many provinces jumped on a bandwagon at the last minute and even a few recalcitrant provinces eventually had to succumb to the centre's preferences, mooting the original intentions of the administrative decentralization.[3]

If an intergovernmental perspective is applied, the process of decollectivization was in fact the aggregated outcome of provincial responses by the three types of implementors: 'pioneers', 'bandwagoners', and 'resisters.'[4] Since the latter two types will be discussed in Chapters 5 and 6, this chapter examines the 'pioneering' pattern of implementation with a case study of Anhui. The peasant-power perspective is best illustrated by this pioneering pattern. Yet, if we rely exclusively on this thesis alone, it becomes difficult to explain why and how local innovations survived and spread at an extremely fast pace in some localities while they completely failed in others. The most crucial intervening variable was the overhead control by higher authorities, whether provincial or commune. Yet, local cadres, provincial and below, did not uniformly respond to the centre, thus producing provincial and sub-provincial variations in the pattern of decollectivization. Some responded to the endogenous economic interests of their localities, and others behaved on the basis of perceived uncertainties, fears, and personal interests.[5] In sum, overhead control was as much a crucial part of the process as peasant initiatives were, even in the most exceptional case like Anhui.

This chapter consists of six sections. The first explores some salient behavioural characteristics of pioneering and presents yearly implementation data that qualify Anhui as a pioneer. The second provides an overview of the key factors that facilitated the genesis and diffusion of local innovations of household farming in Anhui. The third section investigates the question of how radical grass-roots innovations were able to survive in the political and ideological environment extremely antagonistic toward them. The fourth demonstrates the indispensability of political support from the central and provincial authorities in the swift diffusion of decollectivization in Anhui during 1979–80. The fifth examines how Anhui's decollectivization was able to weather the leadership change in 1980–1. The final section offers concluding observations regarding the pioneering pattern of local policy implementation.

ANHUI AS A 'PIONEER' IN THE DECOLLECTIVIZATION REFORM

'Pioneers' refer to the provinces which stand in the forefront of the reform by implementing controversial policies long before the central government begins to push for their popularization and by outpacing most other provinces throughout the process.[6] In the context of post-Mao decollectivization, this category of provinces included Anhui, Gansu, Guangxi, Guizhou, Ningxia, and Sichuan.[7] Pioneering during decollectivization entailed three distinct characteristics: local innovation, provincial support, and central auspices. While local innovation was by no means non-existent in many other provinces, a few provinces like Anhui and Guizhou were particularly well known for early innovations and their swift diffusion. Local innovations in these two provinces had occurred as early as 1978 (i.e. even before the Third Plenum). One immediate question concerns how peasant innovations of household farming in these provinces survived the initial test of obtaining the endorsement of local authorities. The key lay in the active support of the provincial leadership which pre-empted the complex sources of obstruction and blockade located along the administrative hierarchy from the prefecture down to the commune. The next question then concerns the motives of the provincial leadership in supporting such local innovations that were clearly off the policy line of the central government. The most persuasive explanation may be that a reformist coalition within the central leadership provided explicit support for the experiments with and diffusion of household farming in these provinces.[8]

Among the pioneer provinces, Anhui constituted the most interesting case not only because its pace of adopting the household responsibility systems had been the fastest until July 1980 when it was outpaced by Guizhou, but because the province is also widely known to have had the largest number of local innovations related to household farming. Sichuan, another pioneer which is perhaps too casually associated with a fast pace of decollectivization, only had 9.3 per cent of its production teams under the household responsibility systems by August 1980, a performance which was then relatively mediocre among the pioneer provinces (refer to Table 3.1).[9]

Anhui's pace of decollectivization was extremely fast compared to the national average, as shown in Table 4.1. Throughout the entire process of the reform, Anhui consistently outpaced the national average by large margins ranging from 9 per cent in December 1979 to 52.5 per cent in

TABLE 4.1. *Anhui's pace of decollectivization 1979–1982 (percentage of teams under household farming)*

	1979	1980	1981	1982
National average		1: 1.0	6: 28.2	6: 71.9
		12: 14.4	12: 50.0	12: 78.2
Anhui	12: 10.0 (c)	3: 25.0 (c)	6: 69.3	6: 97.0
		7: 30.0 (c)	12: 84.6	12: 98.8
		12: 66.9		

Notes: Figures to left of colon denote month of the respective year; (c) denotes that the figures are for *baochan daohu* only.

Sources: As Table 3.1.

December 1980. By July 1980, even before Central Document No. 75 of 1980 (hereafter CD [80] No. 75), about one third of Anhui's production teams already adopted 'household production quotas' (*baochan daohu*); and by December 1981, even before the dissemination of CD [82] No. 1, about 85 per cent of its teams were under household farming. In sum, Anhui is well qualified as a pioneer.[10]

LOCAL INNOVATIONS IN ANHUI: AN OVERVIEW

Anhui's pioneering was highly contingent upon multiple, simultaneous, and widespread local innovations in the early stage of the reform. Various studies of Anhui's decollectivization list a total of nine different counties as the local sources of policy innovations related to household farming.[11] Whichever version we adopt, local innovations in Anhui were multiple in number, simultaneous in timing, and widespread in scope. Among these nine counties, only three (Fengyang, Laian, and Quanzhao) belonged to the same prefecture (Chuxian), while the remaining six were distributed among six different prefectures and province-administered cities. Geographically, six were located in the middle region (*wanzhong*), with one (Guzhen) in the northern region (*wanbei*: north of Huai River), and two (Dangtu and Wuhu) to the south of the Yangtze River (*jiangnan*).[12]

Available evidence suggests that there were at least three key factors that contributed to the genesis of local innovations in Anhui. First, a meteorological factor specific to Anhui (as well as to some other parts of northern China) was responsible for the local innovations, which were both earlier and more widespread than those in other provinces. A serious drought caused by a ten-month absence of rain in 1978 affected 60 million *mu* of land (i.e. over 90 per cent of Anhui's cultivated land) and made it impossible for peasants to plant rice.[13] Such a grave situation forced the basic-level cadres in some communes (e.g. Mahu commune of Fengyang, Yanchen commune of Laian, and Shannan commune of Feixi) to rent out collective land to work groups and individual households to plant 'life-saving wheat' (*baomingmai*) as well as other dry crops like yellow beans and sorghums. Furthermore, the production outputs from these plots were exempted from the compulsory state procurement. In the process, however, some communes allegedly turned a blind eye to covert implementation of 'household production quotas' (*baochan daohu*) and even 'household farming with fixed levies' (*baogan daohu*) at the lower levels, while others actively supported such deviations.[14]

Second, evidence also suggests that most of the grass-roots units responsible for innovations were among the poorest in the respective locality. For instance, the best-known Xiaogang production team of Liyuan commune in Fengyang, with an average per capita income of 32 *yuan* (about one quarter of the provincial average), was apparently the poorest in the whole commune.[15] Extreme poverty combined with a serious drought forced desperate peasants to search for ways to guarantee subsistence. Such linkages between poverty and innovation seem to have been a general rule in Anhui, as well as in other pioneer provinces like Guizhou.[16] Furthermore, economic hardship as a source of innovation often contributed to its initial survival, as some local cadres became sympathetic and even willing to grant an exemption to those on a subsistence level.[17] On many occasions, basic-level cadres themselves became fervent supporters of household-based responsibility systems.[18]

Poverty very often produces caution rather than innovation as there are so few resources available to save the situation if innovation fails. While poverty may generally create risk-averse attitudes among peasants, the peasants in Anhui still went for radical innovations. What then was their frame of reference? The answer lies in that Anhui peasants had already had experiences with the system of 'household production quotas' in 1961-2 when Zeng Xisheng, provincial first party secretary, had allowed peasants to adopt the controversial system of 'responsibility land' (*zerentian*). As of late 1961 about 85 per cent of Anhui's production teams were under *baochan daohu*, and before the verdict was officially reversed by Mao himself at the 'Seven Thousand Cadres Meeting' in early 1962, about 95 per cent of Anhui's production teams (except those in Huaiyuan and Tongcheng counties where the county leaders stood firmly opposed) reportedly adopted *baochan daohu*. In terms of 'household production quotas', therefore, peasants' reservation and fears must have been significantly mitigated by their previous experiences that the innovation had worked rather successfully.[19]

The decollectivization in Anhui is also characterized by an extremely fast pace at which grass-roots innovations were diffused to neighbouring communes, counties, and prefectures. A typical example would be the spread of *baochan daohu* from Shannan commune to Feixi county and to Liuan prefecture, as illustrated in Table 4.2. A radical and controversial grass-roots innovation initiated by one commune was adopted by almost all production teams in the whole county within less than a year, thus going well beyond the 'experimental' boundary specified by the 1979 central document. A similarly swift pace of diffusion occurred at the prefecture level as well, eventually facilitating an extremely fast province-wide popularization.

Table 4.3 presents data on another prefecture of Chuxian to which the famous Fengyang county belongs. While Fengyang's swift pace of decollectivization is well known along with its Xiaogang team, Laian county's rapid pace sheds interesting light on the process of decollectivization at the sub-provincial level. Within only three months between December 1979 and March 1980, the percentage of the county's production teams under *baochan daohu* jumped from 3 to over 99 per cent. How was something that had begun as a team-level experiment able to get diffused so quickly to other communes, to other counties, and eventually within the entire province? There seem to have been two key factors: provincial support and central auspices which often bypassed the intervening levels of administration to demonstrate support and to enable basic-level cadres and peasants to overcome fears of adopting the household responsibility systems.

THE SURVIVAL OF INNOVATION: THE CASES OF XIAOGANG AND HUANGHUA

The famous Xiaogang production team of Liyuan commune in Fengyang county is most widely viewed as a typical grass-roots pioneer. With twenty households and an average per capita income of 32 *yuan*, the team was well known for its extreme poverty: it had relied on 228 thousand *catties* of 'state-provided grains' (*guojia gongying liang*) and 15,000 *yuan* of 'state subsistence subsidies' (*guojia shengjiukuan*) during 1966–78. A popular story goes that, one day in late November of 1978, eighteen households held a secret meeting where they decided to divide up the collective land. They even made a clandestine pact, according to which the children of the persecuted team cadres were to be supported until the age of eighteen. Secrecy did not last, however, as the commune cadres soon found out Xiaogang's deviant practice. The commune leadership allegedly commented that 'you should know such a practice is in violation of state laws. . . . [Q]uickly go back to the collective system, or we will report to the county party committee.' Allegedly, Chen Tingyuan, the party secretary of Fengyang county,

TABLE 4.2. *Spread of household farming in Liuan prefecture (%)*

	1979	1980	1981
Liuan prefecture[a] (year-end figure)	16	90	98
Feixi county[b]	3: 20		
	6: 37		
	9: 50		
	12: 97		
Shannan commune[c]	3: 97.1		

Sources: [a] Xu Shiqi, 'The Three-Year Implementation of the Household Responsibility System in Liuan Prefecture', 3; [b] Yang and Liu, *Zhongguo nongcun gaige de daolu*, 105–6; [c] Wang Lihang, 'Shannan gongshe tuixing jiating lianchan chengbao zerenzhi jishi' (The Implementation of Household Responsibility Systems in Shannan Commune), *Nongcun gaige de xingqi*, 104.

TABLE 4.3. *Spread of household farming in Chuxian prefecture (%)*

	1979	1980	1981
Chuxian prefecture[a]	1: 0.02[a]	4: 48.4[b]	3: 92.9[d]
	8: 0.4[b]	12: 76.8[c]	12: 99.5[b]
	12: 9.1[b]		
Fengyang county[e] (year-end figure)		95 (g)	
Laian county[f]	3: 1.7	3: 99.5	
	12: 3.1		

Sources: [a] Wang Yuzhao, *Zunzhong nongmin de jueze—Nongcun gaige de shijian he tansuo* (Respecting Peasant Choices: The Practice and Ideas of Rural Reform) (Shanghai: Shanghai renmin chubanshe, 1989), 9. [b] Wang Yuzhao, 'Zhongguo nongmin de weida chuangzhao' (The Great Innovation of Chinese Peasants), *Nongcun gaige de xingqi*, 23, 25. [c] Lu Zixiu, *Nongcun gaige zhexue sikao* (The Philosophical Thoughts on the Rural Reform) (Shanghai: Shanghai renmin chubanshe, 1986), 18. [d] Wang Yuzhao, *Dabaogan yu daqushi* ('Comprehensive Contracts' and the Great Trend) (Beijing: Guangming ribao chubanshe, 1987), 81. [e] This figure is for *baogan daohu*. Despite the degree of publicity it received, data on Fengyang are rare. This figure is from Zhou Yueli, 'Nongye shengchan zerenzhi de fazhan guocheng he shiji xiaoguo' (The Developmental Process of Agricultural Responsibility Systems and Their Actual Effects), *Anhuisheng nongye shengchan zerenzhi: ziliao xuanbian* (Agricultural Production Responsibility Systems in Anhui: Selected Materials) (Internal Publication) (Hefei: Anhui Provincial Rural Work Department, 1983), 81. [f] Zhou Ping and Tang Fuyu, 'Wang Yemei zai tuixing baogan daohu de rizili' (The Days during which Wang Yemei Pushed for *baogan daohu*), *Nongcun gaige de xingqi*, 99–100.

supported the Xiaogang experiment, and later the prefecture and provincial authorities, too, endorsed it.[20]

This widely cited version contains a problem regarding the timing of Xiaogang's experiment with *baogan daohu*. According to the recent compilation of Anhui's decollectivization history, personal recollections by the former party secretary of Fengyang and the team leaders of Xiaogang point to November 1978. On the other hand, other versions suggest spring (some refer to as late as May) of 1979. If the latter date were indeed when the division of collective land had actually taken place, the innovation by Shannan commune of Feixi must have preceded that of Xiaogang.[21] Another problem concerns the reaction by the county leadership. While some official versions indicate that the party secretary of Fengyang, Chen Tingyuan, supported the deviant practice of Xiaogang, the county authorities under Chen's direction were in fact strongly opposed to *baogan daohu*.[22]

How did the Xiaogang experiment then survive in spite of the strong opposition by the county and commune authorities? Various sources point to the support from the Chuxian prefectural authorities and its party secretary, Wang Yuzhao.[23] Yet, these sources indicate Wang's support—in the form of a personal visit to Xiaogang—was given only in late October 1979. This timing of Wang's visit seems to have been manipulated, however, in order to conceal the firm opposition by the county authorities. That is, if the county leadership was diametrically opposed to *baogan daohu* and Wang supported the Xiaogang innovation only in October 1979, how was the team able to resist the county and commune authorities for over half a year? The answer lay in the fact that Wang made his visit to Xiaogang in March 1979 for the purpose of pre-empting potential opposition by county and commune cadres.[24] The Xiaogang experiment was officially endorsed on 24 January 1980, when Wan Li paid a visit to the team.[25]

The case of Huanghua brigade of Shannan commune in Feixi illustrates a different process. Faced with poverty and drought in 1978, peasants of Huanghua brigade demanded 'household production quotas' (*baochan daohu*) on the basis of their memories of the 1960s. In order to cope with the crisis, the commune leadership allowed the brigade to rent out collective land to households who were to plant their 'life-saving wheat'.[26] From late September to late November 1978, many neighbouring brigades also followed suit. As of late 1978, it was an extremely risky practice given the prevailing ideological norms against household-based production and accounting. The experiment thus took the form of a clandestine pact (like the one in Xiaogang) by which every participant was to keep the experiment secret, and if some members were persecuted everyone else would collectively take care of their families.[27]

Secrecy did not last long as neighbouring communes also demanded household farming. As popular demands intensified, fierce opposition was also generated among some local cadres. Despite some opposition and criticism, support came from the Shannan district party committee.[28] Tang Maolin, district party secretary, tacitly supported household farming while convincing the higher authorities that he was making efforts to prevent it.[29] Support also came from the provincial government. On 2 February 1979, Zhou Yueli (then deputy director of the Provincial Agricultural Commission) came to Shannan. During his visit, Zhou did not give explicit support for household farming *per se* but nevertheless commented that '[W]e must respect the innovative spirits of peasants and the methods of farming can be further diversified.' Upon his return to Hefei, Zhou reported to Wan Li on the Shannan situation. Wan Li immediately endorsed the Shannan innovation and designated the commune as an 'experimental spot' (*shidian*). Within two weeks, 200 (97.1 per cent) out of 206 production teams in the commune adopted *baochan daohu*. Continued visits by provincial-level leaders—Wang Guangyu (provincial agricultural secretary) on 18 April and Wan Li on 21 May—effectively pre-empted various sources of opposition and obstruction at the local level.[30]

THE LOCAL–PROVINCIAL–CENTRAL NEXUS IN THE SPREAD OF HOUSEHOLD FARMING IN ANHUI

Peasant innovations were no doubt crucial to the initiation of the decollectivization reform in Anhui. Equally, if not more, important is the fact that grass-roots innovations could have hardly survived, not to speak of their province-wide diffusion, without the support network that linked the sub-provincial authorities, the provincial leadership, and a reformist group at the centre. Although it does not appear that from the outset the reformers at the centre had any concrete plans or alternatives to substitute for the collective system, it is plausible that they were searching hard for some effective solutions to the problems that had plagued the rural economy for so long. In that respect, many provincial leaders appointed by the centre during this period might have considered finding such solutions as one of their key missions.

One of the puzzles that have haunted the students of post-Mao China concerns whether the 'reformers' had a blue-print for their radical schemes of change. Did they from the outset think of 'household responsibility systems' as the effective alternative to the Dazhai system? The assumption that Deng Xiaoping and the reformist coalition had a well thought-out plan regarding the rural reform seems faulty. An interviewee, who had held a vice-ministerial position in the 'agricultural system' (*nongye xitong*) during the period concerned, argued that neither Deng nor Hu Yaobang and Zhao Ziyang had initially favoured household farming: rather, they later took a cue from the popular local innovations. The same interviewee pointed to the initially lagging performance of Sichuan under Zhao as a key piece of evidence for his observation.[31]

Related is the background to Wan Li's assignment to Anhui. If we closely examine Wan Li's career before Anhui, which include deputy director of industry in the South-west China Bureau, deputy mayor of Beijing, Minister of Urban Construction, and Minister of Railways, we find his career to have been heavily urban- and industry-oriented. Given that, why was he assigned to Anhui, a predominantly agricultural province? According to interviews with one of Wan Li's former secretaries, Wan had originally been assigned to Hubei as its governor. Allegedly, however, Deng Xiaoping and Hu Yaobang intervened to assign Wan to Anhui as its first party secretary.[32] This may sound as if there were indeed a reformist plot to make Wan Li the engineer of rural reform in Anhui. Interviewees interpreted the event rather differently, however. According to them, as of 1977 (the year when Wan was assigned to Anhui), neither Deng nor Hu had any idea regarding how to approach the issue of rural reform. Therefore, the designation of Wan as Anhui's party boss had reasons that were more political than economic. Wan was sent to Anhui primarily for the purposes of reducing the military presence in the provincial politics and resolving complex intra-provincial factional bickering.[33] Wan's reputation as 'having the guts to do bold things', which had been fully demonstrated during his tenure as the Minister of Railways, was supposedly the main determinant of his Anhui assignment.[34] Along with Wan (Shandong native), two additional outsiders were injected to clean up factional politics in Anhui: Gu Zhuoxin (Liaoning native) as governor, and Zhao Shouyi (Shaanxi native) as a provincial party secretary.[35]

If Wan's assignment to Anhui had initially had no connection with the reformist blueprint, how did he then get involved in pioneering the rural reform? Two linkages were crucial: one with Wang Yuzhao and the other with Zhou Yueli. Wang Yuzhao, a native of Shandong, had worked in Anhui very long to become the party secretary of Quanzhao county in Chuxian prefecture in 1973. When Wan came to Anhui in 1977, Wang was the director of the prefectural education commission. After sacking the prefectural party secretary who was a military officer, Wan appointed Wang to head the prefectural party committee. Although whether the hometown network (both Wan and Wang were Shandong natives) was a factor is not known, Wang was no doubt the most important channel through which key information on the rural conditions in Chuxian prefecture—the most widely publicized locality in Anhui—was funnelled to Wan. In fact, Anhui's first provincial document on rural policy, known as 'Six Articles' (liutiao), was heavily influenced by the investigations conducted by Wang during early 1977. And his role in provincial policy formulation was to expand rapidly as peasants began to come up with radical innovations.[36]

The other link, Zhou Yueli, had been a secretary to Zeng Xisheng,

Anhui's party boss during the early 1960s. When Mao came out to attack Zeng's experiments with *baochan daohu* in 1962, Zhou fell with his boss. According to an interviewee, Wan Li met Zeng's wife just before his departure for Anhui. At the meeting, Zeng's wife recommended Zhou Yueli as someone who might be able to help Wan. Everyone was allegedly surprised when Wan sought to meet Zhou who at the time was only a division-level (*chuji*) official. During Wan Li's tenure, Zhou was the deputy director of the provincial agricultural commission (1979) and the director of the provincial policy research office (1980). Allegedly, Zhou had a direct access to Wan (some argued that Wan discussed rural issues with Zhou almost on a daily basis). And many in Hefei seem to believe it was Zhou who provided Wan with broad guidance concerning rural reform in Anhui.[37]

Zhou Yueli's contribution to the decollectivization reform in Anhui is threefold. First, he represented Wan Li and the provincial authorities in supporting household farming. During his frequent tours to localities, Zhou actively encouraged local experiments with household responsibility systems. Second, Zhou established communication channels through which key information on grass-roots situations was relayed directly to the provincial government. These channels of communication, utilizing the 'survey and research network' (*diaoyan xitong*), allowed communes to bypass the intermediate authorities in reporting directly to the provincial policy research office under Zhou.[38] Third, Zhou also represented Anhui's position at the 'seven province discussion meeting' (*qisheng zuotanhui*) held in Beijing in March 1979. At this meeting attended by rural-work personnel from Guangdong, Hunan, Sichuan, Jiangsu, Hebei, Jilin, and Anhui, the dominant theme was to criticize *baochan daohu*. Despite the generally hostile atmosphere, Zhou managed to argue in front of Hua Guofeng and Wang Renzhong that *baochan daohu* should be designated as an acceptable form of responsibility system.[39]

Wang Yuzhao, on the other hand, represented the 'reformist spirit' on the local front, especially in Chuxian Prefecture. Wang's contribution to Anhui's decollectivization was also threefold. First, he performed as Wan Li's prefectural agent by relaying key local information to Hefei. Second, Wang constantly toured many teams and brigades in his prefecture to encourage peasant experiments with household responsibility systems. Third, Wang also played a significant role in mitigating the fears of peasants and basic-level cadres who supported household farming. On 15 March 1979, for instance, *People's Daily* published a 'letter from the readers' (*duzhe laixin*) which severely criticized work-group based responsibility systems for destroying the collective system of agricultural production. Wang immediately issued a prefectural party committee document to every county in his prefecture. The document stipulated that 'since spring planting has already started, the current responsibility systems should be maintained by all means'; and that 'those responsibility systems in use have been endorsed by the prefectural party committee which will take full responsibility.' The prefecture's immediate action was strongly supported by Wan Li who endorsed Wang's decision and ordered the provincial party committee to disseminate a similar message to other prefectures.[40] Furthermore, on 17 March, Wan Li, along with Wang Yuzhao, toured the six counties of Quanzhao, Chuxian, Laian, Tianchang, Jiashan, and Dingyuan in order to mitigate the fears of policy reversal among basic-level cadres and peasants.[41]

Despite the swift responses by the provincial and prefectural authorities, the 'reader's letter' left many basic-level cadres and peasants concerned with the political ramifications of their deviation. Some interviewees recalled that the incident had forced many teams in Liuan prefecture to readopt the collective system. In Huoqiu County, for instance, in the immediate aftermath of the publication of the 'readers' letter', the percentage of its teams under the systems based on work groups and households declined from 80 to 28.[42] The incident provided a convenient pretext which conservative local cadres, especially at the prefecture and county levels, utilized to criticize the provincial policy on household farming. Some prefecture- and county-level cadres allegedly went so far as to write letters to Wan Li asking 'where are you leading our province to?'[43]

In addition to the 'readers' letter' incident, opposition continued to come from the centre. Since the divided central leadership was still struggling over the direction of rural policy in 1979, the 'conservative' groups at the centre sought to stem the course of decollectivization. These conservative leaders allegedly made telephone calls to Feixi county officials to criticize their 'serious deviations'.[44] Subsequently, in July 1979, the Feixi county party committee issued County Document Number 46 calling for the redress of the deviation involving household farming. Interestingly, the Anhui provincial party committee was not discouraged by some dissenting views at the centre, probably because of Wan Li's linkage to the reformist coalition and his personal relationship with Deng Xiaoping. The provincial party committee immediately dispatched two high-ranking officials to Feixi—Wang Guangyu, provincial agricultural secretary, and Zhou Yueli—to reaffirm provincial support for the county's experiment. Reassured by provincial support, the county party committee issued County Document Number 50 announcing a further relaxation of control over household-based responsibility systems, accelerating the county-wide popularization of 'household production quotas' in 1979 (see Table 4.2).[45]

What enabled the Anhui provincial authorities under Wan to insist on the household responsibility systems in the face of strong opposition and criticism from both central and local officials?[46] The most crucial factor was Wan's personal relationship with Deng Xiaoping, which provided both political and psychological support for the controversial reform Wan was experimenting with in Anhui.[47] Wan, however, seems to have taken every precaution to inform the central government of the developments in Anhui.

For instance, after his endorsement of the Shannan experiment in February 1979, Wan immediately sent a report to the Centre that some areas of Anhui had already implemented *baochan daohu*.[48] Wan also consulted Deng on key issues of rural reform. Many interviewees who had then participated in the central policy process suggested that generally Deng Xiaoping had not been deeply involved in rural policy-making although he had actively supported the 'liberation of ideas' which made radical local innovations possible.[49] Several interviewees pointed to July 1979 as a turning point. It was around this time that Deng Xiaoping visited the Huang Mountain located in southern Anhui. Throughout the visit, Wan Li accompanied Deng and allegedly discussed many key issues of rural reform in Anhui. One interviewee who then had a direct access to Wan Li argued that Deng had not objected to Wan's experiments with household farming in the province. Otherwise, according to him, Wan must have changed his view on decollectivization given his utmost loyalty to Deng.[50]

Wan Li's personal relationship with Hu Yaobang also helped to maintain the former's confidence in his controversial experiments. Although Hu (along with Deng Xiaoping) was informed only of large issues and initially held a relatively reserved attitude toward decollectivization, the 'very close' relationship between the two (recall Hu's intervention in assigning Wan to Anhui instead of Hubei) allowed Wan to experiment with radical reformist measures.[51] And the inclusion of the 'exception' (*chuwai*) clause—which specified certain regions to be permitted to adopt *baochan daohu*—in the revised document of the Third Plenum decisions was allegedly facilitated by Wan's request to Zhao Ziyang at a Politburo meeting in August 1979, who took part in the redrafting process (*xiugai*).[52]

With tacit support from the key reformist leaders, Wan Li went on to endorse the household responsibility systems in his province. At a provincial rural conference convened in January 1980 which leading cadres of prefectures, cities, and counties attended, heated debates were held among these local leaders. According to a participant, party secretaries of two prefectures, Xu Shiqi of Liuan and Wang Yuzhao of Chuxian, actively supported decollectivization, while those of the remaining seven prefectures either kept silent or strongly opposed *baochan daohu*. According to this interviewee, Wan made the following remark: 'I myself support *baochan daohu* and think it can be fully experimented with. . . . Some are worried that this might violate the Centre's decision, but in fact it is in line with the decision's "spirit" that stresses practice as the only criterion of truth.'[53]

Another watershed was marked by Deng Xiaoping's endorsement. In an 'internal' speech made on 31 May 1980, Deng gave a complete justification for the local experiments in Anhui as follows:

An absolute majority of teams in Anhui's Feixi county adopted household production quotas. . . . A majority of teams in Fengyang county are currently under the household contracts with fixed levies. Both counties experienced rapid growth in just a year. Some comrades are concerned that such practices may adversely affect collective economy. But, as I see it, their worries are largely groundless.[54]

It is not entirely clear from the speech whether Deng's support was confined to the local innovations in Feixi and Fengyang only or to the province as a whole, or whether it could even be extended to other provinces as well. It is very possible that in other pioneer provinces, cadres and peasants alike may have interpreted Deng's speech as supporting their own respective experiments. In any case, local cadres in Anhui took a cue from this speech and carried out the popularization of household responsibility systems.[55] The promotion of Wan Li as a vice-premier in charge of rural policy (replacing Chen Yonggui) and chairman of the State Agricultural Commission (replacing Wang Renzhong) in early 1980 generated a significant boost for the nationwide spread of decollectivization but, at the same time, brought about some problems for Anhui's own decollectivization.[56]

SURVIVING THE LEADERSHIP CHANGE: ANHUI'S DECOLLECTIVIZATION AFTER WAN LI

Much of the decollectivization process has been highly 'romanticized' in China. A predominant majority of the Chinese documentary sources have a tendency to euphemize the local experiences by overemphasizing the voluntary involvement of the peasant masses and by playing down the intensity of policy conflicts and political confrontations involved. Such euphemism is particularly superfluous in characterizing the process in Anhui, the 'model province' of decollectivization.[57] Even many scholarly approaches have also tended to adopt a 'smooth process' perspective with regard to Anhui. Author's interviews with several key figures in the making and implementation of rural policy at the time provide crucial insight on the decollectivization process in Anhui after Zhang Jingfu succeeded Wan Li as the province's party boss in 1980.[58]

While very few documented sources refer to the difficulties created by this leadership change, many interviewees characterized the post-Wan period of 1980–1 as having considerably slowed down the pace of decollectivization in Anhui.[59] The key variable was that the new provincial leader, Zhang Jingfu, was a staunch opponent of the household responsibility systems. As an Anhui native, Zhang had worked extensively in the province during the revolution period in the areas of political and propaganda work. Whether or not he was later linked up with his old networks remains unclear. Several interviewees suggested that after the liberation, Zhang had become one of the core members of the central 'financial system' (*caizheng xitong*) largely under the control of Chen Yun and his lieutenant, Yao Yilin.

Geographically, too, Zhang had been closely linked to Chen Yun's turf by serving as a deputy mayor of Hangzhou, director of the Zhejiang provincial financial and economic commission, and a member of the Zhejiang provincial party standing committee. Since Chen Yun had not been an active supporter of decollectivization (particularly that of *baogan daohu*), Zhang Jingfu might well have adopted the policy line of his patron.[60]

Zhang's reservation toward decollectivization was first manifested at the provincial rural work conference convened in January 1980, where Wan Li personally endorsed the two household-based responsibility systems.[61] Zhang, who had basically agreed to Wan's approach at the conference, suggested on the next day that Wan Li's speech should be put in a provincial party document rather than published in *Anhui Daily*. Zhang's rationale, according to an interviewee, was that provincial party documents were to reach county authorities at the lowest but newspapers could be read by all basic-level cadres and peasants. Wan Li, perhaps out of caution, chose to follow the advice of Zhang who then had already been designated to succeed him.[62]

In the immediate aftermath of Wan's transfer to Beijing in February 1980, Zhang Jingfu allegedly commented that 'cadres at the county level and above should clear their heads in implementing the rural reform', which was then interpreted by many provincial and local officials as an implicit warning against the proponents of household farming. While opinions varied among the interviewees as to whether Zhang had explicitly opposed the household responsibility systems, there was nevertheless a consensus that he had not been a supporter of *baogan daohu*. More importantly, Zhang allegedly cultivated two 'Marxist-Leninist counties' (*malie xian*) in Xucheng and Lujiang, both bordering on Feixi and boasting of their collective economy. Another significant act of sabotage was that Zhang failed to make an internal dissemination of Deng Xiaoping's May 1980 speech.[63]

Zhang's position on the household responsibility systems created serious policy confusion among many local officials, including those in Chuxian prefecture who became increasingly concerned about the possibility of peasants reverting back to the collective system out of fears of persecution. It seems, however, that Zhang's intervention did not have as profound an impact as it had originally intended. Former officials in Chuxian prefecture listed three reasons for this minimized impact. First, Wan Li continued to support Anhui's decollectivization after his transfer to the centre. Despite the fact that he was a vice-premier and chairman of the State Agricultural Commission, Wan was not able to dictate to Zhang Jingfu due to the highly 'horizontal' (*kuaikuai*) nature of rural work and to Zhang's linkages with Chen Yun. Consequently, Wan Li adopted the tactic of 'besieging Anhui from the outside'. For this purpose, Wan utilized various national meetings on agriculture to produce official documents that endorsed the household responsibility systems, thus constraining the room for Zhang's obstruction.

One key example was CD [80] No. 75 which grew out of the September 1980 meeting attended by provincial first party secretaries.[64] Wan also utilized the national media to propagate the effectiveness of household farming. For instance, Wan asked his lieutenants like Wu Xiang and Zhang Guangyou to publish articles in support of decollectivization. Wu Xiang's famous article on the 'log bridge versus wide road' (metaphors for household farming and collective agriculture, respectively) is a good example in point.[65]

Second, while Zhang Jingfu was opposed to household farming, several other provincial leaders of Anhui continued to support decollectivization actively or tacitly at least. Gu Zhuoxin (chairman of the provincial people's congress) and Wang Guangyu (provincial agricultural secretary) provided continued support for local pioneers like Chuxian and Liuan prefectures.[66] Third, many supporters of decollectivization in Anhui came to be linked up with a group of young reformist intellectuals well connected to such high-level leaders as Hu Yaobang and Deng Liqun. This group, later known as the 'Chinese Rural Development Research Group' (*zhongguo nongcun fazhan wenti yanjiuzu*), gave nationwide publicity to Anhui's accomplishments in the decollectivization reform, eventually forcing Zhang to lift his blockade against household farming.[67] Interviewees in Hefei argued that Zhang had then turned himself into a supporter of household farming by mid-1981, after which the spread of decollectivization in Anhui resumed its previous pace under Wan Li.[68]

Tianchang county is an illustrative example of latecomers which adopted the household responsibility systems after Zhang's conversion in 1981. Known as one of the major grain-producing bases in Anhui, Tianchang had boasted of its high agricultural productivity and refused to follow the neighbouring Laian county in adopting household farming during 1979–80. Due to its high level of mechanization and electrification and to the policy uncertainties after Wan's departure, the county authorities were fearful of the potentially adverse impact of household farming. Despite the pressure from the prefecture authorities (Chuxian prefecture, that is), the county refrained from the popular implementation of decollectivization. By September 1980, only 12 per cent of the county's teams were under *baochan daohu* (as opposed to the provincial average of about 40 per cent and the prefecture's average of about 60 per cent). After Zhang's conversion in 1981, however, the spread of household farming was extremely fast in the county so that, by the end of 1981, 96 per cent of its teams adopted the more controversial system of *baogan daohu*.[69]

With the dissemination of CD [82] No. 1 in early 1982, the household responsibility systems became the focus of rural reform. By the time Beijing's preference for household farming became crystal clear, about 90 per cent of Anhui's teams were already under household farming. By mid-1982, with only a very few exceptions (e.g. Tu county near Nanjing), almost all counties adopted the household responsibility systems as the June 1982 data of 97 per cent indicate. By December 1982, 99.8 per cent of the production teams in Anhui adopted the household responsibility systems, almost all of which were *baogan daohu*.

DECOLLECTIVIZATION IN ANHUI: LOCAL INNOVATION, OVERHEAD CONTROL, AND THE POLITICS OF PIONEERING

Much of the foregoing discussion confirms that grass-roots innovations were a crucial propellant of decollectivization in Anhui particularly during the early period of 1978–9. One notable characteristic of local innovations in Anhui was its wide geographical coverage as the result of a natural calamity combined with the peasants' past experiences with household-based responsibility systems. Generic spontaneity played a crucial role, as peasants themselves came up with innovative schemes to meet their serious economic difficulties. Peasant adoption of radical innovations was, however, based upon their prior knowledge and memories of the effectiveness of these innovations. With such a perceptual safety net, 'rational peasants' would not have chosen to stick with the collective system in which they had already lost most of their hopes.[70]

Peasant innovations alone, however, could not have been able to sustain the reform that was then deemed highly sensitive, controversial, and deviant. With the cases of the Xiaogang production team and the Huanghua brigade, the crucial importance of immediate support and continued protection by provincial and other local authorities has been demonstrated. In addition to the generic spontaneity and the peasants' memories of the past experiences, diffusion also played an important role in the spread of decollectivization in Anhui.[71] Diffusion was facilitated in a variety of ways. The most widely used channel was the mass media which offered detailed reports on successful local innovations in a particular region.[72] An alternative channel was through cadres, scholars, and reporters who spread the word on the basis of their field trips and other kinds of encounters with the reform.[73] Still another channel was contingent upon geographical proximity in that being physically closer to the origin of a local innovation made diffusion a lot faster.[74]

In numerical terms, localities involved in innovation were a very small minority as innovation was a very risky business in a system where manifest efforts to deviate from the established routines entailed dangers. Then, how were these innovations initially able to survive and later popularized? The peasant-power perspective would argue that both the survival and popular adoption of grass-roots innovations were the result of conscious institutional choices by peasants, which would then imply a sudden 'evaporation' of the state as a whole. The fact of the matter is that in many cases, local innovations did not survive nor were they popularized as voluntary choices of the peasants.[75] Even in the exceptional case of Anhui for which the teleological argument of the peasant-power perspective and its deterministic view of the transition from innovation to popularization seem more applicable than elsewhere, the provision of political support and protection by the prefecture and provincial authorities was more than indispensable.

The Anhui case shows that there were a variety of factors at work to facilitate the pioneering pattern. A combination of meteorological and economic factors and past history produced multiple, simultaneous, and widespread local innovations. What enabled such radical innovations to survive was the intervention by the provincial authorities to support grass-roots experiments, thus pre-empting potential opposition from the intermediate levels of local administration.[76] Anhui also had few endogenous interests to protect from the potentially adverse effects of decollectivization.[77] Beijing's conditional endorsements also came along in time to support the provincial position. Under such favourable circumstances, peasants maximized their opportunities and the overall outcome was that the peasants constantly stayed ahead of state policy.

NOTES

1. For studies adopting such 'backward mapping' perspectives, see Greg O'Leary and Andrew Watson, 'The Production Responsibility System and the Future of Collective Farming', *Australian Journal of Chinese Affairs*, 8 (1982), 1–34; Justin Yifu Lin, 'The Household Responsibility System Reform in China: A Peasant's Institutional Choice', *American Journal of Agricultural Economics*, 69/2 (1987), 410–15; Daniel Kelliher, *Peasant Power in China: The Era of Rural Reform 1979–1989* (New Haven: Yale University Press, 1992), chs. 1–4; and Kate Xiao Zhou, *How the Farmers Changed China: Power of the People* (Boulder, Colo.: Westview, 1996), chs. 1 and 3.
2. For studies utilizing the 'forward mapping' perspectives, David Zweig, 'Peasants, Ideology, and New Incentive Systems: Jiangsu Province, 1978–1981', in William L. Parish (ed.), *Chinese Rural Development: The Great Transformation* (Armonk, NY: M. E. Sharpe, 1985), 141–63; and Jonathan Unger, 'The Decollectivization of the Chinese Countryside: A Survey of Twenty-Eight Villages', *Pacific Affairs*, 58/4 (1985–6), 585–606.
3. Kelliher, for instance, applies the 'peasant-power' thesis to China as a whole with little geographical and temporal differentiation. See *Peasant Power in China*, 234–6. For a sensible critique of Kelliher, see Joseph Fewsmith, *Dilemmas of Reform in China: Political Conflict and Economic Debate* (Armonk, NY: M. E. Sharpe, 1994), 49 n. 2. Kate Zhou pushes this 'peasant-power' thesis much farther than Kelliher, although it seems that the paucity of the data provided and her excessively unidirectional focus on peasant zeal and successful cases weaken the overall argument. For a critique of Zhou's argument, see David Zweig, 'Rural People, the Politicians, and Power', *China Journal*, 38 (1997), 153–68. For studies that seek a balance between the two competing perspectives, see Tang Tsou, 'The Responsibility System in Agriculture', in *The Cultural Revolution and Post-Mao Reforms: A Historical Perspective* (Chicago: University of Chicago Press, 1986), 194–5; David Zweig, 'Context and Content in Policy Implementation: Household Contracts and Decollectivization, 1977–1983', in David M. Lampton (ed.), *Policy Implementation in Post-*

Mao China (Berkeley and Los Angeles: University of California Press, 1987), 255–83; and Fewsmith, *Dilemmas of Reform in China*, ch. 1. For Chinese material that has a comprehensive coverage with a balanced perspective, see Xu Yong, *Baochan daohu chenfulu* (The Fall and Rise of Baochan daohu) (Zhuhai: Zhuhai chubanshe, 1998), chs. 11–12.

4. Whether endorsing the 'peasant-power' thesis or otherwise, few studies have, differentiated the provincial pace and patterns of decollectivization in any systematic manner. To date, provincial case studies were focused predominantly on Anhui and Sichuan, and even these were mostly presented anecdotally devoid of comprehensive local implemenation data.

5. For differing perceptions of and varied responses by local cadres, see John P. Burns, 'Local Cadre Accommodation to the "Responsibility System" in Rural China', *Pacific Affairs*, 58/4 (1985–6), 607–25.

6. On many occasions in the history of the People's Republic, certain regional and provincial leaders received their 'mission' from Mao who explicitly encouraged them to experiment with and promote some controversial policies locally prior to their national application. For a well-known thesis on the strategic alliance between Mao and his provincial 'lieutenants' during 1956–7, see Parris Chang, *Power and Policy in China* (University Park, Pa.: Penn State University Press, 1978), 14–39. For Sichuan's (i.e. Li Jingquan's) adoption of a 'pioneer' posture in promoting Mao's 'Twelve Year Plan' and other radical policies, see David S. G. Goodman, *Centre and Province in the People's Republic of China: Sichuan and Guizhou, 1955–1965* (Cambridge: Cambridge University Press, 1986), 88–90.

7. All but Ningxia made the top-ten list in terms of their mortality increase during 1956–62, with Anhui and Guizhou ranking first and second. For the mortality rate increase for these provinces, see Dali L. Yang, *Calamity and Reform in China: State, Rural Society, and Institutional Change Since the Great Leap Famine* (Stanford: Stanford University Press, 1996), 38, table 6.

8. While no provinces were officially singled out as testing spots for household farming, political and policy orientations of some provincial leaders and their clientelistic ties to the reformist group at the centre seem to have facilitated the pioneering pattern. Anhui under Wan Li and Sichuan under Zhao Ziyang are but the most well known examples. Chi Biqing of Guizhou also assumed a key role as he firmly represented the cause of decollectivization in the well-known debate over the 'wide road of collective production' (*yangguandao*) versus the 'narrow log bridge of household farming' (*dumuqiao*). A valuable piece of information confirms that some central leaders granted support for household farming in a few select provinces. In April 1980, at a planning conference for long-term development, Deng Xiaoping and Yao Yilin are said to have suggested that Guizhou and Gansu implement 'household production quotas' (*baochan daohu*). See Lu Xueyi, *Lianchan chengbao zerenzhi yanjiu* (Study of Responsibility Systems of Production-Linked Contracts) (Shanghai: Shanghai renmin chubanshe, 1986), 75.

9. On Sichuan, see Chris Bramall, 'Origins of the Agricultural "Miracle": Some Evidence from Sichuan', *China Quarterly*, 143 (1995), 743–6.

10. Anhui's pace of decollectivization served as a semi-model to be studied and emulated in the later stage of the reform. See *Renmin ribao*, 22 and 23 Jan., 28 April, 8 May, 14 June, and 26 Nov. 1981.

11. In his 'Cong Anhuisheng Liuan diqu sannian de shijian kan shuangbao zerenzhi' (The Three-Year Implementation of the Household Responsibility Systems in Liuan Prefecture of Anhui), *Nongye jingji wenti* (Problems of Agricultural Economy), March 1982, 3, Xu Shiqi lists the two counties of Feixi and Liuan. Ma Piao, in his 'Anhui nongcun baochan daohu qingkuang kaocha' (An Examination of the Implementation of *baochan daohu* in Anhui), *Jingji guanli* (Economic Management), February 1981, p. 20, singles out Liuan, Guzhen, Feixi, and Wuwei. Yang Xun and Liu Jiarui point out Feixi for *baochan daohu* and Fengyang for *baogan daohu*. See *Zhongguo nongcun gaige de daolu: zongti shuping yu quyu shizheng* (The Path of China's Rural Reform: An Overview and Local Practice) (Beijing: Beijing daxue chubanshe, 1987), 75. Six counties (Guzhen, Fengyang, Feixi, Laian, Dangtu, and Wuhu) are suggested by Kelliher, *Peasant Power in China*, 60. Four counties of Laian, Feixi, Fengyang, and Wuhu are listed in *Dangdai zhongguo de Anhui* (Contemporary China's Anhui) (Beijing: Dangdai zhongguo chubanshe, 1991), i. 179–86. Feixi, Fengyang, and Laian are suggested in Ou Yuanfang and Deng Jiancheng, 'Anhui nongcun

jiating lianchan chengbao zerenzhi de chansheng yu fazhan' (The Genesis and Development of Household Responsibility Systems in Anhui), in the Historical Archives Commission of the Anhui Provincial Political Consultative Conference (ed.), *Nongcun gaige
de xingqi* (The Rise of Rural Reform) (Beijing: Zhongguo wenshi chubanshe, 1993), 3–5.
Zhou Qiren points out Guzhen county as Anhui's earliest (1977) pioneer for *baochan
daohu*, which was followed by Feixi, Fengyang, Quanzhao, and Wuhu in 1978. See his
'Jiating jingying de zaifaxian' (The Rediscovery of Family Management), in Zhou Qiren
(ed.), *Nongcun biange yu zhongguo fazhan 1978–89* (Rural Change and China's Development) (Hong Kong: Oxford University Press, 1994), 62.

12. Given the geographical distribution of these nine counties, cropping patterns do not seem
to have been a key factor in facilitating the innovations related to household farming. The
cultivated area of northern Anhui (*wanbei*) was hardly planted with rice (2.9 per cent) but
predominantly planted with wheat (45.3 per cent), while that of southern Anhui (*jiangnan*) was predominantly planted with rice (77.8 per cent) but relatively little wheat (12.5
per cent). Six out of these nine counties were located in the middle region (*wanzhong*)
with 53.1 and 29.3 per cent of their land planted with rice and wheat respectively. The data
on the cropping patterns are from Zhang Desheng (ed.), *Anhuisheng jingji dili* (The Economic Geography of Anhui) (Beijing: Xinhua chubanshe, 1986), 108; and Min Yuming
et al., *Anhuisheng dili* (The Geography of Anhui) (Hefei: Anhui renmin chubanshe, 1990),
152–3.

13. Almost all studies of Anhui's decollectivization touch upon the 1978 drought. See, for
instance, Yang and Liu, *Zhongguo nongcun gaige de daolu*, 100; Ma Piao, 'An Examination of the Implementation of *baochan daohu* in Anhui', 20; and Xu Shiqi, 'The Three-
Year Implementation of the Household Responsibility System in Liuan Prefecture of
Anhui Province', 3.

14. The official policy at the time was 'production quotas for work groups' (*baochan daozu*).
For a typical practice of this policy, see the case of Mahu commune of Fengyang county
described in Wang Gengjin, Yang Xun, Wang Ziping, Liang Xiaodong, and Yang Guansan
(eds.), *Xiangcun sanshinian: Fengyang nongcun shehui jingji fazhan shilu, 1949–1983* (The
Countryside over the Last Thirty Years: Records of Social and Economic Development in
Fengyang, 1949–1983) (Beijing: Nongcun duwu chubanshe, 1989), ii. 387–9.

15. Yang and Liu, *Zhongguo nongcun gaige de daolu*, 107, 111; and *Anhui ribao* (*Anhui Daily*;
hereafter *AHRB*), 5 Jan. 1980.

16. For other areas in Anhui, see Ying Daochang, 'Laianxian diyige shixing baochan daohu de
shengchandui' (Laian County's First Production Team in Implementing *baochan daohu*),
Nongcun gaige de xingqi, 90–1; and Xu Shiqi, 'The Three-Year Implementation of the
Household Responsibility System in Liuan Prefecture of Anhui Province', 5–6. For
Guizhou, see Kang Mingzhong, 'Guizhou nongye baochan daohu qianyi' (A Discussion of
the Implementation of *baochan daohu* in Guizhou), *Nongye jingji wenti*, Mar. 1982, 11.

17. In the case of Xiaogang Production Team, the head of the commune is reported to have
said 'Just let them do whatever they want.' Yang and Liu, *Zhongguo nongcun gaige de
daolu*, 113.

18. For the case of Yu Lifan, party secretary of Shaoji commune of Laian county, who actively
encouraged *baochan daohu* within his jurisdiction in late 1978, see Lu Zixiu, *Nongcun
gaige zhexue sikao* (The Philosophical Thoughts on the Rural Reform) (Shanghai:
Shanghai renmin chubanshe, 1986), 44.

19. In this respect, the peasants' innovations of household farming may have been politically
risk-taking but economically risk-averse. Information is from an interview in Hefei in 1994;
and Zhou Yueli, *Jiating chengbaozhi tantao* (Discussion of Household Contract Systems)
(Hefei: Anhui renmin chubanshe, 1985), 36, 43–9. For popular support for 'household production quotas' in 1961–2, see *Dangdai zhongguo de Anhui*, ii. 170–7; 'Guanyu zerentian
wenti de baogao' (Report on the Problems of 'Responsibility Plots'), Research Team on
the Issue of Chinese Rural Development (ed.), *Baochan daohu ziliao xuan* (Selected
Materials on *baochan daohu*) (internal publication) (n.p., 1981), 330–9; and Anhui Provincial Agricultural Commission (ed.), *Anhui zerentian ziliao xuanbian* (Selected Materials
for 'Responsibility Plots' in Anhui) (Hefei: Anhui Provincial Information Bureau, 1987).
For the spread of 'responsibility fields' in Fengyang during 1961–3, see *Xiangcun sanshinian*, ii. 272–365.

20. Yan Junchang and Yan Hongchang (leaders of the Xiaogang team at the time), 'Xiaogang: nongcun jingji tizhi gaige de xianjin dianxing' (Xiaogang: An Advanced Example of the Economic System Reform in the Countryside), *Nongcun gaige de xingqi*, 79–83.

21. For the versions arguing for November 1978, see Chen Tingyuan, 'Zai zhu yuanzhang jiaxiang jueqi de yichang geming' (A Revolution in the Home of Zhu Yuanzhang the Founder of the Ming Dynasty), and Yan Junchang and Yan Hongchang', Xiaogang: An Advanced Example of the Economic System Reform in the Countryside', 44, 80. For those referring to the spring of 1979, see Ou Yuanfang and Deng Jiancheng, 'The Genesis and Development of Household Responsibility Systems in Anhui' and Wang Yuzhao, 'The Great Innovation of Chinese Peasants', 5, 23; and Yang and Liu, *Zhongguo nongcun gaige de daolu*, 112. Interviews in Anhui indicated, both directly and indirectly, that officials affiliated with different localities tended to reflect the interests and reputation of the geographical areas that they had previously served or currently represent. Author's interviews in Hefei also revealed that Xiaogang's *baogan daohu* was first implemented in the spring of 1979 and Shannan, Laian, and Dingyuan were much faster than Fengyang's Xiaogang. A national-level official chronology, too, lists Shannan of Feixi county as the first implementor of decollectivization. See *Dangdai zhongguo de nongye* (Contemporary China's Agriculture) (Beijing: Dangdai zhongguo chubanshe, 1992), 309.

22. For versions arguing for Chen's support, see Yan Junchang and Yan Hongchang, 'Xiaogang: Advanced Example of the Economic System Reform in the Countryside', 82; and Yang and Liu, *Zhongguo nongcun gaige de daolu*, 113. Information on Chen's staunch opposition to the Xiaogang's implementation of *baogan daohu* is from author's interviews in Hefei and Beijing. Chen's initial opposition to household farming (especially *baogan daohu*) can be found in the records of a county party standing committee meeting in 1979 published in *Xiangcun sanshinian*, ii. 402–4.

23. See, for instance, Yan Junchang and Yan Hongchang, 'Xiaogang: Advanced Example of the Economic System Reform in the Countryside', 82–3.

24. If Xiaogang's experiment had taken place in early spring of 1979 (rather than November 1978)—say, early March—Wang's visit in March makes good sense. Author's interview with a former official with Chuxian prefectural party committee in Beijing in 1994.

25. Chen Tingyuan, 'A Revolution in the Home of Zhu Yuanzhang the Founder of the Ming Dynasty' and Yan Junchang and Yan Hongchang, 'Xiaogang: Advanced Example of the Economic System Reform in the Countryside', *Nongcun gaige de xingqi*, 45, 83.

26. For the pioneering role by the commune leadership, see Wang Lihang, 'The Implementation of Household Responsibility Systems in Shannan Commune', 102. For a view that the commune leadership adopted an opportunistic attitude, see Fewsmith, *Dilemmas of Reform in China*, 27. In either case, unlike the Xiaogang case, the commune leadership did not display outright opposition.

27. Kelliher, *Peasant Power in China*, 61; and author's interview in Beijing in 1992.

28. District was the administrative level between the county and the commune.

29. See Wang Yanhai (former reporter for *Anhui Daily*), 'Feixixian shixing baochan daohu de huiyi' (Recollections of Feixi County's Implementation of *baochan daohu*), *Nongcun gaige de xingqi*, 108.

30. Wang Lihang, 'The Implementation of Household Responsibility Systems in Shannan Commune', 103–5; and Yang Xun and Liu Jiarui, *Zhongguo nongcun gaige de daolu*, 102–4. Shannan's designation as an 'experimental spot' must have been a very difficult decision on the part of the provincial authorities not only because Feixi was not a mountainous area with difficulties of access but also because, more importantly, the county bordered on Hefei, the provincial capital. See Wu Xiang, 'Nongcun gaige weishenmo cong Anhui kaishi?' (Why Did the Rural Reform Start in Anhui?), *Zhongguo renli ziyuan kaifa* (Human Resource Development of China), 2 (1994), 33.

31. Interview in Beijing in 1992. Also see Fewsmith, *Dilemmas of Reform in China*, 20 n. 6. For Sichuan's pace of decollectivization, see Table 3.1. For Zhao's reservation toward household-based responsibility systems in 1978–80, see Zhou, *How the Farmers Changed China*, 61, 67.

32. This information, if true, may necessitate a different assessment of Deng's influence over party and government affairs even before his official comeback.

33. According to an interviewee, there were more than five different factions in Anhui at the

time, which included local, Hebei, Shandong, Shanxi, and Subei factions. Interview in Hefei in 1994. For Wan's alleged accomplishments in cleaning up the intra-provincial factional struggles within eight months, see Wu Xiang, 'Why Did the Rural Reform Start in Anhui?', 31; and Zhang Guangyou, *Wan Li zai yijiuqiwu dao yijiubaliu* (Wan Li from 1975 to 1986) (Hong Kong: Qiwen Publishing House, 1995), 147–52.

34. His assignment as the Minister of Railways was presumably masterminded by Deng Xiaoping who was highly appreciative of Wan's abilities as a troubleshooter.

35. Gu had been a deputy minister of the State Planning Commission up to 1963. His first appearance after the Cultural Revolution was in Anhui as a secretary of its provincial revolutionary committee. For backgrounds of Gu and Zhao, see, respectively, Wolfgang Bartke, *Who's Who in the People's Republic of China*, 3rd edn., (Munich: Saur, 1991), 156; and *Zhongguo gongchandang renming dacidian* (Who's Who in the Chinese Communist Party, 1921–1991) (Beijing: Zhongguo guoji guangbo chubanshe, 1991), 544. The provincial leadership group at the time consisted of Wan Li, Gu Zhuoxin, Zhao Shouyi, Wang Guangyu (provincial deputy secretary in charge of agriculture), and Yuan Zhen (secretary-general of the provincial party committee). See Wu Xiang, 'Why Did the Rural Reform Start in Anhui?', 31.

36. Interview with a former official with Chuxian Prefecture in Beijing in 1994. For the 'Six Articles', see Lu Zixiu, *Nongcun gaige zhexue sikao*, 10–15.

37. Interview with a former provincial official in Hefei in 1994.

38. Ibid.

39. Zhou Yueli, 'Baochan daohu shi jiefang sixiang de chanwu' (*Baochan daohu* is the Product of Liberation of Ideas), *Nongcun gaige de xingqi*, 31–2. This bold act was supported by Wan Li as well as Du Runsheng, the deputy chairman of the State Agricultural Commission at the time.

40. See Wang Yuzhao, 'Woguo jingji tizhi gaige de yi xiang lishixing juece' (One Historical Decision in Our Country's Economic System Reform), in State Science and Technology Commission (ed.), *Zhongyao juece shijian yu sikao* (The Practice and Thoughts of Major Decisions) (Beijing: Zhongguo shehuikexue wenxian chubanshe, 1992), i. 4–5; Lu Zixiu (Wang Yuzhao's lieutenant in Chuxian prefecture), 'Wan Li wan dongxing' (Wan Li Goes to the East of Anhui), *Nongcun gaige de xingqi*, 49–50. Also see Zhou Yueli, '*Baochan daohu* is the Product of Liberation of Ideas', 33. The 'letter from the readers' was allegedly prepared in Wang Renzhong's office. And on 20 March, Wang Renzhong also called Wan Li and asked about Anhui's 'deviant activities'. Information from author's interview in Beijing in 1994.

41. Wu Xiang, 'Why Did the Rural Reform Start in Anhui?', 34.

42. Author's interview in Hefei in 1994. The figures for Huoqiu are from Zhou Yueli, '*Baochan daohu* is the Product of Liberation of Ideas', 34.

43. Author's interview in Beijing in 1994.

44. One interviewee identified Wang Dongxing as one of such central leaders who personally called the county party committee. Interview in Beijing in 1992. In another interview in Beijing in 1994, a former deputy secretary-general of Anhui provincial party committee confirmed this and identified Wang Dongxing as having called the Feixi party committee and Wang Renzhong as having called the Chuxian prefectural party committee.

45. See Yang Xun and Liu Jiarui, *Zhongguo nongcun gaige de daolu*, 105–6.

46. Wan Li, during his tenure in Anhui, made numerous comments that were of quite an extraordinary nature. Two examples follow. On 8 September 1978, at a provincial party standing committee meeting, he reportedly said 'if we only care about central documents and instructions from above without due regard for actual conditions, why do we need this level (i.e. provincial level) of leadership?' In September 1979, Wan also said 'those innovations that have not yet been endorsed by the provincial party committee but are in line with the objective conditions, you should courageously implement them. . . . The provincial party committee will soon endorse them but do not wait for them.' See Wu Xiang, 'Why Did the Rural Reform Start in Anhui?', 33, 35.

47. Of course, the most obvious reason for Wan's support for household farming was its effectiveness in raising agricultural productivity. In Fengyang, for instance, its grain output rose by 70 per cent between 1978 and 1980 and its per capita income increased from 61 to 142 *yuan* in the same period. Grain outputs in Dingyuan and Jiashan also rose by 95.3 and

59.2 per cent, respectively, while that of Tianchang (which decollectivized only in 1981) marked only a 12 per cent increase between 1978 and 1980. See Zhou Yueli, *Jiating chengbaozhi tantao*, 183; and Wang Yuzhao, *Dabaogan yu daqushi*, 86–7.

48. Zhou Yueli, *'Baochan daohu* is the Product of Liberation of Ideas', 30.
49. Author's interviews with a former official of the Central Rural Policy Research Office and Wan Li's former secretary in Beijing in 1994.
50. Author's interview with a former Anhui provincial official in Hefei in 1994.
51. Author's interviews in Beijing in 1994.
52. Author's interview with a former Anhui provincial official in Hefei in 1994.
53. Leading cadres of the prefectures like Huizhou are said to have kept silent at the conference. Author's interview with a former Chuxian prefecture official in Beijing in 1994. The content of Wan's speech is from the author's interview with a former Anhui provincial official in Hefei in 1994 and Ou Yuanfang and Deng Jiancheng, 'The Genesis and Development of Household Responsibility Systems in Anhui', 7–8, 31. Also see Yang Xun and Liu Jiarui, *Zhongguo nongcun gaige de daolu*, 126. For the January 1980 provincial rural conference, see Li Debin and Lin Shunbao (eds.), *Xinzhongguo nongcun jingji jishi 1949.10–1984.9* (Chronology of New China's Rural Economy) (Beijing: Beijing daxue chubanshe, 1989), 484.
54. 'Guanyu nongcun zhengce wenti' (On Problems of Rural Policy), *Deng Xiaoping wenxuan* (Selected Writings of Deng Xiaoping) (Beijing: Renmin chubanshe, 1983), 275.
55. While Deng's internal speech was published later in 1983, prefectural-level cadres were permitted to read its content in 1980. Wang Yuzhao, for instance, recollected that he had seen the speech in the summer of 1980 and it had greatly encouraged him and other prefectural officials. See Wang Yuzhao, 'The Great Innovation of Chinese Peasants', 24–5.
56. Wan Li's promotion to the centre and the issuing of CD [80] No. 75 might have been closely related. For Anhui's full endorsement of *baochan daohu* and *baogan daohu* right after the issuing of CD [80] No. 75, see *AHRB*, 17 Oct. 1980.
57. Those subscribing one-sidedly to the peasant-power thesis have tended to accept such highly romanticized versions uncritically. For recent examples of the romanticization, see Li Chaogui, *Zhongguo nongcun daxieyi* (Portrayal of China's Countryside) (Changsha: Hunan wenyi chubanshe, 1993), 1–33; and *Renmin ribao*, 5 June 1994.
58. Neither Kelliher, Zhou, nor Fewsmith touches upon the changing provincial atmosphere in Anhui after Wan's departure. An exceptional mention about intra-provincial debates after Wan's departure is made in Zhou Yueli, *'Baochan daohu* is the Product of Liberation of Ideas', 37.
59. There were 5 and 3.4 per cent increases in the share of teams implementing the household responsibility systems between March and July 1980 and between December 1980 and June 1981, respectively (see Table 4.1). The pace got a lot faster, however, between July and December 1980 (35.9 per cent) probably due to the release of CD [80] No.75 in September.
60. Information on Chen Yun's orientation is from author's interview with ministerial-level officials in Beijing in 1994. Alternatively, however, considering the support given to the household responsibility policy by Yao Yilin (see n. 8) and Song Ping (who supported decollectivization in Gansu), two other proteges of Chen Yun, it may well be that Zhang was simply being opportunistic himself, unsure of the possibility of abrupt policy changes. I was made aware of this possibility by Joe Fewsmith.
61. Zhang began to serve in Anhui as its governor from December 1979. For his background, see Bartke, *Who's Who in the People's Republic of China*, 800–1.
62. Author's interview with a former deputy provincial agricultural secretary in Hefei in 1994.
63. Information based on interviews in Beijing and Hefei in 1994.
64. While about two-thirds of the provinces did not support decollectivization, the meeting nevertheless produced a document that permitted some exceptions which provinces like Anhui, Guizhou, and Gansu utilized to promote household farming. Provinces like Jiangsu strongly opposed household farming at the conference, and its leader, Xu Jiatun, even forbade the dissemination of CD [80] No. 75 within the province. Allegedly, some Jiangsu officials went to Anhui to get hold of the document. Information from an interview in Beijing in 1994.
65. Interview in Beijing in 1994. Wu Xiang's article appeared in *People's Daily* on 5 Nov. 1980.

And for detailed descriptions of this debate, see *Heilongjiang nongye hezuoshi* (History of Agricultural Co-operativization in Heilongjiang; hereafter *Hezuoshi*) (Beijing: Zhonggong dangshi ziliao chubanshe, 1990), 483–5.

66. Interview in Beijing in 1994. With the support from the key provincial leaders, basic-level cadres and peasants managed to resist administrative pressure imposed by the prefecture and county authorities. In Wuwei County in 1980, for instance, peasants boycotted a mass meeting called by the county government designed to criticize *baochan daohu*. See Zhou Yueli, *Jiating chengbaozhi tantao*, 52.

67. For the importance of this group in the process of decollectivization in general and in linking the centre with Anhui, see Fewsmith, *Dilemmas of Reform in China*, 32–43, 46–7.

68. The timing of Zhang's conversion is from interviews in Beijing and Hefei in 1994. Interesting is the fact that Zhang nevertheless continued to play to both groups of supporters and opponents of household farming. One key example is his simultaneous appointment of Wang Yuzhao (a key representative of supporters) and Shi Chun (a key representative of opponents) as members of the provincial party standing committee in 1982 just before his departure for Beijing to become a state councillor and the minister of the State Economic Commission. Information based on an interview with a former provincial official in Hefei in 1994.

69. For economic conditions of Tianchang County, see Administrative Office of the Anhui Provincial Government (ed.), *Anhui shengqing 1949–1984* (Provincial Conditions of Anhui 1949–84) (Hefei: Anhui renmin chubanshe, 1986), 704–6. For the Tianchang case in the decollectivization reform, see Lu Zixiu, *Nongcun gaige zhexue sikao*, 67–70; Zhou Yueli, *Jiating chengbaozhi tantao*, 183; and Wang Yuzhao, *Dabaogan yu daqushi*, 86–7.

70. For the importance of peasant memories, see Barry Naughton, *Growing out of the Plan: Chinese Economic Reform, 1978–1993* (Cambridge: Cambridge University Press, 1995), 140; and Yang, *Calamity and Reform in China*, 144–5, 150. For a Chinese account of this, see *Anhui shengqing 1949–1983*, 290.

71. There is no doubt that the pace of diffusion was contingent upon the effectiveness of a particular innovation. The remarkable accomplishments in Chuxian prefecture—a dramatic increase in grain production from 2.8 billion *jin* in 1979 to 4 billion *jin* in 1981—became known to other localities very fast. For the figures, see Chinese Rural Development Research Group, 'Anhuisheng Chuxian diqu nongcun diaocha zonghe baogao' (Summary Report of the Agricultural Survey on Anhui's Chuxian Prefecture), in Zhou Qiren (ed.), *Zhongguo quyu fazhan chayi* (Survey on Regional Disparities in China's Development) (Hong Kong: Oxford University Press, 1994), 20.

72. For such reports, see *Renmin ribao*, 30 Mar. and 14 Nov. 1979; and *AHRB*, 17 Oct. 1980.

73. For such a case of diffusion from Feixi to Hujiang, see Zhou Yueli, *Jiating chengbaozhi tantao*, 52.

74. The intra-prefecture spread of household farming in Chuxian (see Table 4.3) is particularly illustrative in this regard. Geographical proximity was crucial in spreading the news to Shandong's Heze prefecture which bordered on Anhui (see Chapter 5 for details). Frequent livestock marketing across the border also quickly spread the news about Anhui's innovations to Jiangsu. See Zweig, 'Peasants, Ideology, and New Incentive Systems', 153, 155.

75. The same conclusion was made by Unger, 'The Decollectivization of the Chinese Countryside', 592. More detailed discussions of this issue will be provided in the next two chapters on Shandong and Heilongjiang. In any case, all levels of bureaucratic administration mattered in opposing and supporting the survival and spread of household farming. And individual deal-making between peasants and cadres, if it existed on a large scale at all, was not effective in preventing commune, district, county, prefecture, and provincial authorities from actively intervening.

76. In almost all pioneer provinces, their provincial authorities expressed active support for *baochan daohu* at an earlier point in 1980. Other than Anhui, Guizhou, Neimenggu, and Gansu also held rural conferences in early 1980 to support *baochan daohu*. See *Dangdai zhongguo de nongye*, 310. For Song Ping's support for *baochan daohu* in Gansu in April 1980, see Lu Xueyi, *Dangdai zhongguo nongcun yu dangdai zhongguo nongmin*, 70. For Ningxia's February 1980 decision, see *Dangdai zhongguo de Ningxia* (Contemporary China's Ningxia) (Beijing: Zhongguo shehui kexue chubanshe, 1990), i. 203. And for

Guizhou's March 1980 decision, see *Dangdai zhongguo de Guizhou* (Contemporary China's Guizhou) (Beijing: Zhongguo shehui kexue chubanshe, 1989), i. 117–18.

77. Provinces like Anhui, Sichuan, Gansu, and Guizhou had little incentives to preserve mechanization as their primary strategy of rural development. Anhui with less than 20 per cent of its land under mechanized farming, unlike Shandong and Heilongjiang, had little to be concerned about the negative effects of household farming on its mechanization efforts. Wan Li, as early as November 1977, argued that '[W]hile the policy of mechanization is a correct one, agriculture is fundamentally done with the two hands of the peasant. . . . In the past several years, there were too many policies that did not make any sense.' See Wu Xiang, 'Why Did the Rural Reform Start in Anhui?', 31.

5

The Politics of 'Bandwagoning' in Shandong: Uncertainties, Opportunism, and Compliance

This chapter examines the 'bandwagoning' pattern adopted by a majority of the provinces during the period of decollectivization. These bandwagoners, being uncertain of the centre's intentions and preferences, had initially opted for a highly 'cautious stance of wait and see'. Once Beijing's preference for the household-based systems became crystal clear in late 1982, however, they all quickly bandwagoned to popularize them on a province-wide scale. The pervasiveness of bandwagoning during decollectivization highlights the lingering effects of the Maoist norms and underscores the limited success of the measures of post-Mao administrative decentralization. Such opportunistic behaviour by a majority of the provinces also explains why the level of interprovincial variation in the pace of decollectivization dropped sharply in 1982 compared to that in 1981 (see Table 3.3).

The peasant-power perspective loses much of its explanatory power when it comes to the provinces that shared more in common with the pioneer provinces but lagged far behind them in their pace of decollectivization, and to the provinces that shared more in common with the 'laggards' but quickly complied with Beijing. In the case of decollectivization, a majority of the provinces belonged to this category: Fujian, Guangdong, Hebei, Henan, Hubei, Jiangxi, Neimenggu, Qinghai, Shaanxi, Shandong, Shanxi, and Zhejiang. The prevalence of bandwagoning during decollectivization suggests that there were considerable lingering effects of the Maoist norm that provinces (and lower levels of administration) should avoid pushing ahead with a controversial policy or lagging too far behind in implementing it since both might entail enormous political costs.[1]

Despite some efforts by the centre to mitigate such fears in the early years of the post-Mao era, dominant norms of implementation remained largely unchanged. As peasants relied on their memories of *baochan daohu* of the 1950s and 1960s, cadres, too, had their own recollections of persecutions and purges in the past.[2] Naturally, provincial and local leaders were generally unwilling to opt for an uncontested innovation too hastily but rather chose to wait and see how the centre would respond to a few local pioneers. Thus, the leaders of the bandwagoning provinces neither actively promoted nor consistently prohibited the household responsibility systems, replicating confusion and ambiguity along the administrative hierarchy down to counties, communes, and below. Furthermore, many leaders of these provinces consciously chose to stress what was actually said in central documents over what might be possibly accomplished through the innovative policy.[3]

The fundamental rationale underlying bandwagoning is well captured in the following excerpt from an analysis of Hubei's decollectivization:

In Hubei peasants also pressed toward family farming but made much slower headway in the face of the provincial leadership's caution and intransigence. Official Hubei policy strictly followed whatever was sent down from Beijing. . . . Hubei stayed safely to the rear of the maverick reform provinces. But the prudent leaders of Hubei also avoided emulating [laggard] provinces which later suffered Beijing's wrath for its determined resistance to reform. Hubei was scrupulous about not taking chances or conducting experiments. Thus, from 1977 to 1980, while Anhui, Guizhou, Gansu, and Sichuan moved decisively toward household contracting, Hubei remained committed to collective responsibility systems.[4]

The rationale underlying Hubei's opting for bandwagoning is applicable to most bandwagoner provinces, including Shandong. The data on Shandong's pace in adopting the household responsibility systems, shown in Table 5.1, illustrate the salient characteristics of bandwagoning. The province had initially adopted a passive 'wait and see' attitude in the early period (i.e. January 1980). Its 'inaction' and 'non-decision' resulted in a swift diffusion of household farming in a few poor western prefectures (Heze, Dezhou, Huimin, and Liaocheng—see December 1980 data).[5] This conspicuous pace had to be avoided, however, by such a bandwagoner as Shandong was. Thus, up until the last phase of the reform, the provincial leadership had maintained its tight vigilance over local implementation by 'not actively promoting' (*butichang*) household farming as well as by containing its swift province-wide diffusion.

As the provincial leadership had opted for caution and reservation toward the controversial reform, local cadres and peasants became wary of

TABLE 5.1. *Shandong's pace of decollectivization, 1980–1982*

	Jan. 1980	Dec. 1980	June 1981	Dec. 1981	June 1982	Dec. 1982
A. Nationwide	1.0	14.4	28.2	50.0	71.9	78.2
			(g = 11.3)		(g = 67.0)	
B. Shandong	2.4	27.6	38.2	55.9	69.3	96.8
		(g = 0)	(g = 28.6)	(g = 47.5)	(g = 62.7)	(g = 82.8)
(B) – (A)	1.4	13.2	10.0	5.9	–2.6	18.6

Notes: Figures represent the percentage of production teams under the two household responsibility systems; (g) refers to *baogan daohu* only.

Sources: As Table 3.1.

the possibility of abrupt policy reversal, thus slowing down the overall pace of decollectivization in the province. Consequently, the difference between the national average and Shandong's pace of decollectivization continued to narrow from 13.2 per cent in December 1980 to minus 2.6 per cent in June 1982. That Shandong lagged behind the national average by 2.6 per cent at the time when the more controversial system of *baogan daohu* was being pushed by the centre underscores its reservation toward committing itself too quickly to the uncontested policy. On the other hand, the margin remained relatively small and inconspicuous so that Shandong would not be singled out as a laggard (for instance, compared with Heilongjiang with a total of 8.7 per cent by May 1982). Once Beijing's preference became increasingly manifest in late 1982, the province swiftly popularized the reform. By December 1982, Shandong's pace far exceeded the national average by 19 per cent, clearly distinguishing itself from such laggards as Jilin, Liaoning, and Heilongjiang.[6]

The remainder of this chapter consists of six sections. The first examines the genesis of a local pioneer in Shandong, more specifically the Heze experiment in 1978–80. The second investigates the provincial responses to the local innovations in Heze and explores how they survived and became diffused within the prefecture. The third and fourth sections discuss in detail how decollectivization proceeded in Shandong in chronological and regional terms. The fifth section takes up the puzzle related to mechanization: why did Shandong, with a high level of mechanization and large stocks of agricultural machinery, not put up a fierce fight as Heilongjiang did? Finally, the concluding section provides some observations regarding the pattern of bandwagoning.

THE LOCAL PIONEER IN SHANDONG: THE HEZE 'EXPERIMENT'

While Shandong was no exception to the general pattern that local innovations ignited a chain of reactions which eventually led to province-wide decollectivization, its process of intra-provincial diffusion was clearly much slower and less smooth compared with that of Anhui. Local innovations in Shandong also differed from those in Anhui in two important respects. First, compared with Anhui with multiple (as many as nine) simultaneous local innovations throughout the province, Shandong's local pioneers were fewer in number (two) and located in a much more limited geographical scope (mainly south-western prefectures). Second, while local innovations in Anhui were largely a product of 'generic spontaneity', those in Shandong stemmed from both 'generic spontaneity' and diffusion from the neighbouring province of Anhui.[7]

Shandong's official history of decollectivization singles out Heze prefecture for its pioneering pace. According to this official source, while the systems of 'task rates to the work group' (*baogong daozu*) and 'comprehensive contracts to the work group' (*baogan daozu*) were the dominant responsibility systems in Heze during 1978–9, a 'small number' of production teams were already implementing the system of 'household production quotas', constituting local pioneers for the province as a whole.[8] These 'pioneer' teams were concentrated in Dongming county which had indisputably been the poorest in Heze as well as in Shandong.[9]

According to an official chronology, as early as November 1977, Dongming's county leadership asked the prefecture authorities to provide support for such measures as reallocating 'private plots' (*ziliudi*) to peasants and dividing up barren land for household farming. In February 1978, the prefecture party committee convened an expanded standing committee meeting attended by key figures in the prefectural administration and county party secretaries. At this meeting, three principles were decided upon: (1) those decisions stipulated by the centre before the Cultural Revolution and whose changes had not yet been officially pronounced should be permitted to continue; (2) those decisions which had been criticized during the Cultural Revolution but proved successful through practice should be rehabilitated; and (3) those demands by the masses which did not violate the 'guiding ideas' (*zhidao sixiang*) of the Centre should be accommodated. The key implication was that almost anything could be tried out so far as it had a potential to improve the dire economic situation of the prefecture.[10]

Interviews with former cadres of Heze revealed that the idea of 'household production quotas' (*baochan daohu*) had been raised as early as February 1978 when the Heze prefecture party committee held the so-called 'two thousand people meeting' (*liangqianren dahui*). At this extraordinary meeting, Zhou Zhenxing, the prefectural first party secretary, allegedly made an eight-hour speech, in which he argued that 'production quotas to the work group' (*baochan daozu*) should be popularized and even 'household production quotas' would not be prohibited for poorer units. Zhou also allegedly contended that if he were not allowed to help his prefecture to get rich—even if that meant allotting its collective land to households (referring to *baogan daohu*)—he would quit his position as the party secretary.[11]

With the active support from the prefecture authorities, in March 1978, many production units in Dongming county returned private plots and distributed nearly one hundred thousand *mu* of barren land to peasant households, and even some part of the collective land was distributed to households for their own production.[12] Once this earlier adoption of the innovative measures proved effective in promoting peasant incentives and raising the production outputs, neighbouring units soon followed suit. Not only the explicit support from the prefectural and county authorities, but the spread of the news about the nearby Fengyang county in northern Anhui also contributed to the further acceleration of decollectivization in Dongming.[13] The pace of diffusion was so fast that the share of the county's production teams implementing the household responsibility systems reached 60 per cent by the end of 1979, 78 per cent in March 1980, and 94 per cent in July 1980.[14]

It should be noted that Heze's decollectivization was not a step-by-step transition in which the dominant responsibility system evolved gradually from *baogong daozu* and *baochan daozu* to *baochan daohu* and eventually to *baogan daohu*. *Baochan daohu* had existed even in 1978, and *baogan daohu* became popular as early as 1979. Given the strict prohibition at the time by the central authorities (*baochan daohu* was first allowed on a conditional basis in September 1979) these developments were surely bold. They also testify to the importance of the personal convictions of local (in this case, prefectural) leaders, which mitigated the fears of persecution among basic-level cadres and peasants. With the explicit support from the prefectural and county authorities, commune-level cadres became less motivated to block local innovations, and peasants were more than willing to maximize the widened window of opportunity.[15] By October 1980, 70 per cent of the prefecture's teams were under *baochan daohu*. And as of October 1981, 96.4 per cent of the prefecture's 16,396 production teams were under the more controversial system of *baogan daohu*.[16] Compared with the national and provincial averages at the time of 38 and 48 per cent, respectively, Heze's pace of decollectivization was indeed extremely fast.

PROVINCIAL RESPONSES TO THE HEZE EXPERIMENT

Both the survival and spread of the household responsibility systems in Heze were extraordinary considering the provincial position at the time. In 1978, the first agricultural responsibility system officially allowed in Shandong was that of 'task rates' (*dinge baogong*), with the work group as the primary unit of production and accounting. The positive effects of this system in obliterating excessive egalitarianism embedded in the Dazhai system of remuneration were highly valued so that it was widely popularized for cotton as well as grain production. During much of 1979, the smallest unit of production and accounting any responsibility system could be officially based upon was the work group, and households were not permitted to constitute the primary unit of work or accounting.[17]

Even though the September 1979 document from the Centre did allow conditional implementation of *baochan daohu* for certain geographical areas and production units, such a widespread and swift adoption of the household responsibility systems in Heze prefecture, and Dongming county in particular, clearly went far beyond the 'exceptional' boundary set by the Centre.[18] Consequently, in early 1980 when the popularization of *baochan daohu* and *baogan daohu* in Dongming county generated heated debates all over the province, the provincial authorities officially made known their opposition to such local deviations:

Recently, some localities in our province have contracted out all or part of the land and collective-owned production materials, such as draught animals and farm tools, to individual households. And they consider this system of *baochan daohu* as one of the production responsibility systems. This is wrong. . . . *Baochan daohu* cannot be a fundamental way to relieve poverty . . . [and] we have to rely on the collective economy to achieve this goal.[19]

This quotation poses two interesting questions. First, given that there had not been any earlier reports on the local adoption of *baochan daohu* in Shandong, how could it be that the report warned against the implementation of the controversial system by some localities? Two explanations can be offered: (1) not all of what was happening at the local level was reported in the provincial media; and (2) some localities (such as Dongming county) were bold enough to venture into the policies to which the provincial authorities had not yet been committed. Second, it should be noted that such unconditional opposition to *baochan daohu* expressed in the excerpt was obviously not in line with the Fourth Plenum's 'Decisions Concerning Certain Problems in Rapidly Developing Agriculture', which permitted *baochan daohu* on a conditional basis. Such a rigid stance adopted by Shandong provides a stark contrast with Anhui which officially endorsed both *baochan daohu* and *baogan daohu* at the January 1980 provincial rural work conference. Two explanations can be offered for Shandong's reactive position: (1) there was a unified position of strongly opposing the household responsibility systems among the top provincial officials; or (2) being unsure of the precise intentions of the centre as well as the direction of the controversial reform, the provincial position tilted toward the usually safer bet of 'being a little too "left" than "right"' (*ningzuo huyou*).[20] Available evidence seems to support the latter explanation.

Despite their initial opposition to the household responsibility systems, a high level of uncertainties associated with the fluid policy environment made the provincial authorities opt for bandwagoning, which was then translated into ambivalence. The ambivalent behaviour of key provincial leaders was particularly manifest in their dealing with the local deviations in Heze. Despite the clearly deviant nature of the situation in Heze, where a prefectural party secretary was bold enough to stay far ahead of the central and provincial positions, the provincial authorities took no concrete action to support or redress the deviation. Rather, they adopted a 'wait-and-see' attitude by opting for non-action and non-decision. An interviewee, a former prefecture-level cadre of Heze, provided the following observation concerning the rationale behind the provincial authorities' peculiar reaction to the Heze experiment:

Generally speaking, there was no single unified reaction to speak of from the provincial authorities except that the household-based systems were 'not to be promoted' [*bu tichang*]. This expression [*bu tichang*] we normally understand as a very weak opposition. In the absence of an official provincial position, individual provincial leaders communicated their opinions with the lower levels through personal channels. Some provincial officials would publicly denounce Heze as 'going backward' [*zouhuitou*] while others would either keep silent or privately condone what was taking place in Heze by saying 'why not give it a try?' [*shishikanba*].[21]

Why did the provincial authorities not have any unified reaction to the development in Heze, which was clearly off the policy line set by the central and provincial governments? The same interviewee offered the following observation:

Top provincial officials themselves were not quite sure what to do about the Heze situation. In 1978–80, even the centre was involved in fierce power struggles intertwined with policy conflicts which were largely centred around the rural reform. Naturally, different members of the provincial government would take different policy positions on the basis of their respective political and ideological affiliations. . . . Cadres like Su Yiran would not oppose, cadres like Bai Rubing would keep silent, and cadres like Qin Hezhen would publicly denounce the development in Heze on the basis of their functional affiliation with mechanization.[22]

Interviews with former cadres of the Policy Research Office of the Provincial Agricultural Commission reveal that in early 1980 the provincial leadership made an in-house assessment which positively evaluated the Heze experiment but did not dare to produce written documents in support of it.[23] Apparently, Bai Rubing did not have what Wan Li had: close and powerful connections with the reformist leadership at the centre. Without such protective networks, provincial leaders would have fears of overcommitment to the controversial policy and display reservation and ambivalence. Policy conflicts at the centre were also responsible for amplifying confusion among the provincial and local leaders. When even the centre appeared very cautious about an all-out scheme of decollectivization by adopting such 'formalized expressions' (*tifa*) as 'allowed to implement' (*keyi gao* or *yunxu gao*) with a nuance that 'you may do it but don't make mistakes', they were bound to create fears, ambivalence, and political opportunism among provincial and local implementors.[24]

What further compounded the situation was the open endorsement of Anhui's Feixi and Fengyang experiments by Wan Li in January 1980 and, more importantly, by Deng Xiaoping in May 1980. These endorsements further restrained the provincial authorities in Shandong from delivering a harsh blow against the deviations in Heze. The failure to reach a consensus among the provincial leaders and the resulting absence of concrete actions against Heze were swiftly utilized by the peasants in favour of household farming. They were further assured by the dissemination of CD [80] No. 75 in September 1980, making the prefecture the fastest implementor of the household responsibility systems in Shandong.[25]

What finally legitimized the Heze experiment was a visit to the prefecture by Zhao Ziyang in the autumn of 1980.[26] During his visit, Zhao allegedly characterized the Heze experiment as a correct thing to do and asked other areas in the province to emulate it. After Zhao's visit, Heze was freely allowed to speed up the popularization of the household responsibility systems. Furthermore, Zhao's explicit support for the Heze experiment contributed significantly to the acceleration of the process in which the Heze practice was swiftly diffused to the neighbouring prefectures such as Dezhou, Liaocheng, and Huimin.[27]

Up to this point, the Shandong case and, more specifically, the Heze experiences, closely resemble the pioneering pattern in that initially small-scale local innovations quickly spread within a prefecture and an endorsement was made by a key central leader. Similarities stop there, however, as the Shandong provincial leadership did not come up with immediate official support for the Heze experiment as its Anhui counterpart did for Fengyang and Feixi. While the Heze experiment approximates the peasant-power perspective, the overall process that unfolded in Shandong thereafter was rather significantly different from that of Anhui. In fact, the ambivalent attitudes of key provincial leaders were widely replicated along the administrative hierarchy to contain the swift diffusion of decollectivization beyond Heze and the western prefectures.

THE POLITICS OF BANDWAGONING:
FROM CONTAINMENT TO POPULARIZATION

While Zhao Ziyang's visit might have legitimized the deviant practices in Heze, Shandong's provincial authorities seem to have regarded the Heze experiment as something that should be contained within the prefectural boundary.[28] In other words, the provincial leadership was more willing to follow the written documents from the Centre than personal instructions of a central leader who had only recently entered the central political stage. The dissemination of CD [80] No. 75 (issued on 27 September) constitutes an example in point. In line with CD [80] No. 75—which stipulated that *baochan daohu* and *baogan daohu* could be implemented in certain areas and units specified by the document—Shandong's provincial leadership only partially relaxed its opposition to household farming in late 1980, still maintaining reservation about its wider applicability.[29]

Shandong's overall stance on decollectivization in late 1980 still remained highly cautious, as manifested in its recommendation of *baochan daohu* only for the poor areas. For all other areas, 'specialized-production contract linking income with output' (*zhuanye chengbao lianchan jichou*), which did not have an exclusive focus on the household as the primary unit of production, was 'recommended'.[30] As of early 1981, Shandong's position was still very passive as it held on to the so-called 'three principles': (1) the household-based systems were for the extremely poor teams only; (2) household farming was not to be recommended for areas with advanced collective economy; and (3), more importantly, even in the regions which had long been poor, the household responsibility systems should not be imposed in a standardized fashion.[31]

The provincial leadership's ambivalence and reservation toward household farming were once again manifested in its Provincial Document No. 24 issued on 16 May 1981, which was Shandong's first comprehensive stipulation on the issue of agricultural responsibility systems.[32] According to the document, three responsibility systems were recommended for three categories of regions. First, those regions with advanced levels of production and management 'should actively promote' (*yao jiji tuiguang*) 'specialized production contracts' (*zhuanye chengbao*), with the nature of work determining the size of the primary work unit. Second, the system of 'unified (i.e. collective) management linking output to individual labour' (*tongyi jingying lianchan daolao*) was to 'be actively promoted' in areas with intermediate production levels. Finally, both *baochan daohu* and *baogan daohu* were to be 'allowed' (*yunxu*) in areas which had long been poor and backward.[33]

It seems that policy stipulation was one thing and actual implementation was quite another. That is, the provincial leadership's ambivalence and reservation toward regulating household farming facilitated a situation in which actual local implementation surpassed policy pronouncements, as some peasants in the intermediate-level regions took advantage of policy confusion and provincial inaction. The popularity of the household responsibility systems became increasingly manifest with the fast-rising number of localities adopting the new policy. Not only were the poorer areas—such as Heze county of Heze prefecture, and Bin county and Gaoqing county of Huimin prefecture—singled out as the model cases that demonstrated the positive impact of the household responsibility systems on productivity, but intermediate-level localities like Jining and Weifang prefectures were also identified as having achieved enhanced production due to household farming.[34] Consequently, by October 1981, 96 per cent of Heze's production teams and 65 per cent of Dezhou's teams were under *baogan daohu*, closely followed by Liaocheng and Huimin prefectures. Prefectures with intermediate-level conditions, such as Jining, Taian, and Weifang, also began to witness the household responsibility systems spread at a faster pace.[35]

Towards the end of 1981, in accordance with the decisions made at the national rural work conference (which were later designated as CD [82] No. 1), the provincial authorities made another turn by allowing both *baochan daohu* and *baogan daohu* to be implemented on a fairly popular basis. The following excerpt indicates a significant change in the provincial position:

In areas where the level of agricultural production is relatively high, and diversified production and commercialization are advanced, the major responsibility system currently has been that of the specialized-production contract linking income with output. However, these areas are now allowed [*yunxu*] to adopt household-based systems of production responsibility.[36]

Despite the stipulated permission for the advanced regions to adopt the household responsibility systems, the overall position of the provincial leadership still remained ambivalent well into mid-1982 when Beijing began to apply pressure for their swift popularization. A careful reading of *Mass Daily* suggests an unusually high level of caution in most of Shandong's official policy pronouncements regarding the household responsibility systems. Such caution was, to a considerable extent, the result of opting for a politically safer alternative in order to avoid the conspicuous options of rushing too fast or lagging too far behind others. The very gradual pace at which Shandong's decollectivization proceeded—from 56 per cent in December 1981 to 69 per cent in June 1982 (see Table 5.1)—is supportive of this argument.

Caution was manifested rather explicitly in the province's consistent stress on the 'pluralistic' approach by which a variety of responsibility systems, ranging from 'short-term piece rates' (*xiaoduan baogong*) and 'specialized production contract' (*zhuanye chengbao*) to *baochan daohu* and *baogan daohu*, were all permitted to coexist. For instance, Shandong Provincial Document (*lufa*) No. 23 of 31 August 1982 clearly stipulated the 'principle of allowing multiple systems' (*duozhong xingshi bingcun de yuanze*).[37] One irony was that such a pluralistic approach was taken advantage of by many localities that were vehemently opposed to household farming. That is, as the provincial leadership's ambivalence toward regulating local deviations was utilized by poor prefectures like Heze and Dezhou, its lack of activism in promoting decollectivization was fully maximized by several localities reluctant to decollectivize, most notably Yantai prefecture and Qingdao City.

To draw an analogy with the nationwide situation, Yantai was very similar to Heilongjiang while Heze was to Anhui. Unlike Heze where peasants had very little to divide up except the land, Yantai prefecture in the Jiaodong peninsula region apparently had a lot to lose from the popularization of the household responsibility systems. Not only was Yantai's overall economic status the highest among all prefectures in Shandong but also, more importantly, Yantai was the key region for Shandong's agricultural mechanization and collective-run rural enterprises.[38] Particularly in promoting large-scale mechanization, in addition to Beijing's support, Yantai prefecture made very large investments of its own in sectors related to mechanization, such as iron ore mining, steel manufacturing, and agricultural machinery production. Yantai was so successful in producing steel for the manufacturing of agricultural machinery that it was even singled out by the central government as the model for others to follow.[39]

Due to its superior economic conditions as well as vested interests in mechanization, Yantai's pace of adopting the household responsibility systems was the slowest among all prefectures in Shandong. In 1979, when the western region was experimenting with the systems of 'linking income with output' (*lianchan jichou*), Yantai was just beginning to criticize the Dazhai system. During 1980–1, when both *baochan daohu* and *baogan daohu* became the dominant responsibility systems in Heze and Dezhou, most production teams in Yantai were under the system of 'linking output to the work group' (*lianchan daozu*), and its cadres considered the household responsibility systems unsuitable for Yantai. It was only in January 1982 that, in response to CD [82] No. 1, the Yantai prefectural party committee decided to popularize the system of 'linking output to individual labour' (*lianchan daolao*), and it was only in mid-1982 that a very small number of its teams were permitted to experiment with the household responsibility systems.[40]

To this author's surprise, the slow pace of Yantai's decollectivization was widely known in the agricultural policy community even outside of Shandong. Most interviewees in Beijing singled out Shandong's Jiaodong peninsula region and Yantai in particular for their noticeably slow pace. Many of them specifically referred to mechanization as the core reason for the prefecture's sluggish pace. The issue of mechanization, as it was related to decollectivization, was twofold. First, the sunken cost was too heavy: that is, too much had already been invested in the scheme of across-the-board mechanization based on large- and medium-sized machinery to simply divide up the land and machines to the households. Second, if they were to divide the collective assets under compulsion, the issue of how to distribute, use, and manage the machinery (and other collective production materials) would constitute the core of disagreements and debates.[41]

When the western region and Heze were speeding up their pace of decollectivization, Yantai remained firmly opposed to it. According to an interviewee, during 1980–1 placards and big-character posters were everywhere in Yantai urging its peasants to 'strongly oppose Heze's deviant practice of private farming' (*jianjue fandui Heze danganfeng*).[42] The prefectural authority was in fact taking full advantage of the vague central directive that had recommended *baochan daohu* and *baogan daohu* only for those areas that were distant, peripheral, mountainous, and backward without clearly defining what standards were to be used to determine these special areas. According to a provincial official who at the time had been involved in the collection of provincial data on decollectivization, Yantai consistently justified its sluggish pace by claiming that the prefecture was neither distant, peripheral, mountainous, nor backward.[43]

The general situation in Yantai may be better illustrated by an example of Ye county. Ye county was representative of economically advanced counties in both national and provincial terms: its 'per capita share of grain' (*renjun kouliangshu*) was 490 *jin*, and its per capita income was 120 *yuan* for 1978.[44] The county was also one of the province's experimental sites for agricultural mechanization. In 1978 alone, the county received a priority allocation of 600 large and medium-sized tractors from the province (note that no small or hand tractors were provided). Added were the vague central directives and ambiguous provincial positions regarding the household responsibility systems. The Ye county party committee, in line with the Yantai prefectural party committee, decided in 1980 to prohibit popular implementation of the household responsibility systems and instead to promote 'specialized-production contracts' (*zhuanye chengbao*) focusing on the team or work group as the primary unit of work.[45] As described earlier, this system could in principle be based upon teams, work groups, households, or individual labourers. In practice, however, most of the tasks related to grain production were dependent upon either teams (*zhuanye-dui*) or work groups (*zhuanyezu*), while vegetable production was left largely to specialized households (*zhuanyehu*).[46] The result was that an extremely small percentage of the county's production teams were under household farming by late 1982.

Another example can be offered to explore a microlevel rationale for the delay of decollectivization in Yantai. Yeji brigade of Zhuyou commune in Huang county was one of the many brigades in Yantai which did not popularize the household responsibility systems until the spring of 1983.[47] With an average of 94 horsepower of agricultural machinery available for every 100 *mu* of cultivated land, which was four times larger than the national average, Yeji brigade was well known for its high level of mechanization. The brigade's per capita income distributed within the collective was 460 *yuan* in 1982 and its per *mu* grain productivity was 1,450 *jin* in 1982, more than three times the national average. Furthermore, 53 per cent of the brigade's total labour force was involved in collective-run rural enterprises.

All these factors made the cadres and peasants of Yeji Brigade wonder if household farming could really be applicable without damaging its mechanization, diversified production, and rural enterprises under collective management. Subsequently, they opted for 'specialized-production contract to teams and work groups' rather than household farming. Even in late 1982, 'specialized-production contract' was the most popular responsibility system in Yeji where twelve specialized teams were responsible for grain production, eight specialized teams for vegetable and fruit production, fishery, animal husbandry and agricultural machinery management, and twenty-five specialized groups for rural sideline activities and industrial production. It was only in the spring of 1983 that Yeji began to adopt *baogan daohu* as the position of Yantai prefecture began to shift under the heavy pressure from Beijing and Jinan.[48]

The ambivalent position of the provincial leadership changed rather drastically in late 1982 as Beijing's policy preference was firmly fixed on household farming and it began to put increasing pressure on recalcitrant localities. The Shandong leadership, in its Provincial Document No. 23 of August 1982, made it clear that both *baochan daohu* and *baogan daohu* should be treated equally with other more collective-oriented counter-parts.[49] Especially after Wan Li's famous speech of November 1982, the provincial leadership saw to it that not only the intermediate-level prefec-tures such as Jining, Taian, and Weifang but also, more importantly, such advanced localities as Yantai and Qingdao swiftly popularized the house-hold responsibility systems.[50] A sharp increase in the share of Shandong's production teams under household farming from 69 per cent in June 1982 to 97 per cent in December 1982 can only be attributed to the provincial leadership's bandwagoning.

Once the provincial leadership began to actively reflect the centre's pref-erence for *baogan daohu*, Yantai became the major target of the province's efforts to induce local compliance. In the face of increasing pressure from the provincial leadership, Yantai had to relax its unconditional opposition by initially allowing localities with per capita income lower than 100 *yuan* to adopt *baogan daohu*.[51] Yet, it still took more than two months after the publication of Wan Li's speech before about two-thirds of Yantai's pro-duction teams opted for *baogan daohu*.[52] The resolution of the deadlock and full compliance by Yantai were facilitated only when its prefectural first party secretary, Lu Shengyun, was transferred to Jinan (as a member of the provincial people's procuratorate) and replaced by an outsider, Wang Jifu, in February 1983.[53] Subsequently, by March 1983, 98.4 per cent of Shandong's production teams adopted household farming, a performance that was about 20 per cent higher than the national average and only 1 per cent lower than that of Sichuan.

A short note is due on the attitude of peasants toward household farming in Yantai. In contrast with the common assumption, one that is taken for granted perhaps too casually, that Chinese peasants everywhere at any time preferred household farming to any other type of production, most peas-ants in Yantai initially did not want to decollectivize. In Yantai, household farming was rather 'imposed' on the unwilling peasants by the central and provincial authorities and the adoption of household farming was fairly strongly resisted by a majority of peasants in the early years of decollec-tivization. Furthermore, given the significantly high level of dependence on mechanization and collective-run rural enterprises, it was not as easy to divide up land and production materials in Yantai as it might have been in Heze and Dezhou where almost everyone was farming manually and, therefore, preferred to have his or her own plot, draught animal, and farm tool. A similar observation was offered by interviewees concerning the dominant peasant attitude in Qingdao.[54]

THE SPREAD OF DECOLLECTIVIZATION IN SHANDONG: INTRA-PROVINCIAL VARIATIONS

Shandong constituted a microcosm of China in that Heze typified the pioneering pattern adopted by Anhui and Guizhou, while Yantai was highly analogous to such laggards as Heilongjiang and Liaoning which firmly resisted decollectivization on the basis of their endogenous interests in mechanization. The pioneering pattern adopted by the western prefectures long known for widespread banditry before the 'liberation' and continued poverty under Communist rule is relatively easy to explain given the general nationwide tendency for both the initiation and the spread of household farming to be faster in poorer areas.[55] At the same time, the idiosyncratic factor of an assertive local leader (such as Zhou Zhenxing in Shandong's Heze and Wang Yuzhao in Anhui's Chuxian) also played a significant role in producing local pioneers.[56] It is also relatively easy to understand, as discussed in the previous section, why Yantai had to delay the implementation of decollectivization to such an extent that even its party secretary had to be replaced by an outsider.

The spread of decollectivization in Shandong involved a considerable degree of intra-provincial variation. Interestingly, according to one interviewee, the diffusion of decollectivization 'proceeded from the west to the east' (*congxi wangdong*), and such directionality seemed in close parallel with variations in the key economic conditions of the province's three geographical regions, namely the western (*luxi*), central (*luzhong*), and the eastern peninsula (*jiaodong*) regions. Tables 5.2 and 5.3 provide data on two economic conditions and the decollectivization pace of four—two western (Heze and Dezhou), one central (Jining), and one eastern (Yantai)—prefectures.

Rural economic conditions seem to constitute fairly effective predictors of the pace of decollectivization in these three regions of Shandong. The poor and backward western prefectures, represented by Heze and Dezhou, were pioneers that completed the changes by 1981. On the other hand, the wealthy and advanced eastern prefectures, represented by Yantai, were extremely slow as their decollectivization was not completed even in 1983. The decollectivization pace of the intermediate-level prefectures such as Jining, Taian, Weifang, and Zibo, is problematic. As there are no implementation data available on any of these prefectures, it is difficult to

TABLE 5.2. *Comparison of two economic dimensions of four prefectures (1980)*

	Per capita grain productivity (kg)	Level of mechanization (%)
Heze	223	52.7
Dezhou	269	65.4
Jining	386	66.8
Yantai	475	77.7

Sources: Information on the administrative breakdown of the prefectures is from the Ministry of Civil Affairs, *Zhonghua renmin gongheguo xingzheng quhua jiance* (Abridged Guide to the Administrative Structure of the People's Republic of China) (Beijing: Ditu chubanshe, 1983), 38–40. Figures on per capita grain productivity and levels of mechanization were calculated with the data given in State Statistical Bureau, *Zhongguo fenxian nongcun jingji tongji gaiyao* (A Statistical Survey of Rural Economy in Chinese Counties) (Beijing: Tongji chubanshe, 1989), 238–40, 242–58, 263–5.

TABLE 5.3. *Intra-provincial variation in the pace of decollectivization*

	1980	1981	1982	1983
Shandong[a]	12: 0 (g)	6: 38.2 (g = 28.6)	3: 62.9	3: 98.4
		12: 55.9 (g = 47.5)	5: 69.3 (g = 62.7)	(g = 97.2)
			12: 96.0 (g)	
Heze[b]	10: 70.0 (c)	10: 96.4 (g)	—	—
Dezhou	12: 4.6 (g)[c]	5: 26.8 (g)[c]	—	5: 98.9[d]
		9: 64.5 (g)[c]		
		baogan daohu		
Jining[e]	—	initiated	—	—
Yantai	12: zero[g]	—	*baochan daohu*	2: 70.0 (g)[f]
			initiated[g]	12: 90.0[g]

Sources: [a] As Table 3.1; [b] 'On How Heze Prefecture Implemented *baogan daohu*', *History of Agricultural Co-operativization in Shandong Province*, ii. 299; [c] *DZRB*, 9 Oct. 1981; [d] Ibid. 30 May 1983; [e] Ibid. 29 Oct. 1982; [f] Ibid. 9 Feb. 1983; [g] *Contemporary China's Shandong Province*, i. 301–2.

identify a dominant pattern of implementation in these areas.[57] An informed guess, on the basis of the interviews in Jinan and Qingdao, is that while there were some counties and lower units in these intermediate-level prefectures that took advantage of the ambivalence of the provincial leadership as well as of the vagueness of the central directives, the dominant pattern was still that of bandwagoning.

The data on Shandong's pace of decollectivization in 1982 seem to support the above speculation since the province's performance fell behind the national average with its figures being 55.9 per cent in January 1982 and 69.3 per cent in June 1982, meaning many counties in the central region did not yet go in for household farming.[58] Then, by December 1982, Shandong's performance far surpassed the national average by about 19 per cent, indicating that most localities in the central region decollectivized between June and December 1982 when Beijing's pressure was mounting. Thus, these intermediate-level prefectures displayed conscious restraints until mid-1982 and such restraints reflected the spillover effects of ambivalence and opportunism on the prefectural and county leaders who, like their provincial counterparts, were torn between the competing options of actively promoting household farming and tightly regulating popular demands. Facing the tough choice, they opted for the safer bet—following the written documents from the centre—producing the close parallel between the pace of decollectivization and the levels of economic conditions.

THE MECHANIZATION PUZZLE: A COMPARISON WITH HEILONGJIANG

Having discussed Shandong's pattern of decollectivization and its intra-provincial variation, it is considered necessary to examine a key puzzle related to mechanization. The anomaly is that, despite its equally high level of mechanization, Shandong did not put up a fight with the centre as Heilongjiang did so fiercely (the Heilongjiang case is dealt with in Chapter 6). By 1981, for instance, the total horsepower of Shandong's agricultural machinery was 18.7 million, almost double that of Heilongjiang's 9.6 million, and the share of mechanized area in Shandong's total sown area was 63 per cent while the comparable figure for Heilongjiang was 69 per cent.[59]

The answer to this anomaly may be found in the different scales of agricultural production in the two provinces. One crucial indicator is the average area of land available for cultivation. While it seems natural to associate Heilongjiang (with the largest per capita area of cultivation in China) with a high level of mechanization, we may not intuitively apply the same reasoning to Shandong, whose population density was the second highest only after Jiangsu. Table 5.4 provides a good contrast on this point. In per capita terms (*an renkou pingjun gengdi*), Shandong's area of land under cultivation was a little more than one-third of Heilongjiang's. In terms of per peasant land under cultivation (*an nongye renkou pingjun gengdi*), the ratio was less than one-fourth. And in per-agricultural-labourer terms (*an nongye laodongli pingjun gengdi*), the ratio further dropped to less than one-fifth.

Closely related to the area of land under cultivation is the issue of different mechanization strategies pursued by the two provinces. Table 5.5

TABLE 5.4. *Comparison of the area of land under cultivation in 1980 (mu)*

	Shandong	Heilongjiang
Per capita	1.5	4.1
Per peasant	1.6	6.5
Per agricultural labourer	4.4	22.3

Sources: *History of Agricultural Co-operativization in Shandong Province*, ii. 723; *Heilongjiang jingji tongji nianjian 1989*, 215; and Song Yuansheng, *Heilongjiangsheng nongye jixiehua fazhan yu liangqiannian zhanlue* (The Development of Mechanization in Heilongjiang Province and Its Strategy for the Year 2000) (Harbin: Heilongjiang kexue jishu chubanshe, 1991), 262.

TABLE 5.5. *Indicators of mechanization in Shandong and Heilongjiang*

	Shandong	Heilongjiang
Large and medium-sized tractors		
Number (1,000)	115	68
Horsepower (10,000 hp)	372	370
share of total tractors (%)		
in number	50.5	68.8
in horsepower	72.1	90.5
Average horsepower of large and medium-sized tractors (hp)	32.4	54.0
Small and hand tractors		
Number (1,000)	112	31
Horsepower (10,000 hp)	134	39
share of total tractors (%)		
in number	49.5	31.2
in horsepower	27.9	9.5
Average horsepower of small and hand tractors (hp)	11.9	12.6

Sources: *China Agricultural Yearbook, 1981*, 59; *History of Agricultural Co-operativization in Shandong Province*, ii. 738–9; and *Heilongjiang sishinian jubian*, 221.

illustrates this contrast in terms of the relative shares of large and medium-sized tractors on the one hand, and of small and hand tractors on the other. Shandong's large and medium-sized tractors constituted only a half of its total number of tractors, while Heilongjiang's figure was more than two-thirds. What this meant for the decollectivization in Shandong was that, even if household farming were to be fully implemented, a half of Shandong's tractors, small and hand tractors, could still be utilized if they became necessary at all. An important implication would be that even if Shandong had valued the mechanization option as highly as Heilongjiang (which in itself is an empirical question that will shortly be discussed), it had less incentives to pose as fierce opposition to the centre as Heilongjiang did.

The indicator of average horsepower of large and medium-sized tractors further highlights the differences between the two provinces. The average horsepower of Shandong's large and medium-sized tractors was 32 while that of Heilongjiang was 54. In other words, Shandong's mechanization was geared more toward medium-sized tractors as well as small and hand tractors (which, one must remember, constituted half of the province's total number of tractors), while Heilongjiang depended heavily on very large tractors. This contrast also corresponds well with the different scales of agricultural production in the two provinces; Shandong's medium- and small-sized tractor oriented mechanization was contingent upon its far smaller per peasant and per-agricultural-labourer areas of cultivation (1.6 *mu* and 4.4 *mu* compared to Heilongjiang's 6.5 *mu* and 22.3 *mu*). Related to this is the average size of the production teams in these provinces. The average number of people in a production team in Shandong was only a half (166) of that of Heilongjiang (312), thus suggesting that, compared with Heilongjiang, Shandong had fewer incentives and complexities to prohibit the spread of decollectivization province-wide.[60]

Compared with Heilongjiang, Shandong thus had a sort of 'buffer' by which the potentially devastating effects of the popularization of the household responsibility systems (and *baogan daohu* in particular) on its mechanization could be mitigated. Therefore, the Shandong leadership had much less to be concerned about than its Heilongjiang counterpart. In fact, political opportunism displayed by the Shandong leadership may have been possible under these particular circumstances where its implementation behaviour was not significantly constrained by crucial endogenous interests at stake.

How might we substantiate the above argument empirically? An indicator of 'issue frequency' may be utilized. Issue frequency is defined as being how frequently a policy issue appears in official media. The key assumption is that the more frequently a policy issue is treated in a key provincial newspaper, the more seriously the provincial leadership takes the issue. That is, the more concerned was a province with the adverse effects of household farming on mechanization, the more frequently it would express its concern about mechanization in its official media. Table 5.6 provides the frequency of articles on the issue of mechanization, which appeared in Shandong's *Mass Daily* and Heilongjiang's *Heilongjiang Daily* for the period of 1979–83.[61]

TABLE 5.6. *Salience of mechanization manifested in*
provincial news media

	Mass Daily	Heilongjiang Daily
1979	6/24 (25.0)	35/99 (35.4)
1980	7/33 (21.2)	51/106 (48.1)
1981	5/27 (18.5)	37/68 (54.4)
1982	6/20 (30.0)	17/32 (53.1)
1983	8/24 (33.3)	36/73 (49.3)
AVERAGE	6.4/25.6 (25.6)	35.2/75.6 (48.1)

Notes: Figures on the right of the slash refer to the total
number of articles on mechanization for the respective year;
figures on the left refer to the number of articles on mechanization that appeared on the front page of each issue; and
figures in parentheses refer to the percentages of the two
figures.

Throughout the entire period of 1979–83, during which the overall significance of mechanization was severely downgraded and the household
responsibility systems were popularized, not even once did Shandong score
higher than Heilongjiang on any dimension of this issue frequency scale.[62]
In terms of the total number of articles on mechanization, the total of front-
page articles, and the yearly average, the issue of mechanization was treated
much more frequently and importantly in Heilongjiang's provincial newspaper and, therefore, we may conclude that the Heilongjiang leadership
took the potential impact of decollectivization on mechanization much
more seriously than its Shandong counterpart.

The argument that the Shandong leadership had less vested interests in
mechanization than its Heilongjiang counterpart and, consequently, less
incentives to resist decollectivization, can be further ascertained. First, in
response to the 1979 Fourth Plenum's decision to downgrade the overall
significance of mechanization, Shandong was very quick to discount the
validity of the Maoist scheme of mechanization on the ground that large
machinery-oriented mechanization was not suitable for the provincial situation. The Shandong leadership made frequent calls to stress a gradual pace
of mechanization and the importance of small machinery if mechanization
were needed in a province like Shandong at all.[63]

Second, given its small area of land available for cultivation, Shandong
was also less concerned with the linkage between the collective forms of
production on the one hand and mechanization on the other. An excerpt
from *Mass Daily* well illustrates this point:

At present, our province's level of production is still very low. Whether on the basis of collectives, work groups, or individuals, *most farm work is done manually*. Therefore, except for a few tasks that absolutely require a co-operative framework, all other kinds of production are better left to households and individuals so as to suit manual work [emphasis added].[64]

Third, the shift in the provincial position on mechanization led to some dramatic grass-roots changes totally inconceivable in a province like Heilongjiang. First, it was not until early 1983 that Heilongjiang allowed machinery work to be contracted out to individual households, while in Shandong not only were farm tools and draught animals sold to individual households, but also even large machinery was reportedly contracted out to individuals as early as September 1981.[65] Second, in contrast with Heilongjiang where individual purchases of agricultural machinery were permitted in early 1983, Shandong peasants could buy and own agricultural machinery beginning in 1981. For instance, in late 1981 peasants in Jiaxiang county of Jining prefecture reportedly purchased a total of 217 tractors for their own use.[66]

DECOLLECTIVIZATION IN SHANDONG: OPPORTUNISM, COMPLIANCE, AND THE RATIONALITY OF BANDWAGONING

With no vital provincial interests to protect, the Shandong provincial leadership had little motivation to resist the centre in implementing decollectivization. Nor did it opt for standing in the forefront of the controversial reform, since not only was it gravely concerned about the possibility of abrupt policy reversal but the signals from the centre were also not very clear until very late in the process. Consequently, the Shandong leadership relied on the very familiar and usually safe alternative of bandwagoning. By adopting the bandwagoning option, the Shandong leadership chose to follow the central documents very closely and to proceed at a very modest and inconspicuous pace. With the exception of local pioneers like Heze and three other western prefectures, the peasant-power thesis largely fails to provide a comprehensive explanation for the Shandong case, where peasants in several regions (notably intermediate-level prefectures and the entire Jiaodong peninsula region) were not able to stay ahead of the government policy throughout the process. It was not the demands of the peasants *per se* but rather the perceptions and actions of local cadres that played a more significant role when the centre's preferences remained vague and provincial positions were ambivalent at best.[67]

The case of Shandong as a bandwagoner illustrates how ambivalent and uncertain a provincial leadership could become when central directives were vague and clear stipulations as to the preference of the centre were lacking. Provincial ambivalence in turn generated a complicated situation in which some localities actively promoted the controversial policy, others forfeited their regulatory control only to promote peasant initiatives, and still others opted for their own policy preferences of resisting the reform. Such intra-provincial variations strongly refute the peasant-power thesis, as local governments did not simply 'evaporate' as it would make us believe. Rather, the state (provincial and local levels) adopted an opportunistic attitude of 'calculated neglect' until 1982. That the provincial authorities were not incapable but simply unwilling to regulate peasants too tightly became clear in mid-1982 when they relied on coercive measures to impose Beijing's preference on localities. If the wind had blown the other way, the same coercive measures would have been used to undo the decollectivization carried out in the western prefectures.

In the case of Shandong (and many other provinces as well), the centre managed to influence the provincial implementation of decollectivization in two ways. First, key reformist leaders 'preached' the power of household farming during their tours to various regions in the province. Such figures as Hu Yaobang, Wan Li, and Zhao Ziyang visited Heze, Dezhou, Linyi, and Yantai during 1981–4. On each of these occasions, they conveyed their opinions to the provincial leaders who were accompanying them and ensured the local (county and below) leaders that the new policy would not change. Such messages soon became public information which contributed to the acceleration of decollectivization in certain regions (most notably Heze and Dezhou).[68] Second, the central government required that the provincial leadership report back to Beijing on local implementation of decollectivization at least twice (April and November) in 1983 alone.[69] Such tightened oversight by Beijing must have put considerable pressure on Shandong. In sum, the decollectivization in Shandong was hardly the result of 'peasants confronting the state' as the peasant-power thesis claims.

Bandwagoning is undoubtedly an opportunistic mode of implementation, which generally grows out of leadership concerns for policy change and career-saving calculations. On the other hand, it also contains an element of rationality designed to avoid various problems associated with poorly prepared rushed implementation. Shandong's overall process of decollectivization, which proceeded relatively gradually, conservatively, and modestly, managed to avoid a variety of malpractices associated with standardized implementation prevalent in the pioneer provinces like Anhui where peasants opted for household farming without due preparation and proper guidance, and in the laggard provinces like Heilongjiang where almost all localities were uniformly barred from implementing decollectivization and, later, peasants had to telescope the entire process of decollectivization within a very short period of time. When highly controversial reforms demand a complete structural overhaul, a step-by-step (procedurally as well as spatially) approach may contain a crucial element of rationality since caution provides implementors with sufficient time to assess the new policy for which sufficient information is lacking.

In political terms, cautious players hardly lose their jobs although they are rarely given big promotions either. Key players in Shandong's decollectivization did not get big promotions: Bai Rubing was forced into retirement and Su Yiran succeeded Bai as the provincial first party secretary. Whether the Shandong provincial leadership was being 'pragmatic' (i.e. concerned primarily with the impact of decollectivization on the province) instead of 'opportunistic' (i.e. caring only about their own careers) is difficult to judge, but their choice of response, bandwagoning, seems to have produced a more sound outcome than those of pioneering and resisting in retrospect.

NOTES

1. Such risk-averse behaviour was a predominant choice for provincial implementors in the pre-reform era. Such a pattern is described as 'hanging on'—neither pace-setting nor lagging—in Kenneth Lieberthal and Michel Oksenberg, *Policy Making in China: Leaders, Structures and Processes* (Princeton: Princeton University Press, 1988), 335. Avery Goldstein also uses the concept of 'bandwagon politics' in explaining the sweeping pace of local compliance during agricultural collectivization and the Great Leap Forward of the 1950s, but his rationale differs from the one used in this study in that his bandwagon politics takes place in hierarchical contexts where 'concerns about political survival are not paramount'. See *From Bandwagon to Balance-of-Power Politics: Structural Constraints and Politics in China, 1949–1978* (Stanford: Stanford University Press, 1991), 79–80, 98–9, 108–9.

2. See David Bachman, *Bureaucracy, Economy, and Leadership in China: The Institutional Origins of the Great Leap Forward* (Cambridge: Cambridge University Press, 1991), 5; and William A. Joseph, 'A Tragedy of Good Intentions: Post-Mao Views of the Great Leap Forward,' *Modern China*, 12/4 (1986), 427–8.

3. The Chinese sarcastically call the former category of cadres the 'document group' (*benpai*) who base their policy behaviour exclusively on central instructions stipulated in written documents. The latter category of cadres is described as the 'cat group' (*maopai*) who would pursue any policy that could produce positive results. See Yang Xun and Liu Jiarui, *Zhongguo nongcun gaige de daolu: zongti shuping yu quyushizheng* (The Path of China's Rural Reform: An Overview and Local Practice) (Beijing: Beijing daxue chubanshe, 1987), 76.

4. Daniel Kelliher, *Peasant Power in China: The Era of Rural Reform* (New Haven: Yale University Press, 1992), 65. Kelliher, however, does not provide justifications as to how the peasant-power perspective, which he uses to explain the entire process of decollectivization, bears on the Hubei case where peasants were certainly not able to stay ahead of state policy. For a post-facto Chinese assessment of leadership 'conservatism' in Hubei, see *Dangdai zhongguo de Hubei* (Contemporary China's Hubei Province) (Beijing: Zhongguo shehui kexue chubanshe, 1991), i. 142–3.

5. One source offers a lower figure of 13.5 per cent for December 1980. Given the prevalent tendency during the earlier period to under-report the pace of decollectivization from fears of policy reversal, this study adopts a higher figure suggested by a later publication. See Shandong Provincial Party Committee, *Shandongsheng nongye hezuohua shiliaoji* (History of Agricultural Cooperativization in Shandong Province) (Jinan: Shandong renmin chubanshe, 1990), 732. For the lower figure, see *Dangdai zhongguo de Shandong* (Contemporary China's Shandong Province) (Beijing: Zhongguo shehuikexue chubanshe, 1989), i. 302, table 5.

6. While the figure of 96.8 per cent may be what the province claims to have achieved by December 1982, several pieces of evidence point to lower figures for its real performance. First of all, the considerable degree of resistance put up by Yantai prefecture and Qingdao during the first two months of 1983 questions the reliability of this figure (these two areas had twenty counties accounting for 19 per cent of 104 counties in Shandong). Second, *Contemporary China's Shandong Province* (i. 302, table 5) suggests the figure of 96.8 is for March 1983 rather than for December 1982. In this light, perhaps a mid-80s percentage seems more persuasive for December 1982.

7. On the effects of diffusion from Anhui, see Department of Agriculture and Industry of Heze Prefectural Party Committee, 'Heze diqu nongcun shi zenyang shixing baogan daohu zerenzhi de' (On How Heze Prefecture Implemented *baogan daohu*), *History of Agricultural Cooperativization in Shandong Province*, ii. 299. Also see Dali Yang, *Calamity and Reform in China: State, Rural Society, and Institutional Change since the Great Leap Famine* (Stanford: Stanford University Press, 1996), 156.

8. See 'On How Heze Prefecture Implemented *baogan daohu*', 298–300. It is worth noting that, during the period of decollectivization, it was not Heze but Dezhou that received exclusive attention from the provincial newspaper, *Dazhong ribao* (*Dazhong Daily*). This seems to suggest that Heze's practice was at the time considered so heretic and deviant that its importance had to be downplayed. It was only in the late 1980s that Heze was positively labelled as a 'pioneer'.

9. During 1958–78, Dongming relied on the total of 690 million *jin* of grain provided by the central government, accounting for 27 per cent of the prefecture's total (Heze then had a total of ten counties). As of 1978, per capita income in Dongming was a mere 28.8 *yuan*, 40 *yuan* lower than Shandong's average. See *Contemporary China's Shandong Province*, i. 283–5.

10. See ibid. i. 287; and Research Office of the Shandong Provincial Party Committee, *Shandong sishinian* (Forty Years of Shandong) (Jinan: Shandong renmin chubanshe, 1989), 147.

11. Information from the author's interview in Jinan in 1992. One important question remains: as early as February 1978, obviously in the absence of diffusion from Anhui, how did the prefectural leadership and Zhou come up with such innovative ideas? The answer seems to lie in the locality's past experiences with similar innovations in the early 1960s, a factor that was an important catalyst for the Anhui case as well. See 'Gaoqingxian huagou gongshe liushi niandai chu shixing tudi daohu jingying de qingkuang' (On the Implementation of 'Household Land Contract' in Gaoqing County's Huagou Commune in the Early 1960s), *History of Agricultural Cooperativization in Shandong Province*, ii. 241–3.

12. While one earlier report suggests a much later date—after the Third Plenum—for this dramatic event it may have been a post-factor effort to protect the county as well as the prefecture. For this report, see Work-team dispatched to Dongming County, 'Guanyu dongmingxian baochan daohu de diaocha baogao' (A Report on the Implementation of *baochan daohu* in Dongming County, dated 15 July 1980), *History of Agricultural Cooperativization in Shandong Province*, ii. 286; and 'On How Heze Prefecture Implemented *baogan daohu*', *History of Agricultural Co-operativization in Shandong Province*, ii. 299. For the timing of early 1978, see *Contemporary China's Shandong Province*, i. 288.

13. The seasonal migration of Heze residents—averaged annually at 150,000—must have helped the spread of the news. See ibid. i. 285.

14. 'A Report on the Implementation of *baochan daohu* in Dongming County', *History of Agricultural Cooperativization in Shandong Province*, ii. 286–7.

15. In the spring of 1980, Heze prefectural party committee held a conference on exchanging experiences with various responsibility systems, where the two household-based systems received high priority. See *Contemporary China's Shandong Province*, i. 291.

16. 'On How Heze Prefecture Implemented *baogan daohu*', 299.

17. See *Dazhong ribao* (*Mass Daily*; hereafter *DZRB*), 16 and 18 Jan., 7 and 25 Feb., 24 Mar., 9 Apr., and 16 Nov. 1979. One exceptional report was that several communes in Jihe county of Dezhou prefecture were implementing the system of 'task rates to individual labourers' (*fengong daoren*). See *DZRB*, 1 Aug. 1979.

18. For an official post-facto acknowledgement that the spread of decollectivization in Heze in 1979–80 went far beyond the areas specified by the central document, see *Forty Years of Shandong*, 149.

19. *DZRB*, 20 Mar. 1980.

20. For the prevalence of such norms in Shandong, see *Forty Years of Shandong*, 140.

21. Author's interview in Jinan in 1992.

22. Bai Rubing was the provincial first party secretary during 1974–82; Su Yiran was governor in 1979–82 and later became Shandong's first party secretary; and Qin Hezhen was provincial agricultural secretary. For Qin Hezhen's functional affiliation with mechanization and his position against decollectivization, see *Renmin ribao*, 8 Jan. 1978 and 'Qin Hezhen zai quansheng nongcun gongzuo huiyi shang de jianghua' (Qin Hezhen's Speech at the Provincial Rural Work Conference made on 16 November 1981), *History of Agricultural Co-operativization in Shandong Province*, i. 703, 705.

23. Interviews in Jinan in 1994.

24. I was made aware of the nuances of these expressions by two officials formerly with the Shandong provincial agricultural commission interviewed in Jinan in 1994.

25. It should be noted that even in Heze opposition did exist. An interviewee provided an example in which three teams of a production brigade adopted *baochan daohu* while the fourth team refused to follow suit by arguing that 'we are not going to conduct such capitalist practices'. Author's interview in Jinan in 1992. While such instances were rare in Heze, the case of Qianwanglou brigade in Dongming county is rather well known. Due to its relative wealth and high-level mechanization, the brigade refused to decollectivize until 1983. Information from the interview in Jinan in 1994 and 'Hu Yaobang shicha Heze diqu' (Hu Yaobang Inspects Heze Prefecture), *History of Agricultural Co-operativization in Shandong Province*, ii. 173. For a study on a similar brigade-level case, see Guo Ming and Wang Shuwen, 'Yige dadui shixing duozhong xingshi nongye shengchan zerenzhi de diaocha' (On A Production Brigade Adopting Multiple Types of Production Responsibility Systems), *Jingji yanjiu* (Economic Studies), Sept. 1982, 70–4.

26. This visit, confirmed in interviews, is not documented in the most authoritative *History of Agricultural Co-operativization in Shandong Province*. It is not clear whether the timing of its publication (Dec. 1989 and Jan. 1990 in 2 vols.) might have necessitated the exclusion of any activities associated with Zhao. Given that Hu Yaobang and Wan Li made several extended trips to various places in Shandong during 1981–4, it is not inconceivable that Zhao paid a visit to the province.

27. An interviewee revealed that Zhao had wanted to transplant the Heze experiment to the highly developed Jiaodong peninsula by appointing Zhou Zhenxing as Qingdao's party secretary. Zhou was later promoted to be a vice-governor of Shandong supposedly on the strength of Zhao Ziyang. Author's interview in Jinan in 1992. A question remains with regard to Zhao's attitude toward *baochan daohu*. While Zhao on record opposed *baochan daohu* until June 1980, no documented evidence is available to show he continued to do so after that point. It is quite possible that, after the dissemination of CD [80] No. 75, Zhao might have adopted a much more relaxed position toward the application of *baochan daohu* to poor areas.

28. Interview in Jinan in 1992.

29. For Shandong's conditional approval of *baochan daohu*, see *DZRB*, 6 Nov. 1980; and for that of *baogan daohu*, see Ibid. 18 Dec. 1980.

30. See *DZRB*, 22 Nov. 1980. Under this system of *zhuanye chengbao*, a majority of households were organized into 'specialized teams' (*zhuanyedui*) or 'specialized work groups' (*zhuanyezu*) while only a handful of households were allowed to work on their own. See *DZRB*, 5 Dec. 1980.

31. See the editorial of *DZRB*, 25 Feb. 1981.

32. Such reservation and ambivalence are interesting considering that Shandong was visited by two heavyweight central leaders, Wan Li and Hu Yaobang, who toured Dezhou and Linyi Prefectures respectively in late March of 1981. During their visits, both highly praised the effectiveness of household farming. See 'Wan Li shicha Dezhou' (Wan Li Inspects Dezhou) and 'Hu Yaobang diyici shicha Linyi diqu' (Hu Yaobang Inspects Linyi Prefecture for the First Time), *History of Agricultural Co-operativization in Shandong Province*, ii. 163, 165.

33. As a Central Document is called *zhongfa*, Shandong's provincial document is called *lufa*. For the text, see *Nongcun jingji zhengce huibian 1981–1983* (Collection of Rural Policy Documents for 1981–1983) (internal publication) (Beijing: Nongcun duwu chubanshe, 1984), 350–61, especially 352–4.
34. See *DZRB*, 26 Apr., 14 May, 17 and 26 June, 10 Aug., 10 Sept., and 7 Nov. 1981.
35. For Heze, see *History of Agricultural Co-operativization in Shandong Province*, ii. 299; for Dezhou, *DZRB*, 9 Oct. 1981; for Jining and Weifang, see *DZRB*, 10 Sept. 1981 and 29 Oct. 1982; and for Linyi, see 'Hu Yaobang Inspects Linyi Prefecture for the First Time', *History of Agricultural Cooperativization in Shandong Province*, ii. 165.
36. *DZRB*, 20 Dec. 1981.
37. See the Administrative Offices of the Shandong Provincial Party Committee and Provincial People's Government, 'Guanyu yinfa 'Shandongsheng nongye shengchan zerenzhi shixing banfa' de tongzhi' (Notice on Shandong's Methods of Implementing Agricultural Production Responsibility Systems), *Nongcun jingji zhengce huibian 1981–1983*, 363–6.
38. Research Office of the Shandong Provincial Party Committee, *Shandong Shengqing 1949–1984* (The Provincial Situation of Shandong 1949–1984) (Jinan: Shandong renmin chubanshe, 1986), 15, 17, 19. For Yantai's mechanization, see 'Shandong yantai diqu fazhan nongye jixiehua de diaocha baogao' (A Report on the Survey of the Development of Agricultural Mechanization in Yantai, Shandong), *Hongqi* (*Red Flag*), Nov. 1975, 11–13. For the province's stress on Yantai's development of commune- and brigade-run enterprises, see 'Zhonggong shandongshengwei pizhuan yantai diwei "guanyu dali fazhan shedui qiyie he duozhong jingying de qingkuang baogao"' (The Shandong Provincial Party Committee Circulates the Yantai Prefectural Party Committee's Report on the Development of Commune- and Brigade-Run Enterprises and Diversified Production), *History of Agricultural Co-operativization in Shandong Province*, i. 662–7.
39. The Agricultural Machinery Survey Team of the First Ministry of Machine Building, 'Shandongsheng jiashu nongye jixiehua de diaocha baogao' (A Report on the Survey on Shandong's Acceleration of Agricultural Mechanization), *History of Agricultural Co-operativization in Shandong Province*, i. 589.
40. This paragraph is based upon the information provided in *Contemporary China's Shandong Province*, i. 301.
41. According to a central government cadre who had been dispatched to Dezhou prefecture in Shandong on a survey mission, the day that donkeys were distributed to households they were killed and their meat was put up for sale. Given these negative precedents, local cadres in Yantai were extremely reserved about dividing up machinery that required constant care. Author's interview in Beijing in 1992.
42. Interview in Jinan in 1992.
43. Interview in Jinan in 1992.
44. Comparable figures for Shandong and Yantai (for 1978) were 409 and 484 *jin*, and 69 and 121 *yuan*, respectively. For Shandong figures, see *Contemporary China's Shandong Province*, i. 283; and for Yantai figures, see *Forty Years of Shandong*, 146.
45. *DZRB*, 11 and 19 Mar. 1979, and 22 Oct. 1980.
46. *DZRB*, 5 Dec. 1980.
47. Information on Yeji brigade is from Zhang Lin and Wang Qiang, 'Yejidadui shixing baogan daohu de luogan tedian' (On the Implementation of *Baogan daohu* in Yeji Brigade), *Jingji yanjiu*, July 1983, 66–70.
48. See ibid. 67.
49. For the text, see 'Notice on Shandong's Methods of Implementing Agricultural Production Responsibility Systems', *Nongcun jingji zhengce huibian 1981–1983*, 365.
50. See *DZRB*, 29 Oct., 6 Nov., and 18 Dec. 1982.
51. *DZRB*, 18 Dec. 1982.
52. *DZRB*, 9 Feb. 1983.
53. Interviews in Beijing in 1992 and in Jinan in 1994. No documentary evidence is available to link this personnel change with the sluggish pace of decollectivization, clearly illustrating the inevitable limitations of documentary research. The replacement of Bai Rubing by Su Yiran in December 1982 seems to have been related less to his views on decollectivization than to the overall political framework at the time. As will be discussed in

Chapter 6, the tactic of replacing recalcitrant local leaders was also adopted against provincial first party secretaries in Heilongjiang as well as in Zhejiang.

54. This paragraph is indebted to interviews in Jinan and Qingdao in 1994, and Chen Xiwen, Sun Fangming, and Liu Danhua, 'Yantai diqu nongcun zerenzhi diaocha zonghe baogao' (Summary Report on Rural Responsibility Systems in Yantai Prefecture), in Zhongguo nongcun fazhan wenti yanjiuzu (ed.), *Nongcun, Jingji, Shehui* (Villages, Economy, and Society) (Beijing: Zhishi chubanshe, 1985), iii. 27–36.

55. Several other bandwagoning provinces also went through similar developments—the Shaanbei region of Shaanxi, the Subei region of Jiangsu, etc. For Shaanxi, see *Dangdai zhongguo de Shaanxi* (Contemporary China's Shaanxi Province) (Beijing: Zhongguo shehuikexue chubanshe, 1991), i. 164.

56. By 1978, the Shandong provincial leadership had already been studying ways of improving economic conditions in the four prefectures located in the western plain region. Such a concern might have helped the provincial leadership to turn a 'blind eye' to the Heze experiment and its diffusion to the remaining three prefectures. For the province's concern, see 'Zhonggong shandong shengwei guanyu pizhuan "luxibei siqu nongye fazhan guihua caoan" de tongzhi' (The Shandong Provincial Party Committee's Notice on 'Draft Plan of Agricultural Development in Four Northwestern Prefectures'), *History of Agricultural Co-operativization in Shandong Province*, i. 608–16.

57. Data for Linyi are badly needed; located in the central mountainous region, it was long known for its extreme poverty. Given the Centre's September 1979 document that permitted *baochan daohu* in mountainous areas, how Linyi responded to it may provide an important piece of information about the decollectivization process in this region.

58. The number of counties under Yantai (then encompassing Weihai) and Qingdao accounted for 19 per cent (20 out of 104) of Shandong's total.

59. *Zhongguo nongye nianjian 1981* (China Agricultural Yearbook, 1981) (Beijing: Nongye chubanshe, 1982), 58–9; *Shandongshengqing*, 153; and Heilongjiang Provincial Statistical Bureau, *Heilongjiang sishinian jubian* (Great Changes in Heilongjiang: The Last Forty Years, 1949–1989) (Beijing: Zhongguo tongji chubanshe, 1989), 221.

60. *Zhongguo nongye nianjian 1981*, 10. Different regions had different size criteria for tractors. The most commonly used criterion was: those below 15 or 20 horsepower categorized as 'small'; those between 20 and 50 as 'medium-sized'; and those over 50 as 'large'. Yet, according to an interviewee in Harbin, while a 50 horsepower machine was considered large in Shandong, the same machine was regarded as medium-sized in Heilongjiang where the 75-horsepower Dongfanghong was very popular.

61. Article counting was based upon the following principles: (1) only the articles on the mechanization of primary farm work (*zhongzhiye*) were counted; (2) those on the mechanization of food-processing, irrigation, and electrification were excluded; and (3) those on semi-mechanization focusing on farm tools were included. While a second coder was not utilized, the materials were of public nature (i.e. not private survey materials) so that they are always available for replication.

62. For the downgrading of agricultural mechanization during this period, see Jae Ho Chung, 'The Politics of Agricultural Mechanization in the Post-Mao Era', *China Quarterly*, 134 (June 1993), 264–90.

63. See, for instance, *DZRB*, 24 and 30 Oct. 1979 and 17 July 1980.

64. Ibid. 8 Oct. 1980; also see 17 Mar. and 9 Apr. 1980.

65. See ibid. 10 Sept. and 9 Oct. 1981.

66. Ibid. 7 Nov. 1981, 18 Jan. and 13 Nov. 1982, and 3 July 1983. In Jiangsu, too, peasants were allowed to buy tractors in late 1981 and early 1982. See *Xinhua ribao* (*New China Daily*), 7 Jan. 1982.

67. No clear evidence of 'deal-making' between basic-level cadres and peasants is found. Rather, as some suggest, basic-level cadres were more serious opponents than their superiors in the microlevel cases of Shandong. See, for instance, Kathleen Hartford, 'Socialist Agriculture is Dead: Long Live Socialist Agriculture! Organizational Transformation in Rural China', in Elizabeth J. Perry and Christine Wong (eds.), *The Political Economy of Reform in Post-Mao China* (Cambridge, Mass.: Harvard University Press, 1985), 39–40.

68. For these visits by key central leaders and their activities, see 'Wan Li Inspects Dezhou'; 'Hu Yaobang Inspects Linyi Prefecture for the First Time'; 'Hu Yaobang Inspects Heze

Prefecture'; 'Hu Yaobang Inspects Yantai'; and 'Hu Yaobang Inspects Linyi for the Second Time', *History of Agricultural Co-operativization in Shandong Province*, ii. 163–5, 171–5, 177–80.

69. For the texts of these two progress reports made in 1983, see 'Zhonggong shandong sheng-wei guanyu guanche zhongyang yihao wenjian de qingkuang baogao' (The Shandong Provincial Party Committee's Progress Report on Implementing CD [1983] No. 1), *History of Agricultural Co-operativization in Shandong Province*, i. 722–5 and 728–32.

6

The Politics of Resistance in Heilongjiang: Issue Linkages, Attentive Leadership, and Tactics of Delayed Implementation

The most salient characteristic of the decollectivization reform is that a few provinces dared to resist the centre's preferences in order to protect their endogenous interests. As far as our current understanding of China's policy processes is concerned, such recalcitrance was very rare in the pre-reform era (the post-1957 period in particular) during which provincial compliance with central policy was generally swift, total, standardized, and largely taken for granted.[1] In the context of decollectivization, three north-eastern provinces—Heilongjiang, Jilin, and Liaoning—stood out for their slow, deviant, and resistant pattern of implementation. These 'resister' provinces provide supporting evidence for the effects of administrative decentralization on expanding the scope of policy discretion at least in a few provinces.

Among the 'resisters', Heilongjiang constituted the most outstanding case as its performance constantly lagged far behind the national average throughout the process of decollectivization (see Table 6.1). While Heilongjiang's performance in mid-1981 may not necessarily be regarded as an anti-centre act since Beijing had not yet pushed for the popularization of household farming, it nevertheless indicates that the province was exercising its discretion in determining the pace of decollectivization. Given that, by June 1981, pioneers like Guizhou and Anhui had 95 and 70 per cent, and bandwagoners like Shandong and Hebei had 38 and 36 per cent of their teams under household farming, Heilongjiang's figure of 0.7 per cent suggests that the scope of its decollectivization was limited to only a couple of communes.[2] The Heilongjiang case thus constitutes a strong antithesis to the peasant-power perspective since the provincial authorities were so effective in containing the diffusion of household farming that peasant demands constantly lagged far behind the central policy.[3]

More interestingly, despite Beijing's push for the swift popularization of household farming since mid-1982 and the subsequent compliance by most provinces by the end of the year (as indicated by the national average of 78.2 per cent), Heilongjiang had only 12 per cent of its teams under household farming in December 1982. Furthermore, while other resisters such as Liaoning and Jilin succumbed to the centre's pressure by March 1983 (see Table 3.1), Heilongjiang continued its resistance and it was only toward the

TABLE 6.1. *Heilongjiang's pace of decollectivization, 1981–1984 (% of teams under household farming)*

	1981	1982	1983	1984
National average	6: 28.2	6: 67.0 (g)	8: 93.0	
		12: 78.2	12: 98.3 (g)	
Heilongjiang	9: 0.7	5: 8.7 (g)	2: 73.0 (g)	2: 98.0
		12: 12.0	3: 85.0	
			10: 87.1	
			12: 90+	
Number of provinces that	2	20+	26	26
reached 90% or more				
(year-end figure) (N = 26)				

Notes: Figures to the left of the colon refer to the month of the respective year; (g) refers to figures for *baogan daohu* only.

Sources: As Table 3.1.

end of 1983 that its performance entered a 90 per cent range. Heilongjiang thus managed to delay the popularization of household farming for about twenty months after the first strong manifestation of Beijing's preference in April 1982 and for about one year after most provinces completed the decollectivization reform.

In light of the central–provincial policy dynamics of the pre-reform era, such a defiant act by Heilongjiang supplies a crucial piece of evidence for some positive effects of post-Mao administrative decentralization on the scope of provincial policy discretion.[4] Two conditions facilitated Heilongjiang's resistance to Beijing: (1) crucial endogenous interests were threatened by the decollectivization reform; and (2) a determined provincial leadership was available to protect them. What then were those endogenous interests as the source of conflict between Beijing and Heilongjiang?

A conflict may cross-cut a variety of issue areas and, therefore, a disagreement is often over a package of policies rather than over one single policy. To add a time dimension, conflicts are in most cases more than a one-shot interaction; they are usually the processes that reflect past interactions. Thus, the significance of 'antecedents'—previous interactions whose residual impact is carried over into the next set of interactions—is stressed. In the case of Heilongjiang's conflict with Beijing, it is argued that the previous interactions between the two over the issue of mechanization initially formulated and later reinforced the province's resistance to the centre. Dissatisfaction on the part of Heilongjiang, stemming largely from its 'perceived unfair compensation' for the centre's policy of downgrading the role of mechanization, was carried over into the Beijing–Heilongjiang disagreements over decollectivization.[5]

Endogenous interests alone, however, do not suffice to produce outright provincial resistance. This is where the leadership factor comes in. If the immediate provision of provincial support for grass-roots innovation was the key to the swift diffusion of household farming in Anhui, tight overhead regulation was the principal reason for the delayed decollectivization in Heilongjiang. The Heilongjiang case well illustrates how determined and daring the provincial leadership could become in resisting the centre when its vital endogenous interests were threatened. Its committed defiance speaks for an expanded scope of provincial discretion under administrative decentralization and, at the same time, it challenges the peasant-power perspective as an encompassing explanation of the decollectivization reform.

This chapter consists of six sections. The first describes Heilongjiang's position on the household responsibility systems and illustrates, in comparison with Beijing's evolving position (Chapter 3) and provincial responses by Anhui and Shandong (Chapters 4 and 5), how discernible Heilongjiang's biases were against household farming. The second section discusses the salience of mechanization viewed as the most crucial factor in Heilongjiang's resistance to decollectivization. The third provides detailed backgrounds to the post-Mao reversal of the mechanization policy, which made Heilongjiang the biggest loser and formulated its negative disposition toward household farming. The fourth examines the perceptions and tactics of the provincial leadership in containing the diffusion of household farming. The fifth investigates the unilateral process of conflict resolution, in which Beijing imposed its preference politically to secure swift provincial compliance. The final section offers some observations regarding the generalities and particularities of the Heilongjiang case.

HEILONGJIANG'S POSITION ON THE HOUSEHOLD RESPONSIBILITY SYSTEMS

By 1978, Heilongjiang had not yet ventured into any sort of agricultural responsibility system, although several provinces had already been experimenting with a variety of responsibility systems including 'household production quotas'. The only notable change in Heilongjiang was the shift to a system of 'to each according to his labour' (*anlao fenpei*), which constituted a crucial departure from the Dazhai system of egalitarian remuneration.[6] It was only at the beginning of 1979 that Heilongjiang officially permitted 'task rates' (*dinge baogong*) with the work group as the primary unit.[7] While the provincial leadership endorsed the task-rates system, it was firmly opposed to 'production quotas to the work group' (*baochan daozu*). At a provincial telephone conference in early May of 1979, Zhao Dezun, provincial agriculture secretary, made the provincial position very clear:

Judging on the basis of some experimental practices, this system of 'production quotas to the work group' is full of contradictions and problems. Especially, the system is *not suitable for agricultural mechanization*. In light of our province's situation, it was a totally correct decision for the provincial party committee not to encourage its popularization. [emphasis added][8]

'Some experimental practices' referred to the pilot implementation in the two counties of Zhaoyuan and Fuyu. The Zhaoyuan experiment was conducted under the approval of Bao Zong, first party secretary of Tuohua prefecture, who managed to attain a tacit endorsement from Yang Yichen, provincial first party secretary, on the condition that the geographical scope of the experiment would be significantly reduced. On the other hand, the Fuyu experiment was short-lived since the leadership of Nenjiang prefecture backed down in the face of provincial opposition based upon the assessment that *baochan daozu* was not suitable for counties like Fuyu with high levels of mechanization.[9]

By late 1979, with the exception of Zhaoyuan which the provincial authorities allowed to experiment with *baochan daozu* perhaps out of a token respect for the Third Plenum document, Heilongjiang approved only two responsibility systems of 'task rates to work groups' (*baogong daozu*) and 'work groups for specialized production' (*zhuanyezu*). Only at the provincial work conference held in January 1980 did Yang Yichen allow 'poor' teams (estimated to be 10 to 15 per cent of the province's total) to 'experiment' with *baochan daozu*.[10] This marked a significant contrast with Anhui which officially endorsed both *baochan daohu* and *baogan daohu* at its provincial work conference in January 1980. That the first official report on *baochan daozu* in Heilongjiang appeared in October 1980—one month after the Central Party Secretariat endorsed *baochan daohu* through CD [80] No. 75—also illustrates the degree to which the province had been unwilling to support any responsibility system based on the unit smaller than the production team.[11]

In 1979–80, Heilongjiang's position on the household responsibility systems was unconditional opposition. In 1980, Heilongjiang maintained that 'it is all right to divide into work groups but not into households' (*fenzu bufenjia*).[12] A report of December 1980 listed three acceptable responsibility systems: (1) in areas where the level of mechanization was high, particularly those specializing in wheat and bean production, 'linking payment to output' (*lianchan jichou*), with the brigade as the primary unit, was to be popularized; (2) a system of 'linking payment to output' with the team or the work group as the primary unit would be implemented in poor units; and (3) 'unified farming and household management' (*tongyi jingying fenhu guanli*), a sort of *baochan daohu*, was to be permitted only for the production of commercial crops.[13]

Only in the beginning of 1981 was *baochan daohu* officially endorsed in Heilongjiang, though only conditionally in accordance with CD [80] No. 75. In his report to the Provincial Party Committee's Work Conference, Yang Yichen gave a very reluctant approval:

Our province's agriculture should develop toward a large-scale production on the basis of collectivization, mechanization, specialization, and socialization. . . . [For this purpose,] we must grasp the production brigade as our key link. . . . *Baochan daohu is also allowed but we have to work hard to lead our agriculture to one that is large-scale and collective.* [emphasis added][14]

With *baochan daohu* endorsed, the provincial leadership's concern shifted to *baogan daohu* which was then often identified as 'private farming with individual plots' (*fentian dangan*).[15] After *People's Daily* published an article in August 1981 that defined *baogan daohu* as a socialist responsibility system, *Heilongjiang Daily*, too, carried an article approving it in September 1981.[16] Yet only in November 1981 did the provincial leadership officially permit *baogan daohu* to be adopted by the 'three categories of poor production teams' (*sankaodui*).[17]

It has thus been established that Heilongjiang's provincial leadership officially approved *baochan daohu* in January 1981 and *baogan daohu* in November 1981. Yet, provincial approval was one thing and local implementation was quite another. While, in pioneer provinces like Anhui, local implementation stayed far ahead of provincial approval, the process was quite the other way around in Heilongjiang. In September 1981, for instance, a mere 0.4 per cent of the province's teams were under *baochan daohu*. Furthermore, by December 1982, despite the province having had almost two years and certainly more than one year to implement *baochan daohu* and *baogan daohu*, respectively, only 12 per cent of its teams were under household farming. This suggests that, unlike Anhui, Heilongjiang was utilizing the conditionalities attached to the central directives to contain the diffusion of household farming.

The November 1982 speech by Wan Li, the strongest manifestation of Beijing's preference for household farming (*baogan daohu* in particular), did influence Heilongjiang, although its impact was clearly weaker than anywhere else. The share of Heilongjiang's teams under household farming rose radically from 12 per cent in December 1982 to 70 per cent in February 1983. Yet, it took almost another year before Heilongjiang reached the 90 per cent range in December 1983.[18] Such a sluggish pace was later acknowledged as follows:

Due to the 'backward ideas' of the leadership, Heilongjiang's implementation of the household responsibility systems was delayed for at least a year since the dissemination of CD [82] No. 1. When compared to other advanced provinces,

Heilongjiang's experimentation with and popularization of the policy were slower by two to three years.[19]

What accounts for Heilongjiang's noticeably slow pace of decollectivization? What were the origins of those 'backward ideas' of its leadership? Why did Heilongjiang delay the decollectivization reform even at the expense of standing against Beijing's wishes? Were there crucial provincial interests at stake, on the basis of which its leadership opted for non-compliance? This study argues that Heilongjiang's sluggish pace was closely associated with its endogenous interests in agricultural mechanization and that the provincial leadership maximally utilized its policy discretion in containing the diffusion of household farming.

THE SALIENCE OF MECHANIZATION IN HEILONGJIANG, 1: CONTEXTUAL BACKGROUNDS

Heilongjiang's prioritization of mechanization can be explained by demographic and topographical factors. Heilongjiang has long been known for its low ratio of labour to arable land. In 1980, its per capita area of cultivation was 4.1 *mu*, 2.9 times the national average, while its per-peasant area of cultivation was 6.5 *mu*, 3.6 times the national average.[20] In topographical terms, 84 per cent of its cultivated area was very flat with an average slope of only six degrees. Furthermore, over 70 per cent of its cultivated land consisted of large 'undivided plots' (*lianpian*), each averaging 300 *mu*.[21] Not surprisingly, Heilongjiang has long been a core province in China's mechanization efforts.[22] In 1980, Heilongjiang ranked first in mechanized harvesting, second in mechanized seeding, and fourth in mechanized planting. If we exclude Beijing, Tianjin, and Shanghai, Heilongjiang would rank first in both mechanized planting and harvesting, and second only to Xinjiang in mechanized seeding, constituting the most mechanized province in overall terms.[23]

Table 6.2 presents key indicators of mechanization in Heilongjiang. First, the ratio of Heilongjiang's tractor-ploughed area to its total cultivated area was almost double that of the nation as a whole. Second, its number of large and medium-sized tractors constituted one-tenth of China's total; and in horsepower terms, the share amounted to precisely one-eighth. But its share of small and hand tractors in terms of number and horsepower was only 2.5 and 2.1 per cent, respectively. It is apparent that Heilongjiang relied heavily on large machinery in its mechanization. Within Heilongjiang, 89.2 per cent of the tractors were large and medium-sized (with the average horsepower of 54.9). Given the generally incompatible relationship between the household-based responsibility systems and large-scale mechanization then in China, Heilongjiang would naturally oppose the popularization of household farming that would render most of its large machinery useless.

TABLE 6.2. *Indicators of Heilongjiang's mechanization (1981)*

	Nationwide (A)	Heilongjiang (B)	B/A (%)
Share of tractor-ploughed area (%)	36.8	66.5	—
Large and medium-sized tractors:			
a. number (1,000)	792.0	78.3	9.9
b. horsepower (million)	34.3	4.3	12.5
Small-sized and Hand tractors:			
a. Number (1,000)	2,037	42	2.5
b. Horsepower (million)	23.9	0.5	2.1

Source: State Statistical Bureau, *Statistical Yearbook of China, 1981* (Beijing: China Statistics Publisher, 1982), 173, 176, 185, 186.

The distribution of key crops in Heilongjiang also provides another explanation for its heavy dependence on mechanization. According to 1980 data, about 84 per cent of its cultivated area was sown with various kinds of grains, and grain production was generally much easier to mechanize than commercial crops such as cotton. Furthermore, 87 per cent of its grain-producing area was sown with dry-field crops of wheat (29%), corn (26%), beans (22%), and millet (11%), while only 3 per cent was sown with rice, the least susceptible to mechanization among all grain crops.[24]

Furthermore, state farms (*guoying nongchang*) in Heilongjiang accounted for more than 40 per cent of all the state-farm acreage in China. Beginning with the Tongbei farm established in 1947, Heilongjiang's state farms marked a dramatic growth during 1958–60 when land reclamation drives were pushed hard by Wang Zhen. As a result, by 1965 Heilongjiang already had 103 state farms totalling 16.4 million *mu* accounting for 15 per cent of the province's total cultivated area, and by 1980, the share rose to 22.3 per cent, with mechanization levels of 90 per cent.[25] What merits our attention is the high priority placed on mechanization in the development of state farms specializing in bean and wheat production and land reclamation, as Table 6.3 shows.

THE SALIENCE OF MECHANIZATION IN HEILONGJIANG, 2: POLICY BACKGROUNDS

While the aforementioned contextual factors may have constituted a necessary condition for Heilongjiang's resistance to decollectivization, they did not provide a sufficient condition. For this, we need to look into the policy backgrounds in which Beijing and Heilongjiang clashed over the

TABLE 6.3. *State farms' mechanization compared to the national average*[a]

	National average	State-farm average
Machine-tilled area[b]	33.8	80.6
Machine-ploughed area[b]	12.0	71.9
Machine-harvested area[b]	4.6	55.9
Large and medium-sized tractors[c]	5.6	8.1
Combined harvesters[c]	0.2	2.8

[a] These data are for 1983.
[b] refers to the percentage of the total cultivated land.
[c] refers to the number of the respective machinery per ten thousand *mu* of cultivated land.

Source: *Dangdai zhongguo de nongken shiye* (Contemporary China's Land Reclamation) (Beijing: Zhongguo shehui kexue chubanshe, 1986), 223.

issue of mechanization and the latter's responses to decollectivization were shaped.

Mechanization in Ascendancy and Heilongjiang in the Limelight, 1977–8

In line with the First Dazhai Conference of September 1975 where the target of achieving 'basic mechanization' (*chubu jixiehua*, operationally defined as mechanizing 70 per cent of all farm work) by 1980 had been set, the Third National Conference on Agricultural Mechanization was convened in January 1978.[26] At the Conference, Chen Yonggui, vice-premier in charge of rural policy, stipulated that mechanization would strengthen the rural collective economy and fundamentally transform the 'small producers' mentality' among peasants. The national targets established at the Conference included: (1) an increase in the level of mechanization to 70 per cent of the total sown area; (2) a 70 per cent increase in the number of large- and medium-sized tractors; and (3) a 36 per cent increase in the number of small and hand tractors.[27] The projected target for large and medium-sized tractors was twice as high as that for small and hand tractors, indicating Beijing's preference for large-machinery based mechanization.

While the Maoist principles in many policy areas were challenged and overturned at the Third Plenum of December 1978, mechanization was not one of them. While the Third Plenum document, 'Some Questions Concerning the Acceleration of Agricultural Development (Draft),' downplayed the significance of the Dazhai experiences and the role of the commune, it nevertheless reconfirmed the principal role of mechanization in developing China's agriculture.[28] Expectedly, two themes of collectivization and mechanization constantly echoed in Heilongjiang's rural policy during 1977–8. Heilongjiang's position was justified in the following terms: (1) its low ratio of labour to arable land; (2) the significance of state farms in Heilongjiang where one rural labourer was assigned up to 70 *mu* on average; and (3) the availability of more than 100 million *mu* for reclamation, for which mechanized work was deemed indispensable.[29]

More importantly, there was a special blessing from the central leadership. After becoming the Party Chairman, Hua Guofeng made his first inspection trip to the north-eastern provinces in April 1977. Not only did Hua visit Heilongjiang first, but he also spent three days there out of his five-day trip. Hua reportedly commented that 'Heilongjiang, with few people and vast land, should push hard for mechanization.'[30] Such a blessing from the Party Centre was soon followed by concrete policy measures. First, Heilongjiang was promised not only the centre's financial support for its all-out mechanization but also a priority allocation of new imported farm equipment. According to a project description, around 500 fully 'mechanized agricultural production bases' (*jixiehua nongye shengchan jidi*), each brigade-level base with about 2,000 hectares of land, would be established in Heilongjiang by the end of 1980.[31] Second, the National Work Conference on State Farms convened in January 1978 also stipulated that the priority in financial and material allocations for mechanization was to be assigned to Heilongjiang's state farms.[32] Yang Yichen proudly acknowledged Beijing's pledged support:

The centre has already defined our province as the key province of mechanization and provided enormous support. . . . [And] the centre has committed itself in supplying several thousand large machines every year to enhance the level of our mechanization.[33]

With strong support from the centre, Heilongjiang became quite bold in promoting all-out mechanization. First, it decided to invest more than 70 per cent of all available provincial capital in 'agriculture-aiding industry' (*zhinong gongye*) and especially in the production of large and medium-sized tractors, steel, and diesel engines.[34] Second, Heilongjiang also devised a mega-scale project for reclaiming 20 million *mu* of wasteland in the Three-River Plain by 1980.[35] Third, Heilongjiang became increasingly obsessed with imported machinery in equipping its mechanized work force.[36]

Mechanization Downplayed and Heilongjiang on the Losing Side, 1979–82

Following the intermittent criticisms of the Maoist scheme of all-out mechanization in the first half of 1979, the fatal blow came in September 1979 when the Fourth Plenum passed the 'Decisions Concerning Certain Problems in Rapidly Developing Agriculture'. The document made it clear that the target of completing basic mechanization by 1980 was not realistic. It also stressed the better utilization of already existing machinery rather than the production of new machinery.[37] The Fourth Plenum, however, was not able to resolve the debate over mechanization as it was intertwined with the power struggle and policy conflicts between Hua Guofeng and the 'Dazhai Clique' led by Chen Yonggui on one side and the 'Reformers' (Deng Xiaoping, Wan Li, and Du Runsheng) on the other.[38] While the former group insisted on the supremacy of collective economy based on large-scale mechanization, the latter took up the problem of surplus labour in case of all-out mechanization.[39] The Reformers' victory became clear in July 1980 when Yang Ligong, Minister of Agricultural Machinery, announced the reformulated mechanization policy:

The goal of achieving basic mechanization by 1980 has proved to be impractical. . . . Generally speaking, farm mechanization in China is difficult to achieve even in twenty-five years. . . . China should concentrate its mechanization efforts in the three north-eastern provinces, in some parts of Inner Mongolia and Xinjiang, and in the Yellow and Huai River Valleys.[40]

The official rejection of basic mechanization and the abolition of the across-the-board scheme contributed significantly to the downgrading of mechanization as the key strategy of agricultural development. Expectedly, these changes produced an adverse impact on the mechanization sector as a whole. The total amount of basic construction investment (*jiben jianshe touzi*) in the production and repair of agricultural machinery dwindled from 651 million *yuan* in 1978 to 274 million *yuan* in 1980. As efficient machinery management was stressed over the production of new machinery, tractor production also suffered: the production of large and medium-sized tractors dropped from 113,500 in 1978 to 97,000 in 1980, and that of small and hand tractors from 324,200 to 217,900 for the same years.[41]

The downgrading of mechanization took heavy tolls of Heilongjiang's plans. In stark contrast with its earlier position stressing the superiority of imported machinery, Heilongjiang gradually toned down its demand for imported machinery.[42] Heilongjiang's concession was first manifested in Yang Yichen's sober assessment: 'Merely waiting for imported machinery and simply expecting the state to help—neither of these is desirable.' On 1 April 1979, a decision was announced that all of the 500 'mechanized agricultural production bases' would be equipped with domestic machinery.[43]

Heilongjiang was not much discouraged, however. The protracted policy conflict at the centre enabled Heilongjiang to fight a local war of its own for the cause of mechanization. For instance, Heilongjiang conducted a survey of 37 brigade-level 'testing spots' designated in 1978. According to the survey to which Heilongjiang gave high publicity, 34 of the 37 brigades surveyed were highly successful in enhancing their grain outputs and labour productivity, while only the remaining 3 reported reduced production.[44] Another survey of 86 brigade-level testing spots for mechanized land reclamation designated in early 1979 also reported a remarkable success.[45] On

TABLE 6.4. *Heilongjiang's demand and supply of large and medium-sized tractors*

	1952	1957	1962	1965	1978	1980
Total number allocated	552	3,136	8,365	12,428	46,181	68,473
Total number produced	none	none	none	50	1,100	806

Source: *Heilongjiang sishinian jubian*, 213, 221.

the basis of these successes, Heilongjiang produced an ambitious plan for 1980 during which 705 brigades for mechanized farming and 69 brigades for mechanized reclamation were to be designated and supported.[46]

Heilongjiang's initial fight did not last long. In July 1980 when the reformulated mechanization policy was announced with the rejection of the across-the-board scheme, Beijing designated Heilongjiang as a key-point province in its new scheme of selective mechanization.[47] Subsequently, Heilongjiang came up with a more ambitious long-term plan, according to which it would reach a level of 70 per cent mechanization by 1985 and increase the number of testing spots from 705 in 1980 to 1,333 in 1981.[48] One crucial question remained concerning the centre's financial support and material allocation for Heilongjiang ambitious plan. The most expensive option would have been building agricultural machinery plants in Heilongjiang. Despite its highest mechanization level, Heilongjiang was far from self-sufficient in the production and supply of agricultural machinery. As shown in Table 6.4, the gap between its demand and production of large and medium-sized tractors is too enormous to ignore. The total output value of Heilongjiang's agricultural machinery production constituted only 8.8 per cent of the province's machinery industry.[49] In 1980, Heilongjiang had 16 tractor plants which produced 806 large and medium-sized tractors. That is, each plant produced approximately 31 tractors a year, a production capacity which was almost negligible. Naturally, Heilongjiang had been striving to reduce its heavy dependence on the centre and other provinces for the supply of machinery, parts, and implements.[50]

Although the option of building machinery plants must have been most appealing to Heilongjiang, it was out of the question given the radically downgraded status of mechanization. In fact, regarding agricultural machinery plants, cancellation was the major trend. According to the nationwide data, out of all agricultural machinery plant projects approved in 1978–9, only 5 per cent of large- and medium-scale projects and 12 per cent of small-scale projects were allowed to continue in 1981. Even the total number of China's existing tractor plants decreased from 65 to 45 in 1979–80.[51] The next plausible option would have been equipping Heilongjiang with imported machinery, and this option had already been taken off the list as noted earlier. Another option could have been a functional grant supporting the priority production and allocation of domestically manufactured

TABLE 6.5.   *Beijing's support for mechanization in Heilongjiang*

Year	Financial Support* (in 10 thousand *yuan*)	Increase over the previous year in the stock of large and medium-sized tractors
1977	6,209	572
1978	7,053	6,348
1979	5,312	7,016
1980	4,744	12,173
1981	19,335 (16,001)**	11,124
1982	18,812 (16,000)**	4,627
1983	7,016	5,590

* Financial support includes investments, loans and subsidies.
** Figures in parentheses refer to bank loans.

Source: Song Yuansheng, *Heilongjiangsheng nongye jixiehua fazhan yu erqiannian zhanlue*, 75, 229.

new machinery for Heilongjiang. This alternative, too, was deemed impractical by the central leadership which was then striving hard to reduce the size of new capital investment under the slogan of 'readjustments'.[52]

The least expensive option was interprovincial transfer of used machinery, on which Beijing eventually settled. Around 15,000 large and medium-sized tractors were shipped from other provinces to Heilongjiang in 1980–1 (in addition to the annually planned allocation) as shown in Table 6.5.[53] By downgrading the role of mechanization, Beijing relieved several provinces of the goal of all-out mechanization relying heavily on large and medium-sized tractors unsuitable for local conditions. Subsequently, a majority of large and medium-sized tractors were left unutilized in those provinces, which were then collected and transferred to Heilongjiang.[54] The interprovincial transfer was not free, however. As Table 6.5 indicates, large amounts of bank loans were made to Heilongjiang in 1981–2 mainly to help the province to pay for the tractors transferred. Unlike investments and subsidies, these bank loans had to be paid back to the banks and, fundamentally, to the centre. The tractor transfer, therefore, was hardly a privileged treatment for Heilongjiang. This line of argument that Heilongjiang was by no means a winner becomes more persuasive as we move on to the issues of financial arrangement and materials allocation.

First, financial support for mechanization became increasingly scarce. In November 1980, the State Economic Commission announced a decision to delegate the function of issuing loans for 'plant renovation' to the Construction Bank. The Construction Bank was in turn to determine loan recipients on the basis of two factors—less money spent and quick returns guaranteed—neither of which the mechanization sector satisfied.

Consequently, no new investments were made to renovate the tractor plants or to increase the production capacity of the existing plants in Heilongjiang.[55]

Second, another financial arrangement that adversely affected Heilongjiang's mechanization effort was the sharp increase in the interest rates of loans for agricultural machinery purchase. Since the price of agricultural machinery, despite ten price reductions since 1961, had always been considered high, there was a special category of loans exclusively for the purchase of agricultural machinery (called *nongji zhuanxiang daikuan*).[56] This special loan was issued to collectives and collective-run tractor stations by the People's Bank of China (PBC) and the China Agricultural Bank (CAB). On 1 January 1982, the interest rates doubled from 1.8 per cent to 3.6 per cent for the PBC loans and from 2.16 per cent to 4.32 per cent for the CAB loans.[57] Heilongjiang as a key-point province was not exempted from this change and its mechanization efforts were considerably undermined. The total amount of the loans for agricultural machinery purchase issued to Heilongjiang marked a 20 per cent decrease between 1980 and 1982.[58] Given the enormous size of the estimated investment required to achieve basic and complete mechanization in Heilongjiang, 1.8 and 3.8 billion *yuan* respectively, the overall situation was hardly encouraging.[59]

Third, materials allocation, especially that of diesel oil, was another crucial factor. Even after Heilongjiang was designated as a key-point province, complaints were voiced regarding the insufficient allocation of diesel oil for agricultural machinery. According to a report in October 1980, more than 83 per cent of tractors in Taijia commune of Tuohua county, one of 705 testing spots, were left unused due to fuel shortage; and in Mishan county all tractors reportedly stopped operating for the same reason.[60] Despite the problems, Beijing did almost nothing to mitigate the situation. Instead, in 1982, the centre cancelled the state subsidies on the purchase of diesel oil for agricultural use (*nongyong chaiyou jiage butie*).[61] Furthermore, the amount of diesel oil supplied by the state for agricultural machinery was reduced in 1982 from the usual 5 per cent of the nation's total consumption to merely 3 per cent.[62] The effect of such a reduction was acutely felt in Heilongjiang where the state supply fell 160,000 tons short of the province's demand. Consequently, the amount of diesel oil available for one *mu* decreased from 68 kilograms in 1981 to 40 kilograms in 1982, resulting in at least a 20 per cent decrease of machinery use.[63]

In sum, while financial and material resources for mechanization were rapidly dwindling, the centre did not exempt Heilongjiang from any of these changes. To use a Chinese colloquial expression, it was a typical example of 'only the provision of policy, but not of money for it' (*zhigeizhengce bugeiqian*), which would save the scarce resources of the centre by providing the province largely with nominal support only.

THE POLITICS OF DELAYED IMPLEMENTATION: ISSUE LINKAGES BETWEEN DECOLLECTIVIZATION AND MECHANIZATION

From Heilongjiang's viewpoint, neither the provision of new Chinese-made farm machinery nor the interprovincial transfer of used tractors was as appealing as the establishment of 500 fully mechanized agricultural production bases equipped with imported machinery that Beijing's aborted plan had promised with funds of 1.5 billion *yuan*.[64] Even its designation as a key-point province turned out to be largely nominal given its failure to obtain from the centre any meaningful preferential treatment in promoting mechanization. Under these circumstances, the provincial leadership became keenly aware of the negative effects of the household responsibility reform on its collective economy based on large-scale mechanization.

The Rationale of the Provincial Leadership and the Role of Yang Yichen

Many of the key figures in the provincial leadership of the period concerned had long working experiences in Heilongjiang. Zhao Dezun, provincial agricultural secretary, had worked as a deputy provincial party secretary as early as 1948. Li Li'an, provincial secretary in charge of personnel and organization, started working in Heilongjiang from 1963. Chen Lei began his provincial career in 1947 to become an alternate provincial secretary in 1960–6, vice-chairman of the Provincial Revolutionary Committee in 1977–9, and governor since 1979. The most crucial figure, Yang Yichen, had been a vice-governor during 1954–67, and became provincial first party secretary in 1977.[65] With such long experience in one province, they were generally well versed in the provincial situation and strongly committed to its vital interests.

It is no doubt an overstatement that Heilongjiang's provincial leadership was completely united in its resistance to decollectivization. There were at least nine key players involved in the policy process pertaining to decollectivization. On the basis of interviews, media reports, and official history of the event, they may be placed on a policy-orientation spectrum. According to Table 6.6, only two, Xing Zemin and Xue Lang, supported decollectivization but they held the lowest positions among the nine. On the other hand, with the exception of Li Li'an, all other four members (Yang, Chen Lei, Wang Luming, and Zhao) of the provincial party secretary meetings (*shuji huiyi*) were strong opponents of household farming. Given that at the time the 'view of the superiors' dominated the policy process and 'everything depended on the secretary's decision' (*shuji shuole suan*), the presence of an imposing secretary like Yang made a clear difference.

TABLE 6.6. *Orientations of key provincial leaders toward decollectivization*

Opponents	Middle-of-the-roaders	Supporters
Yang Yichen[a]	Li Li'an[e]	Xing Zemin[h]
Chen Lei[b]	Chen Junsheng[f]	Xue Lang[i]
Zhao Dezun[c]	Wang Yusheng[g]	
Wang Luming[d]		

Notes: The positions listed refer to the respective person's highest position at the time of decollectivization (especially during 1980–3). [a] provincial first party secretary; [b] governor; [c] provincial party secretary in charge of agriculture until retirement in early 1981; [d] provincial party secretary in charge of agriculture from early 1981; [e] provincial party secretary in charge of personnel and organization and a member of the provincial party standing committee; became provincial first party secretary in February 1983; [f] provincial deputy party secretary; [g] director of the provincial rural work department (*nongcun gongzuobu*); [h] secretary-general of the provincial rural work department; [i] deputy director of the provincial rural work department.

When the Fourth Plenum of September 1979 permitted 'peripheral, distant, and mountainous regions' to adopt *baochan daohu*, Heilongjiang's leadership somehow totally exempted the province from this guideline.[66] The Heilongjiang leadership once again exempted itself from CD [80] No. 75, which allowed poor regions to implement *baochan daohu* as well as *baogan daohu*. Regarding whether or not Heilongjiang could have been considered poor, an interviewee in Harbin provided a surprisingly articulate answer:

At the time [referring to the early 1980s], two standards were used to determine whether a locality was poor. One was the 'per capita share of grain' [*renjun kouliangshu*] and areas with less than 300 *jin* (before processing) would be categorized as poor. The other was the 'per capita income under collective distribution' [*gongshenei fenpei de renjun shouru*] and areas with less than 70 *yuan* would be called poor. In Heilongjiang, the yardstick was much higher: 500 *jin* and 100 *yuan*, respectively. . . . It was natural, therefore, that the provincial leadership regarded the household responsibility systems unsuitable for Heilongjiang.[67]

Some historical backgrounds were also closely related to the difficulties of accepting decollectivization in Heilongjiang. Being an early-liberated revolutionary base, Heilongjiang was one of the few provincial units to complete land reform before the pronouncement of the land reform law. Furthermore, China's first collective farm in the form of 'advanced producers' co-operative' (*gaoji hezuoshe*) was Xinghuo farm established in Huachuan county in 1952.[68] Added to this was the personal conviction of Yang Yichen. All the interviewees in Harbin unanimously argued that Yang's opposition to decollectivization was well grounded.[69] They also depicted Yang as a strong proponent of mechanization. They, however, drew a clear line between the Maoist scheme of across-the-board mechanization and the economically sensible scheme of selective mechanization for a few provinces like Heilongjiang. And most of them characterized Yang as a person in pursuit of the second path.[70] Most importantly, they pointed out that Yang had been highly disappointed by the continuing lack of Beijing' support for the province's efforts for mechanization. According to them, under the circumstances where all the promised rewards and support had been withdrawn, and where the household responsibility systems were gradually introduced to undermine its efforts for collective- and large machinery-based mechanization, the provincial leadership had no other choice but to contain their diffusion at all costs.

Yang's commitment to mechanization put him at loggerheads with Beijing on the one hand and with leaders of the pioneer provinces on the other. Yang was a front-line fighter for those which were reluctant to popularize the household responsibility systems. The famous debate of *yang-guandao* (literally 'a wide road', a metaphor for the collective system) versus *dumuqiao* (literally 'a log bridge', a metaphor for the household responsibility systems) in 1980–1 between Chi Biqing of Guizhou and Yang is a well-known example.[71] Yang's commitment to the collective economy and staunch opposition to the household responsibility systems were openly manifested on many occasions:

Our province has one outstanding difference from the rest of the country: that is, our province is a region of 'modernized large-scale agriculture' . . . with a mechanization level of 60 per cent. . . . This explains the primary status mechanization has already taken up in our agriculture, which also indicates the advanced level of our production forces. Therefore, the implementation of responsibility systems should proceed in accordance with this characteristic.[72]

Comrade Hu Yaobang said the two most important keys to agricultural development are the responsibility systems and diversified production [*duozhong jingying*]. This point is correctly taken. Yet, from our province's viewpoint, one more aspect should be added and that is mechanization. . . . In our province, without mechanization neither diversified production nor responsibility systems would be possible.[73]

Both speeches suggested that, given Heilongjiang's level of mechanization, it should be exempted from popularizing household farming. Furthermore, it was also implied that not only Heilongjiang's pace of decollectivization should be very gradual, but also the scope of its application should not exceed 15 per cent of the province's teams.[74] Yang even went so far as to argue that the teams already implementing household farming should be induced to adopt more collective systems and that local leaders should actively intervene in dealing with these 'deviant' teams.[75] The use of administrative measures in containing the diffusion of the household responsibility systems was quite pervasive. For instance, a report on the

Laozhou commune of Zhaodong county revealed that the size of the commune's land under *baogan daohu* had decreased from 8,000 *mu* in late 1981 to 2,000 *mu* in early 1982.[76] Such a drastic decrease must have resulted from the administrative interference by the county authorities which had acted upon the preference of the provincial authorities. Another report revealed that it had been quite common for the peasants under the household responsibility systems to be unable to obtain bank loans as easily as those under the collective system.[77]

There were nevertheless a few deviant localities in Heilongjiang. The first documented pioneer is Dongxing brigade of Yan'an commune in Yanshou county, which implemented *baochan daohu* in the spring of 1979.[78] A more well-known local pioneer is Yonggan second production team of Yixin commune in Duerbote Mongolian autonomous county. As one of the poorest teams in Heilongjiang, with a debt of 110,000 *yuan* to the state, it first adopted *baogan daohu* in the autumn of 1981. Despite pressure from the county authorities, the team continued to hold on to *baogan daohu*, inviting a provincial-level intervention. After an investigation by a work-team headed by Xue Lang, deputy director of the provincial rural work department, the provincial government endorsed the team's experiment, although the endorsement was strictly limited to this one team only.[79] According to an interviewee who had been deeply involved in Heilongjiang's rural work at the time, the provincial endorsement of the Yonggan experiment was a mere gesture of compliance with CD [80] No. 75 by utilizing an insignificant production team from a minority nationality.[80] There is no evidence, however, that this particular experiment was swiftly diffused to the neighbouring units.

Some grass-roots experiments were diffused to the neighbouring units, however, although the scope of diffusion remained highly limited. According to the official history of decollectivization, the adoption of *baogan daohu* by Wanshui brigade of Liushu commune in mountainous Linkou county in the spring of 1981 was quickly emulated by the neighbouring brigades so that, by October 1981, 87 per cent of the commune's teams were under household farming. Here, again, no evidence is available to suggest that the Liushu experiences were swiftly replicated by the neighbouring communes.[81] Until late 1982, the major trend in Heilongjiang was that local experiments were confined to one or two brigades in each county. One key example is Acheng county where the share of its teams under household farming remained 1.3 per cent for both 1980 and 1981.[82]

The case of Jiayin county merits our attention because it illustrates very clearly the provincial leadership's determination to resist decollectivization. Unlike the cases of a Mongolian production team located in a grass area and a production brigade in a hilly region mentioned above, the Jiayin case involved a major grain-producing locality with a large area of per capita land (13 *mu*) and a high level of mechanization (12 horsepower per *mu*).

Since one-third of the county's teams were considered very poor, with the tacit endorsement of the county party committee, fourteen teams from the four communes of Hongguang, Baoxing, Xiangyang, and Hujia adopted *baogan daohu* in late 1981. Due to firm opposition by the provincial authorities, they implemented the controversial system under the name of 'linking income with individual production' (*lianchan daolao*) then permitted by the provincial guideline.[83]

Secrecy did not last, as in January 1982 the public security bureau of Yichun City relayed the information on the 'deviations' in Jiayin to the provincial public security bureau through 'Summary Report No. 4' (*sihao jianbao*). The provincial public security bureau then published the report in issue No. 16 of its internal publication *Reflections on the Current Situation* (*qingkuang fanying*) to catch the provincial leadership's attention. In early February, Yang Yichen and Chen Lei demanded that the communes immediately redress their 'mistakes'. Fortunately, Beijing had just issued CD [82] No. 1 permitting the popular implementation of *baochan daohu* and *baogan daohu*. The provincial leadership then changed its position to a deferred decision pending an investigation. The investigation was again led by Xue Lang. When Xue and his team finished the investigation in mid-March, they concluded that '*baogan daohu* could be an effective measure of relieving poverty in poor communes'. When the official report written in Xue's name was submitted to the provincial leadership, Yang allegedly got infuriated. Subsequently, Yang ignored the report and ordered a scale-down of the experiment in Jiayin as well as a reshuffle of the county leadership. Yang's conviction affected the career of Xue Lang as well since it was not long before Xue was transferred to Liaoning as the director of its provincial policy research office.[84]

As the Jiayin case indicates, Yang Yichen was determined to contain the diffusion of household farming in areas where wheat and bean production was concentrated with high levels of mechanization. For this purpose, he not only ignored the central guidelines endorsing the two household responsibility systems, but he was also willing to remove the provincial and local cadres who had deviated from his policy line. While the provincial leadership endorsed *baogan daohu* in November 1981, the endorsement was merely a pro forma compliance in document form only. In fact, the provincial authorities actively intervened to contain the diffusion process at the grass-roots level. As a result, local experiments in Heilongjiang were generally limited to only a couple of not very significant areas and, consequently, its overall pace of decollectivization constantly lagged far behind.

Provincial Tactics of Delayed Implementation

While the Heilongjiang leadership had been generally successful in limiting the scope of decollectivization, it nevertheless had to face the increasing pressure from the centre. Subsequently, it had to justify its slow pace and to devise various measures to sustain its resistance.

Tactic One: Utilizing the Yindi Zhiyi Principle

As discussed in Chapter 2, the principle of *yindi zhiyi* regained much of its pre-1957 prominence in this period. The observation of *yindi zhiyi*, however, may produce a tricky situation where it becomes difficult for the centre to discern whether and to what extent a given policy is suitable for a particular locale. In 1979–80, for instance, none of the pertinent central directives provided concrete operational definitions of 'peripheral, distant, mountainous, backward, and poor' areas where the household responsibility systems could be implemented on a conditional basis.[85] Heilongjiang took full advantage of this ambiguity by totally banning the controversial policy on the ground that none of these categories applied to Heilongjiang. Another example concerns Heilongjiang's markedly different usage of *yindi zhiyi*. Concerning mechanization, for instance, *yindi zhiyi* was interpreted as follows:

Some comrades view *yindi zhiyi* simply as highlighting unsuitable conditions without trying to overcome them. We should not allow ourselves to take special conditions as a justifiable pretext for not actively implementing mechanization.[86]

In stark contrast is the putting into operation of the same principle regarding decollectivization:

In implementing the responsibility systems, it is extremely crucial to observe *yindi zhiyi*. If we blindly promote a certain responsibility system [i.e. *baochan daohu*], we will certainly not be able to obtain the expected results.[87]

The stress on will and activism in promoting mechanization was turned into the emphasis on caution and passivism to contain the spread of decollectivization. Another piece of evidence is available to support the idea that Heilongjiang utilized *yindi zhiyi* to resist the centre. In the immediate aftermath of the National Rural Work Conference in October–November 1981, from which CD [82] No. 1 originated, *Heilongjiang Daily* published an editorial that read:

[In implementing responsibility systems,] we have only to follow *yindi zhiyi*. . . . A variety of responsibility systems can and should exist simultaneously, and we should not strive for standardization. . . . Regardless of what responsibility systems we adopt, they all should be directed toward maintaining the collective economy.[88]

The use of *yindi zhiyi* was closely linked to the tactic of highlighting Heilongjiang's unique condition, mechanization. In April 1981, despite its endorsement of *baochan daohu* in January, the Heilongjiang leadership stipulated that 'the responsibility systems should be implemented in accordance with local conditions. . . . In our province, it should develop toward maintaining the collective ownership of land, agricultural machinery, and draught animals, and towards promoting mechanization.'[89] According to the summary of the provincial discussion meeting on Agricultural Production Responsibility Systems, not only was the scope of decollectivization to be limited only to poor teams (about 15 per cent) with low levels of mechanization, but the pace of its implementation should also be gradual.[90]

In early 1982, Beijing's preference became manifest with its CD [82] No. 1, and by mid-1982 the household responsibility systems became a mandatory policy with which all provinces were expected to comply. Interestingly, Heilongjiang's reliance on the tactic of issue linkage was not significantly reduced. Rather, the goal of the tactic changed from actively seeking an exemption to passively justifying its slow pace of decollectivization.[91] Even during 1983, this tactic was still in use for the changed goals, which ranged from preventing large farm machinery from being contracted out or sold to individual households to demanding Beijing's support in expanding the province's capacity of producing small and hand tractors.[92] The extent to which Heilongjiang was able to exercise its discretion sheds important light on the changing parameter of central–provincial policy dynamics.

Tactic Two: Manipulating Tifa

It is often very important to pay close attention to 'formalized language in policy stipulations' (tifa) when reading Chinese official publications. Not only does the Chinese leadership seem highly aware of tifa but we scholars should also be sensitive to it.[93] Tifa is particularly important in analysing the process of decollectivization, as it went through the phases of prohibition, experimentation, endorsement, and popularization of various systems.[94] Heilongjiang's tifa is also illustrative of the role rhetorical manipulation played in the decollectivization reform. Most interestingly, during 1979–83, Heilongjiang had never published province-wide data on the percentage of its teams under household farming, although some local-level data were released. It was only in early April 1984, after its performance finally exceeded 90 per cent, that its province-wide data were released for the first time.[95]

While there were several earlier reports on Heilongjiang's pace of decollectivization, all of them were phrased so vaguely that the precise nature of its performance was almost impossible to comprehend. Tifa used in these reports were of three kinds: (1) 'the share of the teams implementing various systems of responsibility [gezhong xingshi de zerenzhi] exceeds 90 per cent'; (2) 'the share of the teams under the contract systems of linking income with output [*lianchan chengbaozhi*] is about 95 per cent'; and (3) 'among more than 95 per cent of the province's teams that adopted production responsibility systems, most have chosen the comprehensive contract system [*dabaogan*]'.[96] It should be noted that the first two *tifa* of 'various systems' and 'the contract systems of linking income with output' could be said of those based on the work group and even the team. Considering Heilongjiang's extremely sluggish pace, these *tifa* were used simply to provide a false sense of compliance. Even the term 'most' (*dabufen*) was employed to refer to 70 per cent (the February 1983 data), while we would normally reserve it for 90 per cent or more.

Tactic Three: Insisting on Agricultural Machinery Responsibility Systems

Heilongjiang's tactics of delayed implementation also included that of insisting on its own preferred system of responsibility, namely 'agricultural machinery responsibility systems' (*nongji zerenzhi*). By popularizing them with the team or the work group as the primary unit, Heilongjiang sought to sustain the collective mode of production based on large-scale mechanization. In March 1980, Heilongjiang presented an agricultural machinery responsibility system with the team as the primary unit as an alternative to the household responsibility systems.[97] In September 1981, an editorial of *Heilongjiang Daily* stipulated that the highest priority should be given to agricultural machinery responsibility systems. Heilongjiang's efforts seemed highly successful since, by September 1981, 56.8 per cent of its teams adopted the agricultural machinery responsibility systems while the share for the household responsibility systems was merely 0.7 per cent. In April 1982 when Heilongjiang had less than 10 per cent of its teams under household farming, three (Heihe, Hejiang, and Nenjiang) of its seven prefectures had an average of 45 per cent of their teams under the agricultural machinery responsibility systems.[98]

The most important characteristic of the agricultural machinery responsibility systems lay in the adoption of the primary production unit larger than the household so as to facilitate a full utilization of large machinery. Table 6.7 well illustrates the bias in favour of large scales of production. Six out of the eight types adopted the team or the work group as the primary unit of production and accounting, and all of them were conceived during 1980–1 when provincial discretion was maximally allowed. It was only after the publication of Wan Li's speech and the dissemination of CD [83] No. 1 that significant changes occurred to take the household as the primary unit. It should be noted however that, in the middle of these changes towards the household-based systems, teams and work groups still remained as the primary unit, indicating Heilongjiang's enduring reservation towards anything that was based on the household.[99]

TABLE 6.7. *Types of agricultural machinery responsibility systems*

Basic unit of work and accounting	Responsibility	Production partner	Origin
nongjidui (team)	*dinge baogong* (task rates)	None	3/1980
nongjidui (team)	*lianhe chengbao* (contract for joint work and distribution)	*nongyedui* (team)	2/1981
nongjidui (team)	*dandu chengbao* (independent contract)	None	2/1981
nongjidui (team)	*fenbie chengbao* (contract for joint work and separate distribution)	*nongyezu* (group)	7/1981
nongjizu (group)	*lianhe chengbao*	*nongyezu* (group)	7/1981
nongjizu (group)	*fenbie chengbao*	*nongyezu* (group)	8/1981
nongji chengbaohu (household)	*dandu chengbao*	None	1/1983
nongji zhuanyehu (household)	*dandu chengbao*	None	2/1983

Sources: *HLJRB*, 28 Dec. 1980; 10 Feb., 27 Apr., 22 July, and 16 Aug. 1981; and 12 Jan. and 28 Feb. 1983. Also see 'Zenyang chengbao nongye jixie' (How to Contract Out Agricultural Machinery?), *Fendou*, Mar. 1983, 37–8.

THE RESOLUTION OF THE CONFLICT: CENTRAL IMPOSITION AND PROVINCIAL SUBMISSION

As the household responsibility reform proved generally successful, the central leadership became eager to accelerate the pace of its popularization. Faced with staunch opposition from a few resisters, the central leadership became concerned with the possibility that their sustained resistance could bog down the entire reform by generating fears of policy change. If such a situation should occur, it could be immediately linked to the question of policy effectiveness and, more importantly, to the legitimacy of the policy creator, the Reformist leadership. The following excerpt typifies such concern on the part of the central leadership:

Deng's faction was pressing the point that it was necessary to abandon rigid dogma and 'seek truth from facts'. But such a premiss implied that the leadership's legitimacy should be judged in terms of its pragmatic accomplishments. Anything less than rapid success for the controversial step away from collective production would provide opponents of Deng's faction with a strong case for bringing down Zhao Ziyang and Wan Li.[100]

According to a former senior cadre with the Central Rural Policy Research Office, another reasoning behind Beijing's push was that speedy decollectivization was closely linked to the plans for the second wave of rural reform—free marketing, hired labour, and so on—all of which presupposed the completion of the decollectivization phase.[101] Given such high political stakes associated with decollectivization as the Reformers' first reform initiative, its swift popularization became a 'superordinate goal' whose overall utility to the central leadership far outweighed some administrative gains from flexible implementation. The rise of the superordinate goal then generated a familiar situation where the centre's priorities prevailed over local preferences. In April 1982, the Administrative Office of the Party Centre (*zhongyang bangongting*) issued a notice that severely criticized 'dogmatic and unliberated ideas' of some provincial officials who still considered household farming as 'going backward'.[102] In October 1982, the Rural Development Research Centre under Du Runsheng voiced discontent with the current pace of decollectivization:

In implementing household responsibility systems, we have to continue to liberate our ideology and relax control. . . . A few regions are still unwilling to act on the demands of the masses by refusing to change the 'one big bowl' situation. Furthermore, some areas which already implemented the responsibility systems are even trying to go back to the old system. All these are wrong.[103]

Beijing's pressure was directed particularly toward Heilongjiang which, by June 1982, had only 8.7 per cent of its teams under household farming. In July 1982, Zhao Ziyang paid a visit to Dalian of Liaoning, another resister province. There, Zhao allegedly demanded an immediate popularization of the household responsibility systems in the sluggish provinces and, more importantly, privately criticized the Heilongjiang leadership. Yet, Zhao's criticism was not well heeded by Yang Yichen. On 13 August 1982, during his visit to Heilongjiang, Hu Yaobang, too, allegedly criticized its extremely sluggish pace of decollectivization.[104]

Initially, the centre's pressure did not have a significant impact. An internal report dated August 1982 provides an important clue as to how determined Heilongjiang was to maintain the collective system based on large-scale mechanization. According to this report prepared by the administrative office of regional planning for mechanization under the provincial agricultural commission, Heilongjiang's efforts were to be concentrated on expanding the scale of production, rather than reducing it. Regarding wheat- and bean-producing areas, the report stressed the centrality of agricultural machinery with 50 to 150 horsepower, which was hardly compatible with household farming. For areas specializing in coarse grains (millet, corn, and sorghum) and also rice an extensive use of large and medium-sized machinery was recommended. Among the total of eight types of machinery recommended for these three regions, only one was small machinery with 12 horsepower.[105]

Only after the speech by Wan Li in November 1982 did Heilongjiang begin to show some real changes, though very grudgingly. Right after the National Agricultural Secretaries Conference where Wan's speech was delivered, the provincial party committee decided to conduct two surveys to determine whether the household responsibility systems could be really applied to the province on a large scale. One survey led by Wang Yusheng, director of the provincial rural work department, was conducted on the experiences of Anhui, Henan, Shandong, Jiangsu, Liaoning, and Jilin. The other survey led by Chen Junsheng, a deputy provincial agricultural secretary, was on the effects of household farming in five counties of highly mechanized Nenjiang prefecture in Heilongjiang. In late December, final reports were completed and they concluded that the household responsibility systems could be an effective means of relieving poverty.[106]

According to the survey on Heilongjiang's counties, the five counties of Gannan, Fuyu, Lindian, Yi'an, and Keshan had an average of 9.6 per cent of their teams under household farming by November 1982 (the provincial average was 12). The projected targets for 1983 set by the report are interesting. First, the targets differed significantly for the five counties, ranging from 26 per cent for Lindian to 60 per cent for Yi'an, indicating the efforts to allow local variations among the counties.[107] Second, the average of the targets for the five counties was 47 per cent, still a very modest figure for the speedy popularization then pushed by Beijing. Third, Keshan County with the highest mechanization level of 90.4 per cent was simply exempted from adopting the household responsibility systems and instead recommended to implement 'specialized production' (zhuanye chengbao). In sum, the report still reflected the province's strong reservation towards a fast and across-the-board popularization of household farming.[108]

Such reservation was manifested in Yang Yichen's speech to the Prefectural, County, and City Party Secretaries' Work Conference held one day after the publication of Wan Li's speech:

In determining which responsibility system to adopt, we have to value the opinions of the masses who will eventually select a system on the basis of their local conditions. Therefore, local conditions should determine whether the contracts are to be made to the teams, work groups, or households.[109]

This speech was in effect a rebuttal of Wan Li's call for the popularization of baogan daohu even in the regions where the per-peasant area of cultivation was large, the history of co-operativization long, and the level of mechanization high. The dissemination of CD [83] No. 1 in January 1983, however, left little room for Heilongjiang's overt resistance as such.[110] Furthermore, the level of publicity given to Jiangsu as a typical well-off province which had extensively adopted household farming significantly reduced the range of options Heilongjiang might otherwise have utilized.[111] Eventually, in late January 1983, the provincial party committee ratified the province-wide implementation of the household responsibility systems.[112]

Subsequently, dozens of articles appeared in *Heilongjiang Daily* in full support of *baogan daohu*, including a report on Mudanjiang prefecture which allegedly increased the share of its teams under household farming from 13 per cent in late 1982 to 93.3 per cent in February 1983.[113] By February 1983, as noted earlier, 73 per cent of Heilongjiang's production teams were under *baogan daohu*.

The timing of February 1983 is crucial because it is not only the very month when Heilongjiang's performance marked a notable leap (by 60 per cent in two months) but also Yang Yichen was transferred to Beijing in that month.[114] The decision to transfer Yang merits our attention in several respects. First, while the decision seemed like a routine personnel reshuffle which affected seven other provinces, it actually reflected Beijing's displeasure with Heilongjiang's consistently sluggish pace of decollectivization. The removal of Tie Ying from Zhejiang was also allegedly associated with his opposition to household farming.[115] Second, Yang was not forced into retirement but appointed as the supreme people's procurator-general (*zuigao jianchayuanzhang*), the bureaucratic rank of which was a half grade higher than that of the provincial first party secretary. Although such a transfer was hardly a 'promotion' in terms of actual power, it seems that Beijing could not simply bury a provincial leader just because he was sincerely representing the interests of the province he was assigned to serve by the very same centre. Third, Yang was replaced by Li Li'an who, among Yang's lieutenants, was known to be sympathetic to the decollectivization reform and, therefore, was deemed more likely to be compliant with the centre.[116]

Despite the provincial endorsement of the household-based systems and the leadership change, efforts for province-wide decollectivization still met with opposition. Some continued to argue that the across-the-board adoption of *baogan daohu* would cause irrecoverable damages to mechanization, while others contended that the household responsibility systems had little to do with mechanization.[117] The resolution of the debate came in September 1983 when the provincial position was redefined as follows:

Since the Third Plenum of 1978, many comrades in our province have worried about the negative effect of *baogan daohu* on mechanization and subsequently delayed its popularization until last winter. . . . Despite its popular adoption, peasants still want tractors, even the large and medium-sized tractors.[118]

Similar changes occurred regarding the agricultural machinery responsibility systems. Under the increasing pressure from the centre, the provincial leadership was no longer able to stress the team or the work group as the only acceptable unit for the responsibility systems. Subsequently, agricultural machinery hitherto managed and used collectively began to be contracted out to individual households (*nongji chengbaohu*).[119] Furthermore, in line with CD [83] No. 1, Heilongjiang permitted individual peasants to buy small agricultural machinery.[120] Compared to Shaanxi, where peasants had been allowed to purchase agricultural machinery as early as July 1982, even before CD [83] No. 1, Heilongjiang was only grudgingly complying with Beijing.[121]

Heilongjiang kept one final card, however: prohibiting the peasants from buying collective-owned large machinery which had constituted the backbone of its scheme for large-scale mechanization. In February 1983, for instance, the provincial leadership made it clear that, unlike small machinery, collective-owned large machinery were not to be sold to individual peasants. It would be almost another one-and-a-half years before Heilongjiang finally reversed its position by permitting individual peasants to purchase collective-owned large machinery in July 1984. Consequently, by September 1984, 80.3 per cent of Heilongjiang's tractors were owned by individual households.[122]

The tide of decollectivization soon spilled over into state farms. While central policy-makers (such as Zhao Ziyang and Du Runsheng) had initially viewed household farming unsuitable for state farms, they later conceded that it could be adopted in state farms only if farm workers wished to do so.[123] In November 1983, Chahayang state farm was widely publicized as having contracted out all of its 600,000 *mu* to individual households. By 1984 the household responsibility systems became a norm for state farms and even the agricultural machinery owned by state farms was sold to individual peasants.[124] Thus, by March 1984, 20 per cent of Heilongjiang's state farms adopted the household responsibility systems, and by the end of the year 32,100 grain-producing family farms were set up in addition to 893 forestry farms and 1,125 animal husbandry farms run by households.[125]

While the province sustained its resistance throughout 1983 (though much less intensely after the departure of Yang), by February 1984 Heilongjiang completely submitted to the centre by popularizing *baogan daohu* in almost all of its production teams (98 per cent). The most frequently utilized tactic of linking its opposition with mechanization was also dropped. For instance, Li Li'an's work report to the January 1984 Provincial Rural Work Conference had no mention at all about mechanization, which was a rarity given the past practices.[126] Heilongjiang's submission became official in April 1984 when Chen Lei, governor of Heilongjiang and a well-known opponent of decollectivization, offered a self-criticism on behalf of the province:

Due to our insufficient understanding, we have been very slow in implementing the household-based responsibility systems, thus lagging far behind other areas with advanced rural economies. Last year, in accordance with CD [83] No. 1, we, too, have popularized the policy so that the percentage of production teams implementing them increased from less than 10 in 1982 to more than 90 last year.[127]

GENERALITIES AND PARTICULARITIES OF
THE HEILONGJIANG CASE

Heilongjiang's implementation pattern is significant in that its pace of decollectivization was consistently slower than all other provinces throughout the entire process of the reform. Despite the mounting pressure from Beijing in 1982, it managed to defy the centre to protect the provincial interests. Even during 1983, Heilongjiang strove to earn as much time as possible to minimize the impact of the colossal change. Such a level of provincial discretion, let alone its enduring resistance to Beijing, was hardly conceivable in the Maoist era. The Heilongjiang case, thus, provides an important clue as to the evolving norms of policy implementation in post-Mao China.

The Heilongjiang case also underscores the crucial role of issue linkages and antecedents. Since most single-policy analyses tend to portray an artificially fragmented world of reality, it often becomes necessary to widen our policy horizon, both spatially and temporally. Regarding tactical actions, while the tactic of issue linkage was fully utilized by Heilongjiang, the tactic of coalition formation seemed virtually non-existent. There is no evidence to support the idea that resister provinces colluded to oppose the centre collectively. The decollectivization case shows that provincial leaders then were still more of a categoric group than of a political group capable of executing collective action.[128]

No evidence is available, either, to suggest that the Heilongjiang leadership was supported by powerful patrons at the centre. While the collusion between Hua Guofeng and the Dazhai Clique on the one hand, and the Heilongjiang provincial leadership on the other was a possibility, no interviewees were able to confirm it. One interviewee argued that Yang's party and government seniority was too high for Hua to become his patron. Another interviewee strongly refuted the collusion thesis by suggesting that if there had indeed been a strategic alliance between the two, not only could Yang's resistance even after the fall of Hua not be explained but also Yang would have been forced into retirement instead of being appointed as the supreme people's procurator-general.[129] If this really were the case, the Heilongjiang case offers an important piece of information as to how provinces came to generate and sustain policy discretion on the basis of their endogenous interests, independent of the politics of central–local clientelism.

The Heilongjiang case also sheds important light on the processes and outcomes of central–provincial conflicts. However salient the concerned policy might have been to the province and whatever novel tactics it might have employed to resist it, when the centre became highly committed to a 'superordinate goal' (in the case of decollectivization, enhancing the new leadership's legitimacy in a relatively short period of time), provincial compliance was simply a matter of time. Stressing *yindi zhiyi* might have expanded the scope of provincial discretion, but the ultimate coercive capacity of the centre was not necessarily weakened, particularly in enforcing its high-priority policies. The outcome of the central–Heilongjiang conflict was more contingent upon the expected payoffs of Beijing than upon the extent of Heilongjiang's leverage.

A brief discussion is due on the attitude of peasants toward household farming in Heilongjiang. According to interviews and published survey reports, a considerable degree of regional variation existed. Peasants in the southern and mountainous regions who specialized in coarse grain with low levels of mechanization were generally more eager to decollectivize. On the other hand, peasants in the northern regions specializing in the production of wheat and beans, most notably, Heihe and Sanjiang, were mostly unwilling to opt for household farming. The 1982 survey of six provinces noted earlier also acknowledged that there were 'areas where peasants still remained unwilling to decollectivize'. A December 1983 survey conducted by Beijing scholars and policy analysts, too, noted that even among poor teams in Heilongjiang some had not demanded household farming and decollectivization was later imposed on them.[130] In Heilongjiang, therefore, peasant zeal for decollectivization was not uniformly distributed and certainly there was no such thing as 'peasant power' that pushed the state. Rather, it was the state that imposed household farming on peasants in Heilongjiang without giving them sufficient time to experiment with and adapt to it.

Beijing's victory over Heilongjiang had its own costs: ironically, the new central leadership repeated the Maoist malpractice of rushed and standardized implementation. Particularly in Heilongjiang, rushed implementation induced an ill-prepared transition to household farming even to the extent that peasants suddenly found it very inconvenient to till and plant.[131] Rushed decollectivization also inflicted enormous losses on Heilongjiang's collective-owned production materials (agricultural machinery in particular) estimated between 900 and 1,600 million *yuan*. In retrospect, household farming turned out to be much less suitable to Heilongjiang than most other provinces. Consequently in 1989, the household responsibility systems became an optional policy in Heilongjiang. Furthermore, once again, agricultural machinery teams were rehabilitated to provide mechanized farming services. By 1991, 8,170 out of Heilongjiang's 14,500 villages, 56 per cent, readopted agricultural machinery responsibility systems with the work group and the team as the primary units of contracted production. In April 1994, during his visit to Harbin, Zhu Rongji pledged a total of 8 billion *yuan* of financial support for Heilongjiang's large-scale mechanization to be pursued in 1995–2000.[132] It is such an irony that Yang Yichen's position proved correct in less than ten years.

NOTES

1. To the best of this author's knowledge, there is no study on the pre-reform era that provides sufficient evidence to support the belief that overt resistance to the centre was a generally available option to the provinces. On the basis of his research on Sichuan and Guizhou for 1955–65, David S. G. Goodman concludes that interprovincial variation in implementation, limited as it was, was not the result of provincial resistance to the centre. See *Centre and Province in the People's Republic of China: Sichuan and Guizhou, 1955–1965* (Cambridge: Cambridge University Press, 1986), 184.
2. In 1981, Heilongjiang had a total of sixty-five counties (including Duerbote Mongolian autonomous county).
3. The intensity of peasant demands for decollectivization in Heilongjiang is an empirical question in itself. Many interviewees in Beijing and Harbin suggested that peasant zeal had been less intense in Heilongjiang than elsewhere in China and that peasants of the areas specializing in wheat and bean production had been particularly lukewarm toward household farming. More details on this are provided later.
4. In the pre-reform era, there was very little overt articulation of provincial interests. See, for instance, Frederick C. Teiwes, 'Provincial Politics: Themes and Variations', in John Lindbeck (ed.), *China: Management of a Revolutionary Society* (Seattle: University of Washington Press, 1971), 135.
5. The role of 'perceived unfair compensation' is noted in David M. Lampton, 'Chinese Politics: The Bargaining Treadmill', *Issues and Studies*, 23/3 (1987), 15.
6. For the implementation of this policy at the national level, see *Renmin ribao*, 22 Oct. 1977. For Heilongjiang's position on this system, see *Heilongjiang ribao* (Heilongjiang Daily; hereafter *HLJRB*), 17 Apr. and 18 Oct. 1978.
7. Ibid. 18 Jan. 1979.
8. Ibid. 11 May 1979.
9. For these two experiments, see *Heilongjiang nongye hezuoshi* (History of Agricultural Co-operativization in Heilongjiang; hereafter *Hezuoshi*) (Beijing: Zhonggong dangshi ziliao chubanshe, 1990), 462–7. In 1982, the share of mechanized land in total sown area was 37 per cent for Zhaoyuan and 46 per cent for Fuyu. These data are from *Zhongguo fenxian nongcun jingji tongji gaiyao* (A Statistical Survey of Rural Economy in Chinese Counties) (Beijing: Zhongguo tongji chubanshe, 1989), 119, 133. It turned out that Fuyu had been very slow in implementing decollectivization as household farming was adopted there only in 1983. See *Fuyuxianzhi* (Fuyu County Gazetteer) (Beijing: Zhonggong dangshi ziliao chubanshe, 1990), 90.
10. *Hezuoshi*, 470.
11. Increased outputs through *baochan daozu* by the Liguang brigade of Qiqihar City were widely publicized on the front page of *HLJRB*, 30 Oct. 1980.
12. It should be noted that Heilongjiang's opposition to household-based systems was directed mainly at grain production dependent on mechanization. As early as March 1980, Heilongjiang officially endorsed the system of 'specialized production households' (*zhuanyehu*) for pig-raising and commercial crops. See *Hezuoshi*, 479–81 and *HLJRB*, 25 May, 20 July, 17 Aug., and 1 Dec. 1980.
13. *HLJRB*, 28 Dec. 1980 and *Hezuoshi*, 485.
14. *HLJRB*, 25 Jan. 1981.
15. Tang Wenbin, 'Zenyang kandai baochan daohu baogan daohu de xingzhi' (How to View the Nature of *Baochan daohu* and *Baogan daohu*), *Fendou* (Struggle), Apr. 1982, 24.
16. It was on 28 April 1981 that *baogan daohu* was first mentioned in *Heilongjiang ribao*. It was not the report of *baogan daohu* in Heilongjiang but about the system in Anhui. For the approval of *baogan daohu*, see *Renmin ribao*, 4 Aug. 1981 and *HLJRB*, 15 Sept. 1981.
17. This was stipulated in 'Quansheng nongye shengchan zerenzhi zuotanhui jiyao de tongzhi' (Notice on the Summary of the Provincial Discussion Meeting Concerning Agricultural Production Responsibility Systems). A summary of the notice is given in *Hezuoshi*, 497–8.
18. By October 1983, the figure was 87.1 per cent. See *Hezuoshi*, 555.
19. *Dangdai zhongguo de Heilongjiang* (Contemporary China's Heilongjiang Province) (Beijing: Zhongguo shehuikexue chubanshe, 1990), i. 168.

20. Heilongjiang Provincial Statistical Bureau, *Heilongjiang sishinian jubian 1949–1989* (Great Changes in Heilongjiang During the Last 40 Years of 1949–1989) (Beijing: Zhongguo tongji chubanshe, 1989), 1, 2, 7.
21. Heilongjiang province's regional planning special group for agricultural mechanization, *Heilongjiangsheng nongye jixiehua quhua* (Regional Planning for Agricultural Mechanization in Heilongjiang) (Harbin: n.p., Oct. 1982), 3.
22. See Benedict A. Stavis, *The Politics of Agricultural Mechanization in China* (Ithaca, NY: Cornell University Press, 1978), 37–8.
23. *Zhongguo nongye nianjian 1980* (Agricultural Yearbook of China, 1980; hereafter *ZGNYNJ*) (Beijing: Zhongguo nongye chubanshe, 1981), 143.
24. For the crop distribution, see Song Yuansheng, *Heilongjiangsheng nongye jixiehua fazhan yu erqiannian zhanlue* (The Development of Mechanization in Heilongjiang and Its Strategy for the Year 2000) (Harbin: Heilongjiang kexue jishu chubanshe, 1991), 8–9. The degrees of susceptibility to mechanization (derived by averaging the four tasks of planting, seeding, tending, and harvesting) for wheat, beans, corn, millet and rice are, respectively, 74.8, 70.0, 42.8, 42.7 and 2.7. This information is from *Heilongjiangsheng nongye jixiehua quhua*, 16.
25. See *Dangdai zhongguo de nongken shiye* (Contemporary China's Land Reclamation) (Beijing: Zhongguo shehui kexue chubanshe, 1986), 14–15, 18, 29, 68, 93–4; and *Heilongjiang sishinian jubian*, 4, 7, 29, 231.
26. For messages on all-out mechanization, see *Renmin ribao*, 19 Jan. and 24 Dec. 1977.
27. See *Quandang dongyuan juezhan sannian wei jibenshang shixian nongye jixiehua er fendou* (Struggle to Accomplish Basic Mechanization in Three Years by Fully Mobilizing the Party; hereafter *Quandang*) (Beijing: Renmin chubanshe, 1978), 11–14, 16–17.
28. *Beijing Review*, 11 Mar. 1979, 9–10.
29. See *HLJRB*, 8 Feb. and 16 Aug. 1977. Also see Yang Yichen's speech in *HLJRB*, 17 Jan. 1978. For the average area of per-peasant land in Heilongjiang's state farms, see *HLJRB*, 8 Feb. 1978. And for the area of land available for reclamation, see ibid. 25 Dec. 1977.
30. For Hua's trip to Heilongjiang, see ibid. 6, 16, and 17 May 1977.
31. For earlier reports on this project, see *Renmin ribao*, 20 Aug. 1977 and *HLJRB*, 26 Jan. 1979.
32. Ibid. 26 Jan. and 15 Feb. 1978.
33. See his report to the Provincial Conference on Learning from the Dazhai, ibid. 3 Mar. 1978.
34. Ibid. 22 Feb. 1978.
35. Ibid. 23 May 1978. This was only the first phase of a more ambitious plan of reclaiming 70 million *mu* by 1985. See ibid. 3 Mar. 1978.
36. Ibid. 27 Dec. 1978. For a detailed discussion of Heilongjiang's plan for all-out mechanization during 1978–80, see *Hezuoshi*, 428–33.
37. *Zhonggong shiyijie sanzhong quanhui yilai zhongyang shouyao jianghua ji wenjian xuanbian* (Selected Speeches and Documents from the Centre Since the Third Plenum of the Eleventh Central Committee of the CCP) (Taibei: Zhonggong yanjiu zazhishe, 1983), 186–9, 195–6.
38. See Jae Ho Chung, 'The Politics of Agricultural Mechanization in the Post-Mao Era, 1977–87', *China Quarterly*, 134 (1993), 275–6.
39. For the latter group's representative view, see the comment by Du Runsheng, vice-chairman of the State Agricultural Commission, in *ZGNYNJ, 1980*, 199.
40. *Renmin ribao*, 20 July 1980.
41. See *Zhongguo guding zichan tuozi tongji ziliao 1950–1985* (Statistical Data on China's Fixed Asset Investment, 1950–1985) (Beijing: Tongji chubanshe, 1987), 43; and *Zhongguo tongji nianjian 1991* (Statistical Yearbook of China; hereafter *ZGTJNJ*) (Beijing: Zhongguo tongji chubanshe, 1991), 427.
42. For the earlier position, see *HLJRB*, 27 Dec. 1978. As late as 13 February, the Heilongjiang provincial bureau for state farm management publicized the superior performance of the agricultural machinery imported from the US firm John Deere. See ibid. 13 Feb. 1979.
43. See ibid. 21 Feb., 20 Mar., and 1 and 11 Apr. 1979.
44. See provincial agriculture secretary Zhao Dezun's report in *HLJRB*, 4 Dec. 1979.

45. Ibid. 18 Oct. 1979 and 3 Mar. 1980.
46. Ibid. 23 Feb. and 29 Mar. 1980.
47. See *Renmin ribao*, 20 July 1980 and *ZGNYNJ, 1981*, 85–6.
48. *HLJRB*, 4 Oct. 1980.
49. Calculated on the basis of information given in *Heilongjiang sishinian jubian*, 204.
50. For the number of tractor plants, see *Heilongjiang tongji nianjian 1987*, 233. According to an interviewee in Harbin, the figure of 806 must have been for medium-sized tractors since at that time Heilongjiang had no capacity for producing large tractors and almost all large tractors, especially Dongfanghong-54 and -76, were made by and shipped from Loyang and Changchun tractor plants. For Heilongjiang's manifested desire for self-sufficiency, see *HLJRB*, 10 Feb. 1977 and 17 Jan. 1978.
51. For project cancellation, see *Dangdai zhongguo de nongye jixie gongye* (Agricultural Machinery Industry in Contemporary China) (Beijing: Zhongguo shehui kexue chubanshe, 1988), 95. And for the number of tractor plants, see *HLJRB*, 9 Nov. 1980.
52. Information on this alternative was obtained from an interview in Beijing in 1992.
53. For the interprovincial transfer of tractors, see Beijing Xinhua, 12 Mar. 1981 in *Foreign Broadcast Information Service: Daily Report-China* (hereafter *FBIS*), 12 Mar. 1981, S1; and *HLJRB*, 8 Dec. 1979, 29 July and 4 Oct. 1980.
54. Under the normal circumstances, the central–Heilongjiang bargaining over the priority allocation of tractors would be of a distributive nature in that there was no way for the centre to give a larger share to Heilongjiang without imposing a smaller share on other provinces. Yet the intervening event of downgrading the all-out mechanization scheme transformed the nature of the bargaining from distributive to integrative so that Heilongjiang got more without necessarily hurting other provinces.
55. See *Renmin ribao*, 21 Nov. 1980 and *Heilongjiang sishinian jubian*, 245.
56. For the price of agricultural machinery, see Ye Zhengzhi, 'Woguo nongye jixie chanpin jiage wenti tantao' (On the Price of China's Agricultural Machinery), *Nongchanpin chengben yu jiage lunwenji* (Collection of Essays on the Costs and Prices of Agricultural Products) (Beijing: Zhongguo kexue chubanshe, 1983), 227–9.
57. For the PBC loans, see *Renmin ribao*, 30 Dec. 1981; and for the CAB loans, see Zhongguo nongye yinhang, *Zhongguo nongcun jinrong tongji 1979–1989* (Statistics on China's Rural Finance 1979–1989) (Beijing: Zhongguo tongji chubanshe, 1991), 1264.
58. *Zhongguo nongcun jinrong tongji 1979–1989*, 406–7. Given that only 12 per cent of Heilongjiang's production teams were under household farming in December 1982, this reduction was not caused by the changes in the size of production units.
59. See Qiu Zhen, 'Heilongjiangsheng nongye jixiehua shudu chutan' (A Preliminary Discussion of Heilongjiang's Pace of Agricultural Mechanization), *Xuexi yu tansuo* (Studies and Explorations), Sept. 1980, 66.
60. See *HLJRB*, 20 Oct. 1980. For other cases, see Heilongjiang Provincial Academy of Social Sciences, 'Shixing lianchan chengbao zerenzhi yu nongye jixiehua' (Implementation of Output-Linking Responsibility Systems and Mechanization), *Xuexi yu tansuo*, 3 (1984), 18.
61. *Dangdai zhongguo caizheng* (Contemporary China's Finance) (Beijing: Zhongguo shehuikexue chubanshe, 1988), i. 311.
62. Yu Guoyao, Cao Mengxiang, and Luo Yousheng, 'Jilinsheng yushuxian nongye jixiehua diaocha' (A Survey on the Agricultural Mechanization in Yushu County of Jilin Province), *Nongye jingji luncong* (Collection of Essays on Agricultural Economy), June 1982, 256.
63. Xu Bu, 'Guanyu Heilongjiangsheng tuixing nongye jixiehua jige wenti de tantao' (A Discussion of Several Problems Regarding the Agricultural Mechanization in Heilongjiang), *Nongye jishu jingji* (Agricultural Technology and Economics), June 1983, 22; and Bing Yushu *et al.*, 'Dui Heilongjiangsheng shangpinliang jidi jianshe de tantao' (A Discussion of Establishing Production Centres of Commercial Crops in Heilongjiang), *Nongye jishu jingji*, Mar. 1983, 10.
64. For the unmaterialized pledge of support, see 'Guowuyuan pizhuan guojia nongwei guanyu dongbei shangpinliang jidi jianshe zuotanhui jiyao' (State Council's Circular on the State Agricultural Commission's Summary of the Discussion Meeting on

Establishing Grain-Production Bases in the Northeast: State Council Document No. 25 issued on 4 August 1980), *Nongcun jingji zhengce huibian 1978–81* (Rural Policy Documents for 1978–81) (Beijing: Nongcun duwu chubanshe, 1982), 96.

65. *Dangdai zhongguo de Heilongjiang*, ii. 420–1, 423, 426–7, 430, 432–5.

66. No interviewees in Harbin seem to have ever thought of Heilongjiang as peripheral as they proudly listed three sectors as number ones in China: the largest producer of grain, timber, and crude oil. Nor did they consider Heilongjiang as distant, which is true compared to the physical distance between Beijing on the one hand and Sichuan, Xinjiang, or even Guangdong on the other. Nor was Heilongjiang regarded as mountainous since few provinces in China are as flat.

67. Interview in Harbin in 1992. Heilongjiang's pride in its economic superiority was once again manifested in 1987 when the provincial party committee set the minimum income level for 'poor counties' (*pinkunxian*) at 300 *yuan* as opposed to the nationwide figure of 250 *yuan*. Interview in Harbin in 1994.

68. According to *People's Daily* of 5 July 1952, among the six great administrative regions, the north-east region was the first to complete land reform, while the other five regions had 81 to 90 per cent of performance rate. For the report's abstract, see Li Debin and Lin Shunbao (eds.), *Xinzhongguo nongcun jingji jishi, 1949–1984* (Chronicles of Rural Economy in New China) (Beijing: Beijing daxue chubanshe, 1989), 49. For Xinghuo farm, see *Hezuoshi*, 204–9.

69. One senior provincial official who had accompanied Yang on several investigative trips to the countryside revealed that Yang's understanding of the rural conditions, especially bean and rice production and animal husbandry, was almost expert. Many interviewees in Harbin strongly endorsed Yang's opposition to decollectivization on the ground that after the province-wide implementation of household farming Heilongjiang's assets in collective production materials (*jiti shengchan ziliao*) marked a huge loss which ranged from 900 million to 1,600 million *yuan*. These views were partly manifested in Bai Wanyin, 'Youguan wanshan lianchan chengbao zerenzhi de jige jishu jingji wenti' (On Some Technological and Economic Problems of Improving Output-Linking Responsibility Systems), *Nongye jishu jingji*, Aug. 1983, 31–2.

70. One interviewee suggested that Yang's obsession with mechanizing Heilongjiang must have been reinforced by his trip to the United States in March 1978. This trip is described in *Hezuoshi*, 428.

71. For details of this debate, see *Hezuoshi*, 483–5.

72. *HLJRB*, 16 Aug. 1981.

73. Ibid. 15 Sept. 1981.

74. This figure of fifteen was derived from a provincial estimate that only 15 per cent of its production teams were categorized as 'poor' (*pinkundui*). See ibid. 16 Aug. 1981. Given that by December 1982 only 12 per cent of Heilongjiang's teams were under household farming, the provincial leadership may have insisted on this formula up to the very last phase of the reform.

75. See ibid. 25 Jan. 1981.

76. Ibid. 4 Feb. 1982. According to the county gazetteer, Zhaodong's pace of decollectivization was extremely slow, a mere 0.2 per cent by 1981. See Zhaodong xianzhi bangongshi, *Zhaodong xianzhi* (Zhaodong County Gazetteer) (Zhaodong, 1985), 98.

77. Li Yang, 'Nongye shengchan zerenzhi bujiushi baochan daohu' (The Agricultural Production Responsibility System Is Not Just *Baochan daohu*), *Fendou*, Feb. 1982, 26.

78. The official history of Heilongjiang's decollectivization, *Heilongjiang nongye hezuoshi*, does not mention this. For Dongxing brigade's pioneering behaviour, see *Yanshou xianzhi* (Yanshou County Gazetteer) (Harbin: Sanhuan chubanshe, 1991), 127.

79. *Hezuoshi*, 500–3.

80. Information obtained from the author's interview in Harbin in 1992.

81. For the Wanshui case, see *Hezuoshi*, 506–8.

82. *Acheng xianzhi* (Acheng County Gazetteer) (Harbin: Heilongjiang renmin chubanshe, 1988), 150.

83. *Hezuoshi*, 515–16.

84. For the Jiayin experiment, see *Hezuoshi*, 516–18. *Hezuoshi* does not reveal the case of Xue Lang and instead provides a conflicting story that the report written by the investi-

gation team found excessive implementation of *baogan daohu* in the county. Author's interviews do confirm Xue Lang's transfer due to his policy conflicts with the provincial leadership. Interviews in Harbin in 1992 and 1994.

85. See 'Zhonggong zhongyang guanyu jiakuai nongye fazhan luogan wenti de jueding' (Decisions Concerning Certain Problems in Rapidly Developing Agriculture: the Fourth Plenum decision), *ZGNYNJ 1980*, 58; 'Zhongyang guanyu jinyibu jiaqiang he wanshan nongye shengchan zerenzhi de jige wenti de tongzhi' (A Notice from the Party Centre Regarding Some Problems on Further Improving Agricultural Production Responsibility Systems: CD [80] No. 75), in Xiang Xiyang and Shen Chong (eds.), *Shinianlai lilun zhengce shijian: ziliao xuanbian* (Theory, Policy, and Implementation in the Last Ten Years: A Selection of Materials) (Beijing: Qiushi chubanshe, 1988), ii. 36; and *HLJRB*, 1 and 28 Dec. 1980.
86. Ibid. 27 Oct. 1978.
87. Ibid. 2 Feb. 1981.
88. Ibid. 25 Dec. 1981. A very similar line of argument was put forward by Yang Yichen, 'Heilongjiangsheng fazhan nongcun jingji de jige wenti' (Some Problems Concerning the Development of Rural Economy in Heilongjiang), *Jingji guanli*, 12 (1981), 3–6.
89. *HLJRB*, 29 Apr. 1981.
90. Ibid. 29 Jan. 1982.
91. See Xiao Mugong, 'Shixing shuangbao buyao shunhai jiti suoyouzhi' (The Implementation of the Household Responsibility Systems Should Not Damage the System of Collective Ownership) and 'Zhengque renshi nongye jitijingji de youyuexing' (Correctly Recognize the Advantages of the Agricultural Collective Economy), *Fendou*, Mar. 1982, 39 and Sept. 1982, 18–19.
92. See 'Zenyang shixing nongji zhuanyedui chengbao' (How to Implement the Agricultural Machinery Contract System?) *Fendou*, July 1983, 37–8; Bai Wanyin, 'Youguan wanshan lianchan chengbao zerenzhi de jige jishu jingji wenti', 31–5; and *HLJRB*, 18 Jan. and 1 and 18 Apr. 1983.
93. See Michael Schoenhals, *Doing Things with Words in Chinese Politics: Five Studies* (Berkeley: Institute of East Asian Studies, 1992), ch. 1.
94. See Guo Shutian, *Zhongguo nongcun gaige yu fazhan shinian* (Ten Years' Development of China's Rural Reform) (Beijing: Nongye chubanshe, 1990), 7; and David Zweig, 'Context and Content in Policy Implementation: Household Contracts and Decollectivization, 1977–1983', in David M. Lampton (ed.), *Policy Implementation in Post-Mao China* (Berkeley: University of California Press, 1987), 259.
95. This constitutes a stark contrast with many provinces which released their province-wide data as early as 1981 and mostly no later than the first half of 1983. For sub-provincial data on some counties and prefectures in Heilongjiang, see *HLJRB*, 11 and 20 Feb. 1983. For the first province-wide data, see Chen Lei's work report to the Provincial People's Congress on 22 Mar. 1984 published in *HLJRB*, 1 Apr. 1984. For other provinces, refer to the provincial newspapers cited in Table 3.1.
96. See, respectively, (1) 'Summary of the Provincial Work Conference on the Production Responsibility System', *HLJRB*, 29 Jan. 1982; (2) ibid. 20 Feb. 1983; and (3) ibid. 15 Mar. 1983.
97. *Hezuoshi*, 481. In the autumn of 1980, Liming brigade of Keshan county (with a mechanization level of 90.4 per cent) adopted an agricultural machinery responsibility system with the production brigade as the primary unit of production and accounting. See ibid. 473.
98. See *Hezuoshi*, 492; and *HLJRB*, 27 Sept. 1981 and 11 Apr. 1982.
99. See ibid. 30 Jan. and 28 Feb. 1983.
100. Jonathan Unger, 'The Decollectivization of the Chinese Countryside: A Survey of Twenty-Eight Villages', *Pacific Affairs*, 58/4 (1985–6), 591.
101. Interview in Beijing in 1994.
102. *Renmin ribao*, 27 Apr. 1982.
103. Ibid. 20 Oct. 1982.
104. Information from Author's interviews in Harbin and Beijing in 1992.
105. This paragraph draws from *Heilongjiangsheng nongtian zuoye jixie xitong* (The Machinery System for Heilongjiang's Agricultural Mechanization) (Harbin: n.p., 28 Aug. 1982),

53–71. The other seven include Longjiang tractors with 100 and 120 horsepower, Dongfanghong-75, Iron Ox-55, Shanghai-50, Dongfanghong-28, and Ningbo-24.

106. Note that the *tifa* of 'the means of relieving poverty' denotes that large-scale popularization was still deemed premature.

107. Of course, such targets were grossly overfulfilled under the centre's pressure. By the end of 1983, Lindian and Yi'an had 96.5 per cent and 97.3 per cent, respectively, of their production teams under household farming. See *Lindianxian zhi* (Lindian County Gazetteer) (n.p., 1988), 99; and *Yi'anxian zhi* (Yi'an County Gazetteer) (Beijing: Zhongguo qingnian chubanshe, 1989), 84.

108. This paragraph is based on author's interview in Harbin in 1992 and 1994, and *Hezuoshi*, 532–42. And for Chen's report on five counties, see 'Guanyu nongye shengchan zerenzhi qingkuang de diaocha baogao' (A Survey Report on the Implementation of the Agricultural Production Responsibility Systems), *Hezuoshi*, 533.

109. *HLJRB*, 25 Dec. 1982.

110. Unlike other central documents on decollectivization (such as CD [80] No. 75 and CD [82] No. 1) which had been passed by the Secretariat, CD [83] No. 1 was ratified by the Politburo. Interview in Beijing in 1994.

111. See *Renmin ribao*, 23 Jan. 1983.

112. Interestingly, this decision was not made public at the time. *Heilongjiang Daily*, for instance, did not carry any report on this meeting or the decision. The information is from *Hezuoshi*, 539.

113. *HLJRB*, 20 Feb. 1983.

114. According to an interviewee in Harbin, Beijing's decision to transfer Yang was made in late December 1982 and therefore gave both the time and freedom for sub-provincial units to carry out decollectivization.

115. A former senior official with the State Agricultural Commission confirmed that Yang's transfer was, above all, related to his 'known' resistance to decollectivization. Interview in Beijing in 1994. For Tie's case, see Keith Forster, 'The Reform of Provincial Party Committee in China: The Case of Zhejiang', *Asian Survey*, 24/6 (1984), 630–1.

116. See *Hezuoshi*, 489. One retired official argued otherwise. He contended that Li had been all along an 'organization man': he had been transferred to Heilongjiang from the Central Organization Department in 1963 and continued to work in that sector ever since. By placing a non-agricultural expert, Beijing wanted to ensure Heilongjiang's swift transition to decollectivization. Interview in Harbin in 1994.

117. See, for instance, *HLJRB*, 18 Jan. and 7 and 11 Feb. 1983. According to a provincial official in Harbin, many in the provincial party and government organizations had been highly sympathetic with Yang's cause, and even Li Li'an, Yang's successor, could not totally ignore the negative effects of decollectivization on mechanization. A former senior provincial official revealed that Chen Lei, governor, had made it clear that the new secretary should not in any way contradict the previous secretary. Interviews in Harbin in 1992 and 1994.

118. *HLJRB*, 27 Sept. 1983.

119. Ibid. 12 Jan. and 11 Feb. 1983. Initially, the practice of contracting out agricultural machinery to households was confined to the areas where the level of mechanization was low. See 'Dui nongji chengbaohu zenyang shixing chengbao?' (On How to Contract out Agricultural Machinery to Households?), *Fendou*, July 1983, 38.

120. *HLJRB*, 3 Feb. 1983.

121. See Shaanxi Provincial Service, 20 July 1982 in *FBIS*, 22 July 1982, T3.

122. See *HLJRB*, 28 Feb. 1983, and 29 July, 13 Aug. and 9 Sept. 1984.

123. Interview in Beijing in 1994.

124. For a recommendation of 'household contracting' (*jiating chengbao*) for state farms, see Zhang Furu, Fan Weichang, and Shen Xingfa, 'Sunke nongchang jingji xiaoyi diaocha' (A Survey of Economic Efficiency of Sunke State Farm), *Xuexi yu Tansuo*, 1 (1984), 71–6. Also see *Dangdai zhongguo de nongken shiye*, 325–7; and *HLJRB*, 16 Nov. and 18 Dec. 1983 and 21 May and 13 Oct. 1984.

125. See Zhou Xun, 'Guoying nongchang jiating chengbao de fazhan qushi' (The Developmental Trend of State Farms' Adopting Household Responsibility Systems), *Xuexi yu tansuo*, 3 (1984), 21; and Fan Weichang, 'Xingban jiating nongchang de jige wenti' (Some Problems with Family Farms), *Xuexi yu tansuo* (1985), 86.

126. See Heilongjiang Provincial Service, 19 Jan. 1984 in *FBIS*, 20 Jan. 1984, S1–3. Beijing lost no time in publicizing its victory over the province. See *Renmin ribao*, 26 Jan. 1984.

127. See his report to the provincial people's congress made on 22 Mar. 1984, published in *HLJRB*, 1 Apr. 1984.

128. On this line of argument, see David S. G. Goodman, 'Provincial Party First Secretaries in National Politics: A Categoric or A Political Group', in David S. G. Goodman (ed.), *Groups and Politics in the People's Republic of China* (Cardiff: University of Wales College of Cardiff Press, 1984), 71.

129. Several central leaders such as Wang Zhen (with special interests in state farms and land reclamation), Xiang Nan (with special interests in mechanization), and Wang Renzhong (former chairman of the State Agricultural Commission who had opposed full-scale decollectivization) were also mentioned as Heilongjiang's potential patrons. But, the author's interviews in Harbin were not able to substantiate Heilongjiang's clientelistic ties with any of these figures. One interviewee in Harbin, a former senior provincial official, hinted at another possibility that Yang might have been very close to Li Xiannian on the basis of their common functional backgrounds in the financial system (*caimao xitong*). According to a former senior official with the State Agricultural Commission, Li Xiannian was a strong opponent of the household responsibility systems. Interviews in Beijing and Harbin in 1992 and 1994.

130. Interviews in Harbin in 1994. For the two surveys, see Heilongjiang Provincial Rural Work Investigation Team, 'Henan Anhui Jiangsu Shandong Liaoning Jilin liusheng lianchan chengbao zerenzhi qingkuang kaocha baogao' (Investigation Report on the Implementation of Output-Linking Contract Responsibility Systems in Six Provinces) (Harbin: Provincial Administrative Office, 13 Jan. 1983), 15–16; and Luo Xiaopeng, Xie Yang, Li Weiqun, and Yu Cunlong, 'Heilongjiangsheng nongye shengchan zerenzhi diaocha baogao' (Investigation Report on Heilongjiang's Rural Production Responsibility Systems), *Nongcun jingji shehui* (Villages, Economy and Society) (Beijing: Zhishi chubanshe, 1985), iii. 123.

131. For a very rare discussion of the problems associated with the rushed decollectivization in Heilongjiang, see 'Nongye lianchan chengbao zerenzhi huibuhui gaibian?' (Will Agricultural Responsibility Systems Change or Not?), *Fendou*, Dec. 1983, 45.

132. Ren Xianliang, 'Zhongguo nongcun xingqi xinxing hezuo zuzhi' (The Rise of New Co-operative Organizations in the Chinese Countryside), *Liaowang zhoukan* (Outlook Weekly; overseas edition), 8 Jan. 1990, 15–16. Interviews in Harbin in 1992 and 1994. For the re-emergence of collective farming in other parts of China, see *South China Morning Post*, 21 Feb. and 6 June 1995; and Wang Ying, *Xinjitizhuyi: xiangcun shehui de zaizuzhi* (New Collectivism: Reorganizing the Rural Society) (Beijing: Jingji guanli chubanshe, 1996).

7

Conclusion

So long as the functioning of the state entails services provided by the territorial units of administration, the central and local governments are inevitably placed in structurally induced dilemmas between general and particular interests. Decentralization may be adopted when the centre recognizes the deleterious long-term effects of central dominance that has indiscriminately sacrificed local interests. The operational effects of decentralization are indeterminate, however, as the centre may often manifest resilient bureaucratic inertia by holding on to the tight control over local behaviour. Furthermore, contrary to our presumption that localities would maximally exploit the discretion granted by decentralization, local implementors are usually much more judicious and prudent. Hence, the operational effects of decentralization become more diluted than we usually take for granted.

The findings of this book are also supportive of the diluted effects of the post-Mao measures of administrative decentralization on the scope of provincial discretion in the decollectivization reform. In the earlier phase of 1979–81, provincial implementors had fairly extensively utilized their discretion in permitting or prohibiting grass-roots innovations and local experiments, producing high levels of interprovincial variation. During 1982–3, however, Beijing reverted to the Maoist norms by administratively imposing standardized implementation of the household responsibility systems irrespective of the provincial conditions. Cross-sectionally, too, the operational effects of the administrative decentralization proved to be limited. While some provinces managed to exercise their discretion in pioneering policy innovations or containing their diffusion, the pervasive fears of policy reversal induced a majority of the provinces to operate under the Maoist norms of opportunistic bandwagoning. Eventually, however, total standardized compliance with little interprovincial variation was the final outcome.

As the case of decollectivization has well demonstrated, implementation of the programmes that are highly prioritized by Beijing, involving few or no tangible resources to allocate and entailing a large number of targets, is generally subject to tight overhead control, leaving little room for local manœuvring. On the basis of the findings, we may specify four conditions under which the provinces may become willing to exercise discretion. First and foremost, systemic norms of local policy implementation must be flexible enough to permit voluntary articulation of provincial endogenous interests. Second, central policy directives must contain some ambiguity so as to facilitate provincial choices and adaptation. Third, the given policy must be salient to the province to the extent that immediate unconditional compliance would inflict enormous losses on it. Finally, the provincial leadership must be highly committed to the province's endogenous interests even at the expense of risking its own political survival.[1]

Given the diluted and volatile effects of decentralization, this concluding chapter discusses the limitations of both central control and local discretion as the monolithic explanations of China's intergovernmental dynamics in the post-decollectivization phase. The first section identifies the conditions under which the powerful centre may be forced to opt for 'benign neglect' of local initiatives, discretion, and deviations. The second explores the limits of local autonomy by examining the structural attributes embedded in the 'strong state' that are likely to induce the 'centralizing paradox' to occur. The third section then shifts its analytical focus from impersonal organizations to human agency, which this book has argued to be the most crucial intervening variable in shaping the processes and outcomes of the implementation game. The final section offers some general observations regarding the changes and continuities of central–local policy dynamics in the 'post-movement' regime of China.

LIMITS OF CENTRAL CONTROL IN THE POST-DECOLLECTIVIZATION ERA

More often than not, a central government has overriding powers, constitutionally or politically, over local governments. Such centripetal tendencies were particularly strong in state socialism and other 'dictatorial' regimes where local governing bodies operated more as the centre's agents than local representatives. The prevalent use of ideology and coercion in manufacturing compliance further suffocated local initiatives and discretion, producing pro forma compliance and reducing the regime's responsiveness.[2] As a structural remedy, decentralization was often adopted. However, decentralization in state socialism was more often than not something of a façade behind which, paradoxically, lay strong forces reverting back to centralization. Only when the systemic crisis of shortage and inefficiency reached an unsustainable point, as in the late 1970s in China, did the centre opt for genuine decentralization by providing localities with a 'voice' option which would hold their potential 'exit' at bay.[3]

By permitting localities the voice option (i.e. adaptive implementation), Beijing has in fact opened a Pandora's box full of potential deviations. This has in turn engendered a turbulent process in which the conventional rules of implementation (i.e. bandwagoning) were condemned and alternative modes (i.e. pioneering and resisting) were contested. Yet, the centre was 'forced' to remain benevolent toward local deviations for the sake of hoped-for gains at the system level. Beijing's tolerance was 'forced' since it was based upon the leadership's painful realization that implementation was the key to successful reforms and enlisting local support was indispensable. In Atul Kohli's term, the centre made a strategic choice to promote the 'developmental power' (i.e. the capacity to bring about socio-economic development) at the expense of its 'centralizing power' (i.e. the capacity to enforce sanctions against localities).[4]

Once the economic logic of reform prevailed over the political rationale of control, the range of the centre's tolerance of local initiatives, discretion, and deviation was expanded. As long as local initiatives and discretion contributed to the improvement of the overall economic conditions at the system level, Beijing was willing to tolerate some local deviations. In the post-decollectivization era (1984–), the pattern of China's central–local relations has increasingly diversified into that of coercion, collision, collusion, co-ordination, and competition. The magnitude of local discretion, variation, and deviations has also been such that scholars began to characterize China's central–local relations as 'federalism, Chinese style', or 'behavioural federalism'.[5] So far as the centre's assessment indicates that the overall benefits of permitting local discretion has outweighed the total costs of local deviations, Beijing may continue to allow local initiatives and leeway in implementation. This is the most important rationale for post-Mao decentralization as Beijing's strategic concessions for the sake of system-level gains.[6]

LIMITS OF LOCAL DISCRETION IN THE POST-DECOLLECTIVIZATION ERA: CAPABILITIES VERSUS CHOICES IN THE STRONG STATE

It is erroneous to infer that the range of the centre's tolerance is in any way fixed or constant across the board. No central government bureaucracy would simply let go of its power unprepared. As the Soviet experiences suggest:

[P]rocesses of decentralization dictated by demands for greater efficiency are constantly counterbalanced with attempts to impose new checks . . . lest any unit (be it economic, territorial, or functional) become so effective as to be able to follow its own set of objectives.[7]

Thus, the tension between the general and particular interests continues even under decentralization. More often than not, however, the centre remains capable of delineating the boundaries of permissible local discretion by way of improving its capacity to monitor local behaviour and threatening to apply coercive sanction.

Most importantly, in unitary systems, the central government almost always reserves the right to change the rules of the implementation game. Particularly in China, where the transitional reform has proceeded very gradually under the close guidance of Beijing, most critical decisions have still depended very much on the planning governance structure embedded in the centre. Thus, the durability of the arrangements governing the allocation of authority, resources, and responsibilities has been highly contingent upon the discretion of Beijing, not the provinces.[8] In the case of the decollectivization reform, the centre altered the rules of implementation in 1982 so that the adoption of the household responsibility systems became mandatory on all provincial implementors. In the post-decollectivization era, too, arbitrary rule changes were often made by Beijing in order to regain its control over the provinces in the areas of fiscal, personnel, and investment management.[9] Thus, in systems where political discretion of the centre is not constrained legally or institutionally, the durability of decentralization is closely tied to the strategic choices of the centre.

It seems that 'administrative decentralization may coexist with political centralization, and it is wrong to infer ... that administrative decentralization implies some degree of political self-control among subsidiary units.'[10] In state-socialist systems like China, centralized political control may remain relatively intact despite the radical measures of economic decentralization. Even locally initiated pilot programmes generally require strong support from the centre in order for them to survive and be later popularized as national policies, as the case of Anhui is illustrative for the decollectivization reform.[11] In the post-decollectivization era, the centre was given another very effective instrument of local control—preferential policies. Beijing's provision or withdrawal of preferential designations such as special economic zones and various development zones has constituted a very useful means of inducement and sanctions against localities.[12]

Local deviations and perversities generated under decentralization should not be construed as the core characteristics of the changes that have occurred in systems like those of China. However extensive its scope may be, administrative decentralization cannot fundamentally transform the penetrative capacity of the 'strong state'. To borrow LaPalombara's terms, decentralization reforms and the weakened role of ideology in post-Mao China may have diminished Beijing's capacity to 'breed voluntary compliance' among local implementors, but its capacity to coerce them into compliance remains relatively unchanged particularly with regard to national priority policies. Heilongjiang's eventual submission to Beijing further underscores the point.[13]

THE INTERVENTION OF NORMS AND AGENCY:
BUREAUCRATIC CAREERISM, OPPORTUNISTIC
BANDWAGONING, AND PUBLIC ENTREPRENEURS

Outcomes of central–local policy dynamics are shaped by the factors of human agency as much as by institutional constraints. The intricate dilemma of the centre—that it needs local adaptation and, at the same time, seeks to limit it—is further compounded by differing preferences, interests, and choices of the actors involved. Problems occur precisely at this intervening level consisting of what are usually called agents, implementors, or middlemen. While decentralization may in theory grant them considerable leeway in interpreting and implementing central policy so as to allow *de facto* 'local policy-remake', local agents at this intervening level do not necessarily respond to such incentives in the same way. Much of when, how, and why the local agents engage in innovation, resistance, or opportunism depend heavily on the norms that govern their perceptions and choices of action.

These norms constitute the dominant frame of reference from which local implementors derive 'culturally rational' choices in the case of conflicts between the centre's general interest and their endogenous interests.[14] Culturally rational choices are more often dictated by the survival imperative embedded in bureaucratic careerism, and bureaucratic careerism makes it perfectly rational for local implementors to comply with the centre irrespective of local endogenous interests. This view, however, may lead to a faulty generalization that local implementors are always quick to adopt whatever is demanded by the centre. Yet, under the circumstances where the centre's priorities have constantly oscillated, local implementors generally prefer to remain cautious until they are assured that the swift implementation of the given policy would entail no serious risk. In China where the policy cycles were frequent and the costs of non-compliance high, provincial leaders had good reasons not to put confidence in the centre's policy stipulations and instead to opt for bandwagoning. A scholar notes on the perceptual source of bureaucratic careerism:

There is too much at stake, especially one's career, for implementors to become closely identified with any one policy. . . . No career-minded bureaucrat wants to be identified as a zealot for a state policy, despite its popularity or unpopularity, if there is a strong chance that he or she will be left out on the limb of that policy long after its creators and the agency chiefs have turned to other endeavors.[15]

While there may always be a small number of local agents who choose to execute central policy faster than most others, their calculus of the risks associated with pioneering may be significantly adjusted by the clientelistic ties they have with the policy advocates at the centre. The decollectivization case highlights the crucial importance of such protective networks, as the contrast between Anhui and Shandong has demonstrated. Interesting are some unusual modes of implementation. As the cases of Heilongjiang and Yantai typify, some local implementors dared to defy the central and provincial authorities on the basis of their strong sense of mission in protecting local interests. Administrative decentralization may generate incentives as well as opportunities for local implementors to display 'strategic entrepreneurial behaviour', which Heilongjiang's Yang Yichen and Yantai's Lu Shengyun had manifested. In the post-decollectivization era as well, as the overall framework of decentralization has proved relatively durable, an increasing number of provincial and sub-provincial officials have opted for strategic entrepreneurship.[16]

CENTRAL–LOCAL POLICY DYNAMICS IN THE 'POST-MOVEMENT' REGIME: CHANGES, CONTINUITIES, AND UNCERTAINTIES

In the aftermath of Mao's death in 1976 China began to finally concede on ideological grounds and seek economic rationality in its management of development programmes. The drastically reduced role of ideological control supplies an important clue to the characteristics of the post-Mao regime. It seems that the regime has made a crucial transition from a totalitarian rule to an authoritarian administration although there were few fundamental structural changes to speak of.[17] If the Chinese regime has indeed departed from its totalitarian phase, it means that its bureaucracy is now immersed more in the conventional routine management fairly independent of ideological constraints. Should we then expect these changes to *ipso facto* expand the scope of provincial autonomy and to promote local deviations? The answer is a negative for the short run at least since, despite some notable local deviations reported in the post-Mao era, the fundamental transformation of systemic norms is an arduous time-consuming process. Furthermore, the task also presupposes repeated demonstrations of Beijing's genuine commitment to the rules of decentralization. In the longer run, on the other hand, each cycle of decentralization may 'leave residues of policies, structures and interests, which prevent a return to point zero' and leave the conditions fertile for further decentralization. If we subscribe to this 'spiral' model of changes, we may then predict that local deviations are likely to be more frequent and widespread in proportion with the duration of the economic reform.[18]

It should be noted that, in state-socialist systems, the decline of ideology may not necessarily constitute a sign of decay but rather of the revitalization of the regime.[19] If that were indeed the case, the prevalent discourses on the collapse of China might be building a man of straw. It should not be forgotten that the strong state, which the post-Mao Chinese regimes still is, may continue to possess the right and capacity to impose its priorities on

localities, society, and its people. Reported local deviations may not necessarily be the proof of a regime on the verge of collapse. Rather, they may
simply reflect the side effects of a transition from dispersed domination to
integrated domination. That is, while during the transitional reforms the
central state strategically shares its powers and responsibilities with local
authorities as well as with segments of the society, once the reformist phase
is successfully completed, the overall structure may paradoxically become
more state- and centre-oriented.[20]

Most importantly, despite decentralization, the reformist centre in China
still retains considerable powers in the management of local officials. In
addition to Beijing's strengthened capacity of local monitoring, the *nomenklatura* control over local government personnel constitutes the ultimate
antinomy of provincial discretion and autonomy. As long as the key local
decision-makers are appointed and dismissed solely by the central party
apparatus, the boundary of permissible discretion is almost always delineated by the centre. The vulnerability of local implementors thus further
reinforces the stability of regime power.[21] In this regard, the fundamental
transformation of central–local policy dynamics has crucial bearings upon
democratization.[22] But this is far beyond the purview of the book.

In conclusion, this book has found that the operational effects of the early
post-Mao administrative decentralization were only partial and diluted
during the decollectivization period. The volume has also specified the conditions under which each of the three patterns of local policy implementation is likely to be adopted. These patterns, though differing in their
respective 'mixes', seem applicable to most cases of policy implementation.
A critical question remains, however, regarding how to predict the particular mix at a given time as the predisposition of human agents does not
lend itself to easy generalization. Generally speaking, as China's systemic
reforms further deepen with the intensification of decentralization, mar-
ketization, and privatization—i.e. as Beijing becomes increasingly more
dependent on the local supply of key information—the dominant mix is
likely to include more pioneers and resisters, while the number of bandwagoners may gradually decrease. Yet, the centre may continue to commute
intermittently between the political and economic logic of reform, often
making the norms of decentralization less durable and reliable. This would
in turn render the long-term predictions about China's central–local relations both more difficult and uncertain.

NOTES

1. The lack of overt provincial resistance during the Maoist era may thus be attributed
   to the absence of the first and fourth conditions. In the case of the decollectivization
   reform, the interprovincial variations stemmed largely from the absence of the third (in

the case of pioneers like Anhui and many of the bandwagoners like Hubei and Shandong) and the fourth (in the case of resisters like Liaoning and Jilin).

2. See John A. Hall, *Coercion and Consent: Studies on the Modern State* (Cambridge: Polity Press, 1994), ch. 3.

3. John R. Firn, 'Devolution: An Exit-Voice Model of Regional Policy', in Edward Nevin (ed.), *The Economics of Devolution* (Cardiff: University of Wales College of Cardiff Press, 1978), 112–29.

4. See Atul Kohli, *Democracy and Discontent: India's Growing Crisis of Governability* (Cambridge: Cambridge University Press, 1990), 397–9.

5. For a wide range of new patterns, see Jae Ho Chung, 'The Expanding Space of Provincial Politics and Development: Thematic Suggestions for the Future Research Agenda', *Provincial China*, 4 (1997), 4–18. For the use of federalism concepts, see Gabriella Montinola, Yingyi Qian, and Barry R. Weingast, 'Federalism, Chinese Style: The Political Basis for Economic Success', *World Politics*, 48/1 (1995), 50–81; and Yongnian Zheng, 'Perforated Sovereignty: Provincial Dynamism and China's Foreign Trade', *Pacific Review*, 7/3 (1994), 309–21.

6. See Vivienne Shue, 'Powers of State, Paradoxes of Dominion in China', in Kenneth Lieberthal, Joyce Kalgren, Roderick MacFarquhar, and Frederic Wakeman (eds.), *Perspectives on Modern China: Four Anniversaries* (Armonk, NY: M. E. Sharpe, 1991), 222–3; and Susan Shirk, *The Political Logic of Economic Reform in China* (Berkeley and Los Angeles: University of California Press, 1993).

7. Ferenc Feher, Agnes Heller, and György Markus, *Dictatorship over Needs: An Analysis of Soviet Societies* (New York: Blackwell, 1983), 63.

8. See David Stark and Victor Nee, 'Towards an Institutional Analysis of State Socialism', in Victor Nee and David Stark (eds.), *Remaking the Economic Institutions of Socialism: China and Eastern Europe* (Stanford: Stanford University Press, 1989), 31; and Steven L. Solnick, 'The Breakdown of Hierarchies in the Soviet Union and China: A Neoinstitutional Perspective', *World Politics*, 48/2 (Jan. 1996), 209–38.

9. See, for instance, Jae Ho Chung, 'Beijing Confronting the Provinces: The 1994 Tax-Sharing Reform and Its Implications for Central–Provincial Relations in China', *China Information*, 9/2/3 (1994/5), 1–23; John P. Burns, 'Strengthening Central CCP Control of Leadership Selection: The 1990 Nomenklatura', *China Quarterly*, 138 (1994), 458–91; and Yasheng Huang, *Inflation and Investment Controls in China: The Political Economy of Central–Local Relations During the Reform Era* (Cambridge: Cambridge University Press, 1996).

10. Brian C. Smith, *Decentralization: The Territorial Dimension of the State* (London: Allen and Unwin, 1985), 11.

11. For the vital role of central support in ensuring the survival of local pilot programmes, see David F. Pyle, 'From Pilot Project to Operational Program in India: The Problems of Transition', in Merilee S. Grindle (ed.), *Politics and Policy Implementation in the Third World* (Princeton: Princeton University Press, 1980), 123–44.

12. See Dorothy J. Solinger, 'Despite Decentralization: Disadvantages, Dependence and Ongoing Central Power in the Inland—The Case of Wuhan', *China Quarterly*, 145 (1996), 1–34; and Jae Ho Chung (ed.), *Cities in China: Recipes for Economic Development in the Reform Era* (London: Routledge, 1999).

13. Joseph LaPalombara, 'Penetration: A Crisis of Government Capacity', in Leonard Binder *et al.*, *Crises and Sequences in Political Development* (Princeton: Princeton University Press, 1971), 208–9. This is also what Michael Mann has called 'infrastructural power'. See 'The Autonomous Power of the State', in Marvin E. Olsen and Martin N. Marger (eds.), *Power in Modern Societies* (Boulder, Colo.: Westview, 1993), 315.

14. For the centrality of conventions and culture, see Gary J. Miller, *Managerial Dilemmas: The Political Economy of Hierarchy* (Cambridge: Cambridge University Press, 1992), ch. 10.

15. Joel S. Migdal, *Strong Societies and Weak States: State–Society Relations and State Capabilities in the Third World* (Princeton: Princeton University Press, 1988), 241.

16. For public entrepreneurship, see Mark Schneider and Paul Teske, *Public Entrepreneurs: Agents for Change in American Government* (Princeton: Princeton University Press, 1995), ch. 2–3. For its manifestation at the provincial and sub-provincial levels, see Peter T. Y.

Cheung, Jae Ho Chung, and Lin Zhimin (eds.), *Provincial Strategies of Economic Reform in Post-Mao China: Leadership, Politics and Implementation* (Armonk, NY: M. E. Sharpe, 1998).

17. The rigid dichotomy of totalitarianism and authoritarianism based solely on their structural attributes is misleading. It is rather the degree of emphasis on ideology as the key control mechanism that defines regime characteristics. In this regard, Maoist rule should be viewed as the 'totalitarian era of authoritarianism'. See Amos Perlmutter, *Modern Authoritarianism: A Comparative Institutional Analysis* (New Haven: Yale University Press, 1981), 67, 71; and Jacques Rupnik, 'Totalitarianism Revisited', in John Keane (ed.), *Civil Society and the State* (London: Verso, 1988), 269–72.

18. For this concept of spiral changes, see Jude Howell, *China Opens Its Doors: The Politics of Economic Transition* (London: Lynne Rienner, 1993), 5–6.

19. See Samuel P. Huntington, 'Social and Institutional Dynamics of One-Party Systems', in Samuel P. Huntington and Clement H. Moore (eds.), *Authoritarian Politics in Modern Society: The Dynamics of Established One-Party Systems* (New York: Basic Books, 1970), 26–7, 40–3; and Richard Lowenthal, 'Development and Utopia in Communist Policy', in Chalmers Johnson (ed.), *Change in Communist Systems* (Stanford: Stanford University Press, 1970), 112.

20. See Joel S. Migdal, 'The State in Society: An Approach to Struggles for Domination', in Joel S. Migdal, Atul Kohli, and Vivienne Shue (eds.), *State Power and Social Forces: Domination and Transformation in the Third World* (Cambridge: Cambridge University Press, 1994), 8–18.

21. See Yan Huai, 'Organizational Hierarchy and the Cadre Management System', in Carol Lee Hamrin and Suisheng Zhao (eds.), *Decision-Making in Deng's China: Perspectives from Insiders* (Armonk, NY: M. E. Sharpe, 1995), 48–50; and Huang, *Inflation and Investment Controls in China*, ch. 9.

22. See, for instance, Tamara J. Resler and Roger E. Kanet, 'Democratization: The National-Subnational Linkage', in Ilpyong J. Kim and Jane Shapiro Zacek (eds.), *Establishing Democratic Rule: The Reemergence of Local Governments in Post-Authoritarian Systems* (Washington: Paragon, 1993), 17–34.

APPENDIX: POSITIONS OF THE INTERVIEWEES IN CHINA

Interviewees	Positions	Affiliations
1 (r)	above minister level	State Agricultural Commission
2 (r)	vice-minister	Research Centre for Rural Development
3 (r)	vice-minister	As above
4 (r)	unkown	Wan Li's secretary
5	bureau director	Ministry of Agriculture
6	deputy bureau director	Ministry of Agriculture
7	researcher	CASS
8	researcher	CASS
9	professor	Beijing Agricultural University
10 (r)	governor	Anhui
11	deputy provincial agricultural secretary	Anhui
12 (r)	deputy party secretary	Chuxian Prefecture in Anhui
13 (r)	director	Anhui provincial rural research office
14 (r)	county party secretary	Fengyang County in Anhui
15	section chief	Provincial Agricultural Commission in Anhui
16 (r)	director	Shandong provincial rural research office
17 (r)	deputy director	Shandong provincial rural research office
18 (r)	party secretary	Heze Prefecture in Shandong
19	bureau chief	Shandong Agricultural Commission
20	deputy chief	Shandong provincial bureau of agricultural machinery management
21	section chief	Shandong Agricultural Commission
22	director	Shandong provincial agricultural mechanization research institute
23	bureau chief	Qingdao Agricultural Commission
24	party secretary	Jiashi Commune of Dezhou in Shandong
25 (r)	deputy director	Heilongjiang Agricultural Commission

(cont.)

Interviewees	Positions	Affiliations
26	deputy director	Heilongjiang Agricultural Commission
27 (r)	bureau chief	Heilongjiang Bureau of Agriculture
28	director	Songhuajiang Prefecture Agricultural Commission
29	director	Heilongjiang research centre for rural development
30	director	Heilongjiang provincial agricultural mechanization research institute
31	bureau chief	Heilongjiang bureau of state farm management
32	section chief	Heilongjiang Agricultural Commission

Note: The names of all interviewees are withheld. (r) denotes that the respective individual had retired by the time of interviewing.

Bibliography

Aberbach, Joel D., *Keeping a Watchful Eye: The Politics of Congressional Oversight* (Washington: The Brookings Institution, 1990).

Acheng xianzhi (Harbin: Heilongjiang renmin chubanshe, 1988).

Adler, Michael, and Asquith, Stewart, 'Discretion and Power', in Michael Hill (ed.), *The Policy Process: A Reader* (New York: Harvester Wheatsheaf, 1993), 399–406.

Administrative Office of the Anhui Provincial Government (ed.), *Anhui shengqing 1949–1984* (Hefei: Anhui renmin chubanshe, 1986).

Almond, Gabriel A. and Genco, Stephen J., 'Clouds, Clocks and the Study of Politics', *World Politics*, 29/4 (1977), 489–522.

Anhui Provincial Agricultural Commission (ed.), *Anhui zerentian ziliao xuanbian* (Hefei: Anhui Provincial Information Bureau, 1987).

Anhui ribao (Anhui Daily).

Anhuisheng nongye shengchan zerenzhi: ziliao xuanbian (Hefei: Anhui Provincial Rural Work Department, 1983).

Aryeetey, Ernest, 'Decentralization for Rural Development: Exogenous Factors and Semi-Autonomous Program Units in Ghana', *Community Development Journal*, 25/3 (1990), 206–14.

Ash, Robert F., 'The Evolution of Agricultural Policy', *China Quarterly*, 116 (1988), 767–822.

Ashford, Douglas, 'Theories of Local Government: Some Comparative Considerations', *Comparative Political Studies*, 8/1 (1975), 90–107.

Axelrod, Robert, 'An Evolutionary Approach to Norms', *American Political Science Review*, 80/4 (1986), 1095–111.

Bacharach, Samuel B., and Lawler, Edward J., *Power and Politics in Organizations: The Social Psychology of Conflict, Coalitions, and Bargaining* (San Francisco: Jossey-Bass, 1980).

——— *Bargaining: Power, Tactics, and Outcomes* (San Fracisco: Jossey-Bass, 1981).

Bachman, David, *Bureaucracy, Economy and Leadership in China: The Institutional Origins of the Great Leap Forward* (Cambridge: Cambridge University Press, 1991).

Bai, Renpu and Liu, Tianfu, 'Lun nongye jixie de heli toufang wenti', *Nongye jishu jingjixue wenxuan* (Beijing: Nongye chubanshe, 1981), 99–110.

Bai, Wanyin, 'Youguan wanshan lianchan chengbao zerenzhi de jige jishu jingji wenti', *Nongye jishu jingji*, Aug. 1983, 31–5.

Bardach, Eugene, *The Implementation Game* (Cambridge, Mass.: MIT Press, 1977).

Barker, R. and Rose, B. (eds.), *The Chinese Agricultural Economy* (Ithaca, NY: Cornell University Press, 1982).

Barnett, A. Doak, *Cadres, Bureaucracy, and Political Power in Communist China* (New York: Columbia University Press, 1967).

Baron, Robert A., 'Conflict in Organizations', in Kevin R. Murphy and Frank E. Saal (eds.), *Psychology in Organizations: Integrating Science and Practice* (Hillsdale, NJ: Lawrence Erlbaum Associates, 1990), 197–216.

Barrett, Susan and Hill, Michael, 'Policy, Bargaining and Structure in Implementation', in Michael J. Goldsmith (ed.), *New Research in Central–Local Relations* (Aldershot: Gower, 1986), 34–59.

Bartke, Wolfgang, *Who's Who in the People's Republic of China*, 2nd edn. (New York: K. G. Saur, 1987).

Baum, Richard, 'Elite Behavior under Conditions of Stress', in Robert A. Scalapino (ed.), *Elites in the People's Republic of China* (Seattle: University of Washington Press, 1972), 540–74.

——*Burying Mao: Chinese Politics in the Age of Deng Xiaoping* (Princeton: Princeton University Press, 1994).

Beijing Review.

Berman, Paul, 'The Study of Macro- and Micro-Implementation', *Public Policy*, 26/2 (1978), 157–84.

Bhalla, A. S., *Economic Transition in Hunan and Southern China* (New York: Macmillan, 1984).

Binder, Leonard, 'National Integration and Political Development', *American Political Science Review*, 58/3 (1964), 622–31.

Bing, Yushu, Dai, Moan, Xu, Bu, Yan, Banggui, Yan, Zehong, Zhou, Wenbao, Wang, Jiali, Yang, Rongqiu, and Yu, Hong, 'Dui Heilongjiangsheng shangpinliang jidi jianshe de tantao', *Nongye jishu jingji*, Mar. 1983, 6–10.

Blau, Peter M., 'Decentralization in Bureaucracies', in Mayer N. Zald (ed.), *Power in Organizations* (Nashville: Vanderbilt University Press, 1970), 150–74.

Blondel, Jean, *Political Leadership: Towards a General Analysis* (London: Sage, 1987).

Bo, Yibo, *Ruogan zhongda juece yu shijian de huigu* (Beijing: Zhonggong zhongyang dangxiao chubanshe, 1993), two vols.

Boeckelman, Keith, 'The Influence of States on Federal Policy Adoptions', *Policy Studies Journal*, 20/3 (1992), 365–75.

Bramall, Chris, 'Origins of the Agricultural "Miracle": Some Evidence from Sichuan', *China Quarterly*, 143 (1995), 731–55.

Brown-John, C. Lloyd (ed.), *Centralizing and Decentralizing Trends in Federal States* (Lanham, Md.: University Press of America, 1988).

Brzezinski, Zbigniew, 'The Soviet Political System: Transformation or Degeneration', *Problems of Communism*, 15/1 (1966), 1–15.

Bünger, Karl, 'Concluding Remarks on Two Aspects of the Chinese Unitary State as Compared with the European State System', in Stuart R. Schram (ed.), *Foundations and Limits of State Power in China* (London: University of London Press, 1987), 313–23.

Bunker, Douglas R., 'Policy Science Perspectives on Implementation Processes', *Policy Science*, 3/1 (1972), 71–80.

Bunker, Stephen G., 'Policy Implementation in an Authoritarian State: A Case from Brazil', *Latin American Research Review*, 18/1 (1983), 33–58.

Burns, John P., 'Local Cadre Accommodation to the "Responsibility System" in Rural China', *Pacific Affairs*, 58/4 (1985–6), 607–25.

——'China's Nomenklatura System', *Problems of Communism*, 36/5 (1987), 36–51.

——'Strengthening Central CCP Control of Leadership Selection: The 1990 Nomenklatura', *China Quarterly*, 138 (1994), 458–91.

Campbell, Robert W., *The Socialist Economies in Transition: A Primer on Semi-Reformed Systems* (Bloomington: Indiana University Press, 1991).

Carroll, David J., Rosati, Jerel A., and Coate, Roger A., 'Human Needs Realism: A Critical Assessment of the Power of Human Needs in World Society', in Roger A. Coate and Jerel A. Rosati (eds.), *The Power of Human Needs in World Society* (Boulder, Colo.: Lynne Rienner, 1988), 257–74.

Chan, Alfred, 'The Campaign for Agricultural Development in the Great Leap Forward: A Study of Policy-Making and Implementation in Liaoning', *China Quarterly*, 129 (1992), 52–71.

Chan, Anita, Madsen, Richard, and Unger, Jonathan, *Chen Village: The Recent History of A Peasant Community in Mao's China* (Berkeley and Los Angeles: University of California Press, 1984).

Chandler, J. A., *Public Policy-Making for Local Government* (London: Croom Helm, 1988).

Chang, Maria Hsia, 'China's Future: Regionalism, Federation, or Disintegration', *Studies in Comparative Communism*, 25/3 (1992), 211–27.

Chang, Parris C., 'Research Notes on the Changing Loci of Decision-Making in the CCP', *China Quarterly*, 44 (1970), 169–81.

—— 'Provincial Party Leaders' Strategies of Survival During the Cultural Revolution', in Robert A. Scalapino (ed.), *Elites in the People's Republic of China*, 501–39.

—— 'Peking and the Provinces: Decentralization of Power', *Problems of Communism*, 21/4 (1972), 67–74.

Chen, Xiwen, Sun, Fangming, and Liu, Danhua, 'Yantai diqu nongcun zerenzhi diaocha zonghe baogao', in Zhongguo nongcun fazhan wenti yanjiuzu (ed.), *Nongcun, Jingji, Shehui* (Beijing: Zhishi chubanshe, 1985), iii. 27–36.

Cheng, Xingchao, *Zhongguo difangzhengfu* (Xianggang: Zhonghua shuju, 1987).

Cheung, Peter Tsan-yin, 'The Case of Guangdong in Central–Provincial Relations', in Jia Hao and Lin Zhimin (eds.), *Changing Central–Local Relations in China: Reform and State Capacity* (Boulder, Colo.: Westview, 1994), 207–37.

China Geographical Society, *Nongye buju yu nongye quhua* (Beijing kexue chubanshe, 1982).

Chu, Han, *Sannian ziran huihai changbian jishi* (Chengdu: Sichuan renmin chubanshe, 1996).

Chung, Jae Ho, 'The Politics of Agricultural Mechanization in the Post-Mao Era', *China Quarterly*, 134 (1993), 264–90.

—— 'Beijing Confronting the Provinces: The 1994 Tax-Sharing Reform and Its Implications for Central–Provincial Relations in China', *China Information*, 9/2–3 (1994/5), 1–23.

—— 'Studies of Central–Provincial Relations in the People's Republic of China: A Mid-Term Appraisal', *China Quarterly*, 142 (1995), 487–508.

—— 'Central–Provincial Relations', in Lo Chi Kin, Suzanne Pepper, and Tsui Kai-Yuen (eds.), *China Review 1995* (Hong Kong: Chinese University Press, 1995), 3.1–45.

—— 'The Expanding Space of Provincial Politics and Development: Thematic Suggestions for the Future Research Agenda', *Provincial China*, 4 (1997), 4–18.

—— Cheung, P. and Lin, Z. (eds.), *Provincial Strategies of Economic Reform in Post-Mao China: Leadership, Politics and Implementation* (Armonk, NY: M. E. Sharpe, 1998).

Chung, Jae Ho (ed.), *Cities in China: Recipes for Economic Development in the Reform Era* (London: Routledge, 1999).

Claval, Paul, 'Center-Periphery and Space: Models of Political Geography', in Jean Gottmann (ed.), *Center and Periphery: Spatial Variation in Politics* (Beverly Hills: Sage, 1980), 63–71.

Crook, Frederick W., 'The *Baogan Daohu* Incentive System: Translation and Analysis of a Model Contract', *China Quarterly*, 102 (1985), 298–303.

Dangdai zhongguo caizheng (Beijing: Zhongguo shehuikexue chubanshe, 1988).

Dangdai zhongguo de nongken shiye (Beijing: Zhongguo shehuikexue chubanshe, 1986).

Dangdai zhongguo de nongye (Beijing: Dangdai zhongguo chubanshe, 1992).

Dangdai zhongguo de nongye jixie gongye (Beijing: Zhongguo shehuikexue chubanshe, 1988).

Dangdai zhongguo publications on various provinces (Beijing: Zhongguo shehuikexue chubanshe, various years).

Dazhong ribao (*Mass Daily*).

deB. Mills, William, 'Leadership Change in China's Provinces', *Problems of Communism*, 34/3 (1985), 24–40.

DeHoog, Ruth H., 'Competition, Negotiation, or Cooperation?: Three Alternative Models for Contracting for Services', in Miriam K. Mills (ed.), *Conflict Resolution and Public Policy* (New York: Greenwood Press, 1990), 155–76.

Deng Xiaoping wenxuan (Beijing: Renmin chubanshe, 1983).

Devereux, Stephen and Hoddinott, John (eds.), *Fieldwork in Developing Countries* (Boulder, Colo.: Lynne Rienner, 1993).

Diao, Tianding, *Zhongguo difang guojia jigou gaiyao* (Beijing: Falu chubanshe, 1989).

Diermeier, Daniel, Ericson, Joel M., Frye, Timothy, and Lewis, Steven, 'Credible Commitment and Property Rights', in David Weimer (ed.), *The Political Economy of Property Rights: Institutional Change and Credibility in the Reform of Centrally Planned Economies* (Cambridge: Cambridge University Press, 1997), 20–42.

Dittmer, Lowell, 'Political Development: Leadership, Politics and Ideology', in Joyce E. Kallgren (ed.), *The People's Republic of China After Thirty Years: An Overview* (Berkeley: Center for Chinese Studies, University of California Press, 1979), 27–43.

Domenach, Jean-Luc, *The Origins of the Great Leap Forward: The Case of One Chinese Province* (Boulder, Colo.: Westview, 1995).

Donnithorne, Audrey, 'China's Cellular Economy: Some Economic Trends since the Cultural Revolution', *China Quarterly*, 52 (1972), 605–19.

——'Centralization and Decentralization in China's Fiscal Management: Comment', *China Quarterly*, 66 (1976), 328–54.

——'New Light on Central–Provincial Relations', *Australian Journal of Chinese Affairs*, 10 (1983), 97–104.

Dorris, Carl E., 'Peasant Mobilization in North China and the Origin of Yenan Communism', *China Quarterly*, 68 (1976), 697–720.

Du Runsheng, *Zhongguo nongcun jingji gaige* (Beijing: Zhongguo shehuikexue chubanshe, 1985).

Duara, Prasenjit, 'Provincial Narratives of the Nation: Centralism and Federalism in Republican China', in Harumi Befu (ed.), *Cultural Nationalism in East Asia* (Berkeley: Institute of East Asian Studies, University of California Press, 1993), 9–35.

'Dui nongji chengbaohu zenyang shixing chengbao', *Fendou*, July 1983, 37–8.

Durasoff, Douglas, 'Conflicts between Economic Decentralization and Political Control in the Domestic Reform of Soviet and Post-Soviet Systems', *Social Science Quarterly*, 69/2 (1988), 381–98.

Dyker, David A., 'Decentralization and the Command Principle—Some Lessons from Soviet Experiences', *Journal of Comparative Economics*, 5/2 (1981), 121–48.

Echeverri-Gent, John, 'Between Autonomy and Capture: Embedding Government Agencies in Their Societal Environment', *Policy Studies* Journal, 20/3 (1992), 342–64.

Edwards, III, George C., *Implementing Public Policy* (Washington: Congressional Quarterly Press, 1980).

Elmore, Richard F., 'Backward Mapping: Implementation Research and Policy Decisions', *Political Science Quarterly*, 94/4 (1979–80), 601–16.

—— 'Forward and Backward Mapping', in Kenneth Hanf and T. Toonen (eds.), *Policy Implementation in Federal and Unitary Systems* (Dordrecht: Martinus Nijhoff, 1985), 33–70.

Falkenheim, Victor C., 'Peking and the Provinces: Continuing Central Predominance', *Problems of Communism*, 21/4 (1972), 75–83.

—— 'Provincial Leadership in Fukien: 1949–66', in Robert A. Scalapino (ed.), *Elites in the People's Republic of China*, 199–244.

Feher, Ferenc, Heller, Agnes, and Markus, György, *Dictatorship over Needs: An Analysis of Soviet Societies* (New York: Blackwell, 1983).

Feldman, David, Peretz Jean H., and Jendrucko, Barbara D., 'Policy Gridlock in Waste Management: Balancing Federal and State Concerns', *Policy Studies Journal*, 22/4 (1994), 589–603.

Ferdinand, Peter, 'Regionalism', in Gerald Segal (ed.), *Chinese Politics and Foreign Policy Reform* (London: Royal Institute of International Affairs, 1990), 135–58.

—— and Wang, Yongjiang, 'Central–Provincial Financial Relations in China and the Role of the Ministry of Commerce', in John Child and Martin Lockett (eds.), *Advances in Chinese Industrial Studies: Reform Policy and the Chinese Enterprise* (Greewich, Conn.: JAI Press, 1990), 15–35.

Fewsmith, Joseph, *Dilemmas of Reform in China: Political Conflict and Economic Debate* (Armonk, NY: M. E. Sharpe, 1994).

Firn, John R., 'Devolution: An Exit-Voice Model of Regional Policy', in Edward Nevin (ed.), *The Economics of Devolution* (Cardiff: University of Wales College of Cardiff Press, 1978), 112–29.

Fitzgerald, John, 'Reports of My Death Have Been Greatly Exaggerated: The History of the Death of China', in David S. G. Goodman and Gerald Segal (eds.), *China Deconstructs: Politics, Trade, and Regionalism* (London: Routledge, 1994), 21–58.

Food and Agriculture Organization, *Learning from China: A Report on Agriculture and the Chinese People's Commune* (Rome: FAO, 1978).

Foreign Broadcast Information Service: Daily Report—China.

Forster, Keith, 'The Reform of Provincial Party Committees in China: The Case of Zhejiang', *Asian Survey*, 24/6 (1984), 618–36.

Forster, Keith, *Rebellion and Factionalism in A Chinese Province: Zhejiang, 1966–1976* (Armonk, NY: M. E. Sharpe, 1990).

Friedman, Edward, 'China's North-South Split and the Forces of Disintegration', *Current History*, 575 (1993), 270–74.

Furniss, Norman, 'Northern Ireland as A Case Study of Decentralization in Unitary States', *World Politics*, 27/3 (1975), 387–404.

Fuyuxianzhi (Beijing: Zhonggong dangshi ziliao chubanshe, 1990).

Geddes, Barbara, *Politician's Dilemma: Building State Capacity in Latin America* (Berkeley and Los Angeles: University of California Press, 1994).

Geertz, Clifford, 'The Integrative Revolution', in Clifford Geertz (ed.), *Old Societies and New States* (New York: Praeger, 1964), 105–57.

Godwin, Kenneth, 'Policy Formation and Implementation in Less Industrialized Countries: A Comparative Analysis of Institutional Effects', *Western Political Quarterly*, 45/2 (1992), 419–39.

Goldsmith, Michael J. (ed.), *New Research in Central Local Relations* (Aldershot: Gower, 1986).

—— 'Centre and Locality: Functions, Access and Discretion', in Edward C. Page and Michael J. Goldsmith (eds.), *Central and Local Government Relations: A Comparative Analysis of West European Unitary States* (London: Sage, 1987), 1–11.

—— 'Local Autonomy: Theory and Practice', in Desmond S. King and Jon Pierre (eds.), *Challenges to Local Government*, Sage Modern Politics Series, 28 (London: Sage, 1990).

Goldstein, Avery, *From Bandwagon to Balance-of-Power Politics: Structural Constraints and Politics in China, 1949–1978* (Stanford: Stanford University Press, 1991).

Goldstone, Jack A., 'The Coming Chinese Collapse', *Foreign Policy*, 99 (1995), 35–52.

Goodman, David S. G., 'The Provincial First Party Secretaries in the People's Republic of China, 1949–1978: A Profile', *British Journal of Political Science*, 10/1 (1980), 39–74.

—— 'Li Jingquan and the South-West Region, 1958–1966: The Life and "Crimes" of a "Local Emperor"', *China Quarterly*, 81 (1981), 66–96.

—— 'The Provincial Revolutionary Committee in the People's Republic of China, 1967–1979: An Obituary', *China Quarterly*, 85 (1982), 49–79.

—— 'Provincial Party First Secretaries in National Politics: A Categoric or a Political Group?', in David S. G. Goodman (ed.), *Groups and Politics in the People's Republic of China* (Cardiff: University of Wales College of Cardiff Press, 1984), 68–82.

—— 'The Methodology of Contemporary Chinese Studies: Political Studies and the PRC', in Yu-ming Shaw (ed.), *Power and Policy in the PRC* (Boulder, Colo.: Westview, 1985), 340–52.

—— *China's Provincial Leaders, 1949–1985: Directory* (Cardiff: University of Wales College of Cardiff Press, 1986).

—— *Centre and Province in the People's Republic of China: Sichuan and Guizhou, 1955–1965* (Cambridge: Cambridge University Press, 1986).

—— (ed.), *China's Regional Development* (London: Routledge, 1989).

—— 'Provinces Confronting the State?' in Kuan Hsin-chi and Maurice Brosseau (eds.), *China Review, 1992* (Hong Kong: Chinese University Press, 1992), 3.2–19.

——and Gerald Segal (eds.), *China Deconstructs: Politics, Trade, and Regionalism* (London: Routledge, 1994).

Gottmann, Jean (ed.), *Center and Periphery: Spatial Variations in Politics* (Beverly Hills: Sage Publications, 1980).

Graham, Lawrence S., 'Centralization versus Decentralization Dilemmas in the Administration of Public Service', *International Review of Administrative Sciences*, 46/2 (1980), 219–32.

Grindle, Merilee S. (ed.), *Politics and Policy Implementation in the Third World* (Princeton: Princeton University Press, 1980).

Gui, Shiyong, *Zhongguo jihua tizhi gaige* (Beijing: Zhongguo caizheng jingji chubanshe, 1994).

Guo, Ming and Wang, Shuwen, 'Yige dadui shixing duozhong xingshi nongye shengchan zerenzhi de diaocha', *Jingji yanjiu*, Sept. 1982, 70–4.

Guo, Shutian, *Zhongguo nongcun gaige yu fazhan shinian* (Beijing: Nongye chubanshe, 1990).

Hall, John A., *Coercion and Consent: Studies on the Modern State* (Cambridge: Polity Press, 1994).

Halpern, Nina, 'Information Flows and Policy Coordination in the Chinese Bureaucracy', in Kenneth G. Lieberthal and David M. Lampton (eds.), *Bureaucracy, Politics and Decision Making in Post-Mao China* (Berkeley and Los Angeles: University of California Press, 1992), 125–48.

Hamrin, Carol Lee, *China and the Challenge of the Future: Changing Political Patterns* (Boulder, Colo.: Westview, 1990).

Hanf, Kenneth and Scharpf, F. W. (eds.), *Interorganizational Policy-Making: Limits of Coordination and Central Control* (London: Sage, 1978).

Harding, Harry, 'The Study of Chinese Politics: Toward A Third Generation of Scholarship', *World Politics*, 36/2 (1984), 284–307.

——'Competing Models of the Chinese Communist Policy Process: Toward a Sorting and Evaluation', *Issues and Studies*, 20/2 (1984), 13–38.

——*China's Second Revolution: Reform After Mao* (Washington: The Brookings Institution, 1987).

Hartford, Kathleen, 'Socialist Agriculture Is Dead: Long Live Socialist Agriculture! Organizational Transformation in Rural China', in Elizabeth J. Perry and Christine Wong (eds.), *The Political Economy of Reform in Post-Mao China* (Cambridge, Mass.: Council on East Asian Studies, Harvard University Press, 1985), 31–61.

Heaphey, James J. (ed.), *Spatial Dimensions of Development Administration* (Durham, NC: Duke University Press, 1971).

Heilongjiang jingji tongji nianjian (Beijing: Zhongguo tongji chubanshe, various years).

Heilongjiang nongye hezuoshi (Beijing: Zhonggong dangshi ziliao chubanshe, 1990).

Heilongjiang Province's Regional Planning Special Group for Agricultural Mechanization, *Heilongjiangsheng nongye jixiehua quhua* (Harbin: n.p., 1982).

Heilongjiang ribao (Heilongjiang Daily).

Heilongjiangsheng nongtian zuoye jixie xitong (Harbin: n.p., Aug. 1982).

Heilongjiang shengqing 1986 (Harbin: Heilongjiang renmin chubanshe, 1987).

Heilongjiang shengshi tansuo (Harbin: Heilongjiang renmin chubanshe, 1983).

Heilongjiang sishinian (Harbin: Heilongjiang renmin chubanshe, 1986).

Heilongjiang sishinian jubian 1949–1989 (Beijing: Zhongguo tongji chubanshe, 1989).

Heilongjiang tongji nianjian (Harbin: Heilongjiang renmin chubanshe, various years).

Hinton, Willian, *The Great Reversals: The Privatization of China, 1978–1989* (New York: Monthly Review Press, 1990).

Historical Archives Commission of the Anhui Provincial Political Consultative Conference (ed.), *Nongcun gaige de xingqi* (Beijing: Zhongguo wenshi chubanshe, 1993).

Hogwood, Brian W. and Gunn, Lewis A., *Policy Analysis for the Real World* (New York: Oxford University Press, 1984).

Hoogerweft, Andries, 'Policy and Time: Consequences of Time Perspectives for the Contents, Processes and Effects of Public Policies', *International Review of Administrative Sciences*, 56/4 (1990), 671–92.

Howlett, Michael, 'Policy Instruments, Policy Styles, and Policy Implementation: National Approaches to Theories of Instrument Choice', *Policy Studies Journal*, 19/2 (1991), 1–21.

Huang, Yasheng, 'Information, Bureaucracy, and Economic Reform in China and the Soviet Union', *World Politics*, 47/1 (1994), 102–34.

—— 'Administrative Monitoring in China', *China Quarterly*, 143 (1995), 828–43.

—— *Inflation and Investment Controls in China: The Political Economy of Central–Local Relations During the Reform Era* (Cambridge: Cambridge University Press, 1996).

Hubei nongcun jingji, 1949–1989 (Beijing: Zhongguo tongji chubanshe, 1990).

Humes, IV, Samuel, *Local Governance and National Power: A Worldwide Comparison of Tradition and Change in Local Government* (New York: Harvester Wheatsheaf, 1991).

Huntington, Samuel P., 'Social and Institutional Dynamics of One-Party Systems', in Samuel P. Huntington and Clement H. Moore (eds.), *Authoritarian Politics in Modern Society: The Dynamics of Established One-Party Systems* (New York: Basic Books, 1970), 3–47.

—— 'The Change to Change', *Comparative Politics*, 3/3 (1971), 283–322.

Jackman, Robert W., *Power without Force: The Political Capacity of Nation-States* (Ann Arbor: University of Michigan Press, 1993).

Jia, Hao and Lin, Zhimin (eds.), *Changing Central–Local Relations in China: Reform and State Capacity* (Boulder, Colo.: Westview, 1994).

Jianming nongye jingji cidian (Nanchang: Jiangxi renmin chubanshe, 1983).

Jilin ribao (Jilin Daily).

Jin, Ji, *Banglianzhi: Zhongguo de zuijia chulu* (Hong Kong: Baixing Publishing Co., 1992).

Johnson, Chalmers, 'Chinese Communist Leadership and Mass Response: The Yenan Period and the Socialist Education Campaign', in Ping-ti Ho and Tang Tsou (eds.), *China in Crisis* (Chicago: University of Chicago Press, 1968), i. 397–437.

—— 'Political Science and East Asian Studies', in Lucian Pye (ed.), *Political Science and Area Studies: Rivals or Partners?* (Bloomington: Indiana University Press, 1975), 78–97.

Johnson, Graham E., 'The Production Responsibility System in Chinese Agriculture: Some Examples from Guangdong', *Pacific Affairs*, 55/3 (1982), 430–51.

Jones, Bryan D., *Leadership and Politics: New Perspectives in Political Science* (Lawrence: University Press of Kansas, 1989).

Jones, G. W. (ed.), *New Approaches to the Study of Central–Local Government Relationships* (Farnborough: Gower, 1980).

Joseph, William A., 'A Tragedy of Good Intentions: Post-Mao Views of the Great Leap Forward', *Modern China*, 12/4 (1986), 419–57.

Kang, Mingzhong, 'Guizhou nongye baochan daohu qianyi', *Nongye jingji wenti*, 3 (1982), 8–12.

Kelliher, Daniel, *Peasant Power in China: The Era of Rural Reform 1979–1989* (New Haven: Yale University Press, 1992).

Khorev, B. S., 'Economic Decentralization and Regionalism', *Soviet Geography*, 31/7 (1990), 509–16.

Kiggundu, Moses N., *Managing Organizations in Developing Countries: An Operational and Strategic Approach* (West Hartford, Conn.: Kumarian Press, 1989).

Kohli, Atul, *Democracy and Discontent: India's Growing Crisis of Governability* (Cambridge: Cambridge University Press, 1990).

Kojima, Reeitsu, 'Agricultural Organizations: New Forms, New Contradictions', *China Quarterly*, 116 (1988), 706–35.

Kornai, János, *Highway and Byways: Studies on Reform and Postcommunist Transition* (Cambridge, Mass.: MIT Press, 1995).

Krane, Dale, 'The Evolutionary Patterns of Federal States', in C. Lloyd Brown-John (ed.), *Centralizing and Decentralizing Trends in Federal States* (Lanham, Md.: University Press of America, 1988), 39–62.

Krug, Barbara, 'Regional Politics in Communist China: The Spatial Dimension of Power', *Issues and Studies*, 21/1 (1985), 58–78.

Kueh, Yak-Yeow, 'China's New Agricultural-Policy Program: Major Economic Consequences, 1979–1983', *Journal of Comparative Economics*, 8/4 (1984), 353–75.

Lampton, David M., 'The Implementation Problem in Post-Mao China', in David M. Lampton (ed.), *Policy Implementation in Post-Mao China* (Berkeley and Los Angeles: University of California Press, 1987), 3–24.

——'Chinese Politics: The Bargaining Treadmill', *Issues and Studies*, 23/3 (1987), 11–41.

LaPalombara, Joseph, 'Penetration: A Crisis of Government Capacity', in Leonard Binder *et al.*, *Crises and Sequences in Political Development* (Princeton: Princeton University Press, 1971), 205–32.

Lardy, Nicholas R., 'Centralization and Decentralization in China's Fiscal Management', *China Quarterly*, 61 (1975), 25–60.

——'Economic Planning in the People's Republic of China: Central–Provincial Relations', in Joint Economic Committee of the US Congress, *China: A Reassessment of the Economy* (Washington: Government Printing Office, 1975).

——'Prospects and Some Policy Problems of Agricultural Development in China', *American Journal of Agricultural Economics*, 68/2 (1986), 451–7.

——'Dilemmas in the Pattern of Resource Allocation in China, 1978–1985', in Victor Nee and David Stark (eds.), *Remaking the Economic Institutions of*

Socialism: China and Eastern Europe (Stanford: Stanford University Press, 1989), 278–305.

——*Foreign Trade and Economic Reform in China, 1978–1990* (Cambridge: Cambridge University Press, 1992).

Latham, Richard J., 'The Implication of Rural Reforms for Grass-Roots Cadres', in Elizabeth J. Perry and Christine Wong (eds.), *The Political Economy of Reform in Post-Mao China* (Cambridge, Mass.: Council on East Asian Studies, Harvard University Press, 1985), 151–73.

Levitt, Brian and March, James G., 'Organizational Learning', in *Annual Review of Sociology* (Palo Alto, Calif.: Annual Review Press, 1988), 319–40.

Li, Chaogui, *Zhongguo nongcun daxieyi* (Changsha: Hunan wenyi chubanshe, 1993).

Li, Cheng and Bachman, David, 'Localism, Elitism and Immobilism: Elite Formation and Social Change in Post-Mao China', *World Politics*, 42/1 (1989), 64–94.

Li, Debin and Lin, Shunbao (eds.), *Xinzhongguo nongcun jingji jishi 1949.9–1984.9* (Beijing: Beijing daxue chubanshe, 1989).

Li, Huicun, *Zhongguo tongjishi* (Beijing: Zhongguo tongji chubanshe, 1993).

Li, Linda C., *Centre and Provinces: China 1978–1993* (Oxford: Oxford University Press, 1998).

Li, Rui, *Dayuejin qinliji* (Shanghai: Shanghai yuandong chubanshe, 1996).

Li, Yang, 'Nongye shengchan zerenzhi bujiushi baochan daohu', *Fendou*, Feb. 1982, 25–6.

'Lianchan chengbaozhi zai Xinjiang xunshu fazhan', *Nongcun gongzuo tongxun*, (1983), 44.

Lieberthal, Kenneth, *Central Documents and Politburo Politics in China* (Ann Arbor: Center for Chinese Studies, University of Michigan, 1978).

——'China and Political Science', *Political Science*, 19/1 (1986), 70–8.

——and Oksenberg, Michel, *Policy Making in China: Leaders, Structures, and Processes* (Princton: Princeton University Press, 1988).

——and Lampton, David M. (eds.), *Bureaucracy, Politics and Decision Making in Post-Mao China* (Berkeley and Los Angeles: University of California Press, 1992).

Light, Paul C., *Thickening Government: Federal Hierarchy and the Diffusion of Accountability* (Washington: The Brookings Institution, 1995).

Lin, Justin Yifu, 'The Household Responsibility Reform in China: A Peasant's Institutional Choice', *American Journal of Agricultural Economics*, 69/2 (1987), 410–15.

Lin, Sen, 'A New Pattern of Decentralization in China: The Increase of Provincial Powers in Economic Legislation', *China Information*, 7/3 (1992–3), 27–38.

Lindianxian zhi (n.p., 1988).

Lo, Chuhua, 'Nongye shengchan zerenzhi fazhanxingshi he shijianzhong tichu de jige wenti', *Nongye jingji wenti*, 3 (1983), 11–14.

Lockhart, Charles, *Bargaining in International Conflicts* (New York: Columbia University Press, 1979).

Lowenthal, Richard, 'Development and Utopia in Communist Policy', in Chalmers Johnson (ed.), *Change in Communist Systems* (Stanford: Stanford University Press, 1970), 33–116.

Lu, Xueyi, *Lianchan chengbao zerenzhi yanjiu* (Shanghai: Shanghai renmin chubanshe, 1986).

——*Dangdai zhongguo nongcun yu dangdai zhongguo nongmin* (Beijing: Zhishi chubanshe, 1991).

Lu, Zixiu, *Nongcun gaige zhexue sikao* (Shanghai: Shanghai renmin chubanshe, 1986).

Luo, Xiaopeng, 'Rural Reform and the Rise of Localism', in Jia Hao and Lin Zhimin (eds.), *Changing Central–Local Relations in China: Reform and State Capacity* (Boulder, Colo.: Westview, 1994), 113–34.

Lyons, Thomas, *Economic Integration and Planning in Communist China* (New York: Columbia University Press, 1987).

—— and Wang, Yan, *Planning and Finance in China's Economic Reforms* (Ithaca, NY: Cornell University, East Asia Papers No. 46, 1988).

Ma, Piao, 'Anhui nongcun baochan daohu qingkuang kaocha', *Jingji guanli*, 2 (1981), 19–22.

MacFarquhar, Roderick, *The Origins of the Cultural Revolution*, 2 vols. (New York: Columbia University Press, 1974 and 1983).

Majone, G. and Wildavsky, Aaron, 'Implementation as Evolution', in Howard Freeman (ed.), *Policy Studies Review Annual* (Beverly Hills: Sage, 1978), 103–17.

Maynard-Moody, Steven, 'Beyond Implementation: Developing an Institutional Theory of Administrative Policy-Making', *Public Administration Review*, 49/2 (1989), 137–43.

McMillen, Donald H., *Chinese Communist Power and Policy in Xinjiang, 1949–1977* (Boulder, Colo.: Westview Press, 1979).

Meisner, Maurice, *Mao's China: A History of the People's Republic* (New York: Free Press, 1977).

Migdal, Joel S., *Strong Societies and Weat States: State–Society Relations and State Capabilities in the Third World* (Princeton: Princeton University Press, 1988).

Miller, Gary J., *Managerial Dilemmas: The Political Economy of Hierarchy* (Cambridge: Cambridge University Press, 1992).

Min, Yaoliang and Li, Bingkun, *Zhongguo nongcun jingji gaige yanjiu* (Beijing: Zhongguo nongye chubanshe, 1988).

Ministry of Civil Affairs, *Zhonghua renmin gongheguo xingzheng quhua jiance* (Beijing: Ditu chubanshe, 1983).

Mitnick, Barry M. and Backoff, Robert W., 'The Incentive Relation in Implementation', in George C. Edwards (ed.), *Public Policy Implementation* (Greenwich, Conn.: JAI Press, 1984), 59–122.

Mohr, Lawrence B., 'Organizations, Decisions and Courts', *Law and Society Review*, 10/4 (1976), 621–42.

—— 'The Reliability of the Case Study As A Source of Information', in Lee S. Sproull and Patrick D. Larkey (eds.), *Advances in Information Processing in Organizations*, vol. 2 of Robert F. Coulam and Richard A. Smith (eds.), *Research on Public Organizations* (Greenwich, Conn.: JAI Press, 1985), 65–94.

Montinola, Gabriella, Qian, Yingyi, and Weingast, Barry R., 'Federalism, Chinese Style: The Political Basis for Economic Success', *World Politics*, 48/1 (1995), 50–81.

Moody, Peter, 'Policy and Power: The Case of Tao Chu, 1956–66', *China Quarterly*, 54 (1973), 267–93.

Moses, Joel C., 'Regionalism in Soviet Politics: Continuity As A Source of Change, 1953–1982', *Soviet Studies*, 37/2 (1985), 184–211.

Mu, Wei-chin, *Provincial–Central Government Relations and the Problem of*

National Unity in Modern China, doctoral diss., Princeton University, 1948, reproduced by the University Microfilms, 1965.

Mueller, Keith J., 'Local Implementation of National Policy', *Policy Studies Review*, 4/1 (1984), 86–98.

National Foreign Assessment Center, *Directory of Chinese Officials: Provincial Organizations* (Washington: Government Printing Office, Dec. 1981 and Aug. 1983).

Naughton, Barry, 'The Decline of Central Control over Investment in Post-Mao China', in David M. Lampton (ed.), *Policy Implementation in Post-Mao China* (Berkeley: University of California Press, 1987), 51–80.

——'The Third Front: Defence Industrialization in the Chinese Interior', *China Quarterly*, 115 (1988), 351–86.

——*Growing out of the Plan: Chinese Economic Reform, 1978–1993* (Cambridge: Cambridge University Press, 1995).

Nee, Victor and Stark, David (eds.), *Remaking the Economic Institutions of Socialism: China and Eastern Europe* (Stanford: Stanford University Press, 1989).

Nelson, Harvey, *The Chinese Military System* (Boulder, Colo.: Westview, 1977).

Nongcun jingji zhengce huibian 1978–1981 (Beijing: Nongcun duwu chubanshe, 1982).

Nongcun jingji zhengce huibian 1981–1983 (Beijing: Nongcun duwu chubanshe, 1984).

Nongmuyuyebu sheduiqiye guanliju, 'Jinyibu wanshan nongye zerenzhi', *Nongye jingji wenti*, 10 (1982).

Nongye de genben chulu zaiyu jixiehua (Beijing: Nongye chubanshe, 1976).

Nongye jishujingji shouce (Beijing: Nongye chubanshe, 1984).

Nongye jishu jingjixue wenxuan (Beijing: Nongye chubanshe, 1981).

Nongye shengchan zerenzhi lunwenji (Beijing: Renmin chubanshe, 1986).

Nongye xiandaihua (Beijing: Kexue puji chubanshe, 1983).

North, Douglas, *Institutions, Institutional Change and Economic Performance* (Cambridge: Cambridge University Press, 1990).

Nove, Alec, *The Economics of Feasible Socialism* (London: Allen and Unwin, 1983).

Oi, Jean, *State and Peasant in Contemporary China* (Berkeley: University of California Press, 1989).

Oksenberg, Michel, 'Local Government and Politics in China, 1955–58', *Journal of Development Studies*, 4/1 (1967), 25–48.

——'Local Leaders in Rural China, 1962–65: Individual Attributes, Bureaucratic Positions, and Political Recruitment', in A. Doak Barnett (ed.), *Chinese Communist Politics in Action* (Seattle: University of Washington Press, 1969), 155–215.

——'Methods of Communication within the Chinese Bureaucracy', *China Quarterly*, 57 (1974), 1–39.

——and Tong, James, 'The Evolution of Central–Provincial Fiscal Relations in China, 1971–1984: The Formal System', *China Quarterly*, 125 (1991), 1–32.

O'Leary, Greg and Watson, Andrew, 'The Production Responsibility System and the Future of Collective Farming', *Australian Journal of Chinese Affairs*, 8 (July 1982), 1–34.

Oszlak, Oscar, 'Public Policies and Political Regimes in Latin America', *International Social Science Journal*, 108 (1986), 219–35.

O'Tool, Jr., Lawrence J., and Montjoy, Robert S., 'Interorganizational Policy Implementation: A Theoretical Perspective', *Public Administration Review*, 44/6 (Nov.–Dec. 1984), 491–503.

Paddison, Ronan, *The Fragmented State: The Political Geography of Power* (Oxford: Blackwell, 1983).

Page, Edward and Goldsmith, Michael (eds.), *Central and Local Government Relations* (Beverly Hills: Sage Publications, 1987).

Parish, William L. (ed.), *Chinese Rural Development: The Great Transformation* (Armonk, NY: M. E. Sharpe, 1985).

Perkins, Dwight and Yusuf, Shahid, *Rural Development in China* (Baltimore: The Johns Hopkins University Press, 1984).

Perlmutter, Amos, *Modern Authoritarianism: A Comparative Institutional Analysis* (New Haven: Yale University Press, 1981).

Petrick, Richard L., 'Policy Cycles and Policy Learning in the People's Republic of China', *Comparative Political Studies*, 14/1 (1981), 101–22.

Policy Research Office of the State Planning Commission, 'Woguo zhongyang yu difang jingji guanli quanxian yanjiu', *Jingji yanjiu cankao*, 434/435 (1994).

Pressman, Jeffrey L. and Wildawsky, Aaron, *Implementation*, 3rd expanded edn. (Berkeley: University of California Press, 1984).

Prime, Penelope B., 'Central–Provincial Investment and Finance: The Cultural Revolution and Its Legacy in Jiangsu Province', in William A. Joseph, Christine P. W. Wong, and David Zweig (eds.), *New Perspectives on the Cultural Revolution* (Cambridge, Mass.: Harvard University Press, 1991), 197–215.

Pruitt, Dean G., *Negotiation Behavior* (New York: Academic Press, 1981).

—— and Lewis, Steven A., 'The Psychology of Integrative Bargaining', in Daniel Druckman (ed.), *Negotiations* (Beverly Hills: Sage, 1977), 161–92.

Pryor, Frederic, *Property and Industrial Organization in Communist and Capitalist Nations* (Bloomington: Indiana University Press, 1973).

—— 'When Is Collectivization Reversible?', *Studies in Comparative Communism*, 24/1 (Mar. 1991), 3–24.

Pyle, David F., 'From Pilot Project to Operational Program in India: The Problems of Transition', in Merilee S. Grindle (ed.), *Politics and Policy Implementation in the Third World* (Princeton: Princeton University Press, 1980), 123–44.

Qiu, Zhen, 'Heilongjiangsheng nongye jixiehua shudu chutan', *Xuexi yu tansuo*, Sept. 1980, 65–71.

Quandang dongyuan juezhan sannian wei jibenshang shixian nongye jixiehua er fendou (Beijing renmin chubanshe, 1978).

'Quanguo nongye shengchan zerenzhi wenti taolunhui jiyao', *Nongye jingji wenti*, 2 (1982).

Ragin, Charles C., *The Comparative Method: Moving Beyond Qualitative and Quantitative Strategies* (Berkeley: University of California Press, 1987).

Rangarajan, L. N., *The Limitation of Conflict: A Theory of Bargaining and Negotiation* (London: Croom Helm, 1985).

Renmin ribao (*People's Daily*).

Research Office of the Shandong Provincial Party Committee, *Shandong Shengqing 1949–1984* (Jinan: Shandong renmin chubanshe, 1986).

Research Office of the Shandong Provincial Party Committee, *Shandong sishinian* (Jinan: Shandong renmin chubanshe, 1989).

Research Team on the Issue of Chinese Rural Development (ed.), *Baochan daohu ziliao xuanbian* (n.d., n.p., 1981).

Rhodes, R. A. W., 'Power Dependence Theories of Central–Local Relations: A Critical Assessment', in Michael J. Goldsmith (ed.), *New Research in Central–Local Relations* (Aldershot: Gower Publishing Company, 1986), 1–33.

Ricci, David, *The Tragedy of Political Science: Politics, Scholarship and Democracy* (New Haven: Yale University Press, 1984).

Rich, Michael J., 'Distributive Politics and the Allocation of Federal Grants', *American Political Science Review*, 83/1 (1989), 193–213.

Riskin, Carl, 'Neither Plan Nor Market: Mao's Political Economy', in Joseph, Wong, and Zweig (eds.), *New Perspectives on the Cultural Revolution* 133–52.

Rondinelli, Dennis A., Nellis, John R., and Cheema, G. Shabbir, *Decentralization in Developing Countries: A Review of Recent Experiences* (Washington: World Bank, 1984).

Rose, Douglas D., 'National and Local Forces in State Politics: The Implications of Multiple-Level Policy Analysis', *American Political Science Review*, 67/4 (1973), 1162–73.

Ross, Cameron, *Local Government in the Soviet Union* (London: Croom Helm, 1987).

Rousseau, Mark O., and Zariski, Raphael, *Regionalism and Regional Devolution in Comparative Perspective* (New York: Praeger, 1987).

Rupnik, Jacques, 'Totalitarianism Revisited', in John Keanne (ed.), *Civil Society and the State* (London: Verso, 1988), 263–91.

Sabatier, Paul A., 'Top-Down and Bottom-Up Approaches to Implementation Research: A Critical Analysis and Suggested Synthesis', *Journal of Public Policy*, 6 (1986), 21–48.

Samoff, Joel, 'Decentralization: The Politics of Interventionism', *Development and Change*, 21/3 (1990), 513–24.

Samuels, Richard J., *The Politics of Regional Policy in Japan: Localities Incorporated?* (Princeton: Princeton University Press, 1983).

Schneider, Mark and Teske, Paul, *Public Entrepreneurs: Agents for Change in American Government* (Princeton: Princeton University Press, 1995).

Schoenhals, Michael, 'Elite Information in China', *Problems of Communism*, 34/5 (1985), 65–71.

——*Doing Things with Words in Chinese Politics: Five Studies* (Berkeley: Institute of East Asian Studies, 1992).

Schram, Stuart R., 'Decentralization in a Unitary State: Theory and Practice, 1940–1984', S. R. Schram (ed.), *The Scope of State Power in China* (London: University of London Press, 1985), 81–125.

Schroeder, Paul E., 'Territorial Actors as Competitors for Power: The Case of Hubei and Wuhan', in Kenneth G. Lieberthal and David M. Lampton (eds.), *Bureaucracy, Politics and Decision Making in Post-Mao China* (Berkeley and Los Angeles: University of California Press, 1992), 283–307.

Schultz, Ann, *Local Politics and Nation-States: Case Studies in Politics and Policy* (Oxford: Clio Books, 1979).

Schurmann, Franz, *Ideology and Organization in Communist China*, enlarged 2nd edn. (Berkeley: University of California Press, 1968).

Scott, James C., 'Resistance without Protest and without Organization: Peasant

Opposition to the Islamic Zakat and the Christian Tithe', *Comparative Studies in Society and History*, 29/4 (1987), 417–52.

—— *Domination and the Arts of Resistance: Hidden Transcripts* (New Haven: Yale University Press, 1990).

Segal, Gerald, *China Changes Shape: Regionalism and Foreign Policy*, Adelphi Paper, no. 287 (London: International Institute for Strategic Studies, 1994).

Selden, Mark, *The Yenan Way in Revolutionary China* (Cambridge, Mass.: Harvard University Press, 1971).

Shandong Provincial Party Committee, *Shandongshengnongye hezuohua shiliaoji* (Jinan: Shandong renmin chubanshe, 1989 and 1990), 2 vol.

'Shandong Yantai diqu fazhan nongye jixiehua de diaocha baogao', *Hongqi*, Nov. 1975.

Shao, Bingren, 'Lun jianli nongye shengchan zerenzhi yihou nongye jixiehua de fazhan qiantu', *Nongye jingji luncong*, 3 (1982), 280–5.

Sheridan, James E., *China in Disintegration: The Republican Era in Chinese History, 1912–1949* (New York: Free Press, 1975).

Shirk, Susan, 'The Domestic Political Dimensions of China's Foreign Economic Relations', in Samuel S. Kim (ed.), *China and the World: Chinese Foreign Policy in the Post-Mao Era* (Boulder, Colo.: Westview, 1984), 57–81.

—— 'Playing to the Provinces: Deng Xiaoping's Political Strategy of Economic Reform', *Studies in Comparative Communism*, 23/3–4 (1990), 227–58.

—— *The Political Logic of Economic Reform in China* (Berkeley: University of California Press, 1993).

Shou, Xiaohe, Li, Xiongfan, and Sun, Xuyu (eds.), *Zhongguo shengshizizhiqu ziliao shouce* (Beijing: Shehuikexue wenxuan chubanshe, 1990).

Shue, Vivienne, *The Reach of the State: Sketches of the Chinese Body Politic* (Stanford: Stanford University Press, 1988).

Sichuansheng nongye hezuo jingji shiliao (Chengdu: Sichuan kexue jishu chubanshe, 1989).

Sicular, Terry, 'Agricultural Planning and Pricing in the Post-Mao Period', *China Quarterly*, 116 (1988), 671–705.

Siu, Helen F., *Agents and Victims in South China: Accomplices in Rural Revolution* (New Haven and London: Yale University Press, 1989).

Skinner, William and Edwin Winckler, 'Compliance Succession in Rural Communist China: A Cyclical Theory', in Amitai Etzioni (ed.), *Complex Organizations: A Sociological Reader*, 2nd edn. (New York: 1969), 410–38.

Slater, David, 'Debating Decentralization', *Development and Change*, 21/3 (1990), 501–12.

Smith, B. C., 'Measuring Decentralisation', in G. W. Jones (ed.), *New Approaches to the Study of Central–Local Government Relationships* (Westmead: Gower, 1980), 137–51.

—— *Decentralization: The Territorial Dimension of the State* (London: Allen and Unwin, 1985).

Solinger, Dorothy J., *Regional Government and Political Integration in Southwest China, 1949–1954* (Berkeley: University of California Press, 1977).

—— 'Some Speculations on the Return of the Regions: Parallel with the Past', *China Quarterly*, 75 (1978), 623–38.

Solinger, Dorothy J., 'Politics in Yunnan Province in the Decade of Disorder', *China Quarterly*, 92 (1982), 628–62.

—— 'The Fifth National People's Congress and the Process of Policy-Making: Reform, Readjustment and the Opposition', *Asian Survey*, 22/12 (1982), 1,244–58.

—— 'China's New Economic Policies and the Local Industrial Political Process: The Case of Wuhan', *Comparative Politics*, 18/4 (1986), 379–99.

—— 'City, Province, and Region: The Case of Wuhan', in Ilpyong J. Kim and Bruce J. Reynolds (eds.), *Chinese Economic Policy: Economic Reform at Midstream* (New York: Paragon House, 1988), 233–84.

—— 'Despite Decentralization: Disadvantages, Dependence and Ongoing Central Power in the Inland—The Case of Wuhan', *China Quarterly*, 145 (1996), 1–34.

Solnick, Steven L., 'The Breakdown of Hierarchies in the Soviet Union and China: A Neoinstitutional Perspective', *World Politics*, 48/2 (Jan. 1996), 209–38.

Song, Xinzhong, *Zhongguo caizheng tizhi gaige yanjiu* (Beijing: Zhongguo caizheng jingji chubanshe, 1992).

Song, Yuansheng, *Heilongjiangsheng nongye jixiehua fazhan yu erqiannian zhanlue* (Harbin: Heilongjiang kexue jishu chubanshe, 1991).

State Science and Technology Commission (ed.), *Zhongyao juece shijian yu sikao* (Beijing: Zhongguo shehuikexue wenxian chubanshe, 1992).

State Statistical Bureau, *Guomin shouru tongji ziliao huibian 1949–1985* (Beijing: Zhongguo tongji chubanshe, 1987).

State Statistical Bureau, *Statistical Yearbook of China* (Beijing: China Statistics Publisher, various years).

State Statistical Bureau, *Zhongguo fenxian nongcun jingji tongji gaiyao* (Beijing: Tongji chubanshe, 1989).

Stavis, Benedict A., *The Politics of Agricultural Mechanization in China* (Ithaca, NY: Cornell University Press, 1978).

Stephenson, Jr., Max O. and M. Pops, Gerald, 'Conflict Resolution Methods and the Policy Process', *Public Administration Review*, 49/5 (1989), 463–73.

Stern, Lewis M., 'Politics without Consensus: Center–Province Relations and Political Communication in China, January 1976–January 1977', *Asian Survey*, 19/3 (1979), 260–80.

Stewart, John, 'Dilemmas', in Stewart Ranson, George Jones, and Kieron Walsh (eds.), *Between Centre and Locality: The Politics of Public Policy* (London: George Allen and Unwin, 1985), 23–35.

Sun, Qitai and Xiong, Zhiyong, *Dazhai hongqi de shengqi yu duoluo* (Huixian: Henan renmin chubanshe, 1990).

Szelenyi, Ivan, *Socialist Entrepreneurs: Embourgeoisement in Rural Hungary* (Madison: University of Wisconsin Press, 1988).

Tam, On Kit, *China's Agricultural Modernization: The Socialist Mechanization Scheme* (London: Croom Helm, 1985).

Tang, Wenbin, 'Zenyang kandai baochan daohu baogan daohu de xingzhi', *Fendou*, Apr. 1982, 24.

Tant, A. P., 'The Politics of Official Statistics', *Government and Opposition*, 30/2 (1995), 254–66.

Tarrow, Sidney, 'Local Constraints on Regional Reform: A Comparison of Italy and France', *Comparative Politics*, 7/1 (1974), 1–36.

——*Between Center and Periphery* (New Haven: Yale University Press, 1977).

Taylor, Jeffrey R., 'Rural Employment Trends and the Legacy of Surplus Labour, 1978–86', *China Quarterly*, 116 (1988), 736–66.

Teiwes, Frederick, 'The Purge of Provincial Leaders, 1957–1958', *China Quarterly*, 27 (1966), 14–32.

——'Provincial Politics in China: Themes and Variations', in John M. H. Lindbeck (ed.), *China: Management of A Revolutionary Society* (Seattle: University of Washington Press, 1971), 116–89.

——*Politics and Purge in China: Rectification and the Decline of Party Norms* (New York: M. E. Sharpe, 1979), 349–74.

——'Establishment and Consolidation of the New Regime', in Roderick MacFarquhar and John K. Fairbank (eds.), *The Cambridge History of China*, xiv. *The People's Republic of China*, pt. 1, *The Emergence of Revolutionary China 1949–1965* (Cambridge: Cambridge University Press, 1987), 51–143.

——and Sun Warren (eds.), *The Politics of Agricultural Cooperativization in China: Mao, Deng Zihui, and the 'High Tide' of 1955* (Armonk, NY: M. E. Sharpe, 1993).

Thomas, John W. and Grindle, Merilee S., 'After the Decision: Implementing Policy Reforms in Developing Countries', *World Development*, 18/8 (1990), 1163–81.

Thomas, Robert D., 'Implementing Federal Programs at the Local Level', *Political Science Quarterly*, 94/3 (1979), 419–35.

Thompson, Frank, 'Policy Implementation and Overhead Control', in George C. Edwards, III (ed.), *Public Policy Implementation* (Greenwich, Conn.: JAI Press, 1984), 3–26.

Thurston, Anne F., *Enemies of the People: The Ordeal of the Intellectuals in China's Great Cultural Revolution* (Cambridge, Mass.: Harvard University Press, 1987).

——and Pasternak, Burton (eds.), *The Social Sciences and Fieldwork in China: Views from the Field* (Boulder, Colo.: Westview, 1983).

Tong, James, 'Fiscal Reform, Elite Turnover and Central-Provincial Relations in Post-Mao China', *Australian Journal of Chinese Affairs*, 22 (1989), 1–30.

——'Effects of Fiscal Reforms on Interprovincial Variations in Medical Services in China, 1979–1984', in Donna L. Bahry and Joel C. Moses (eds.), *Political Implications of Economic Reform in Communist Systems* (New York: New York University Press, 1990), 109–30.

Tsou, Tang, 'The Responsibility System in Agriculture,' in Tang Tsou, *The Cultural Revolution and Post-Mao Reforms: A Historical Perspective* (Chicago: University of Chicago Press, 1986), 189–218.

——Bletcher, Marc, and Meisner, Mitch, 'National Agricultural Policy: The Dazhai Model and Local Change in the Post-Mao Era', in Mark Selden and Victor Lippit (eds.), *The Transition to Socialism in China* (Armonk, NY: M. E. Sharpe, 1982), 266–99.

Tucker, Robert C., *The Marxian Revolutionary Idea* (New York: W. W. Norton, 1969).

Unger, Jonathan, 'The Decollectivization of the Chinese Countryside: A Survey of Twenty-Eight Villages', *Pacific Affairs*, 58/4 (1985–6), 585–606.

Unger, Jonathan, 'The Struggle to Dictate China's Administration: The Conflict of Branches *vs.* areas *vs.* Reform', *Australian Journal of Chinese Affairs*, 18 (1987), 15–46.

Van Meter, Donald S. and Van Horn, Carl E., 'The Policy Implementation Process: A Conceptual Framework', *Administration and Society*, 185 (1974), 1124–31.

Vengroff, Richard and Ben Salem, Hatem, 'Assessing the Impact of Decentralization on Governance: A Comparative Methodological Approach and Application to Tunisia', *Public Administration and Development*, 12 (1992), 473–92.

Vogel, Ezra, *Canton under Communism* (Cambridge, Mass.: Harvard University Press, 1969).

—— *One Step Ahead in China: Guangdong under Reform* (Cambridge, Mass.: Harvard University Press, 1989).

Wakeman, Jr., Frederick, *The Fall of Imperial China* (New York: Free Press, 1975).

Waldron, Arthur, 'Warlordism Versus Federalism: The Revival of A Debate', *China Quarterly*, 121 (1990), 116–28.

Walker, David B., 'Decentralization: Recent Trends and Prospects from A Comparative Governmental Perspective', *International Review of Administrative Sciences*, 57/1 (1991), 113–29.

Walker, Kenneth R., 'China's Agriculture during the Period of Readjustment', *China Quarterly*, 100 (1984), 783–812.

Wan, Jieqiu, *Zhengfu tuidong yu jingji fazhan: Sunan moshi de lilun sikao* (Shanghai: Fudan University Press, 1993).

Wang, Gengjin, Yang, Xun, Wang, Ziping, Liang, Xiaodong, and Yang, Guansan (eds.), *Xiangcun sanshinian: Fengyang nongcun shehui jingji fazhan shilu, 1949–1983* (Beijing: Nongcun duwu chubanshe, 1989).

Wang, Lixin and Fewsmith, Joseph, 'Bulwark of the Planned Economy: The Structure and Role of the State Planning Commission', in Carol Lee Hamrin and Suisheng Zhao (eds.), *Decision-Making in Deng's China: Perspectives from Insiders* (Armonk, NY: M. E. Sharpe, 1995), 51–65.

Wang, Shaoguang, 'The Rise of the Regions: Fiscal Reform and the Decline of Central State Capacity in China', in Andrew G. Walder (ed.), *The Waning of the Communist State: Economic Origins of Political Decline in China and Hungary* (Berkeley and Los Angeles: University of California Press, 1995), 87–113.

—— and Hu, Angang, *Zhongguo guojia nengli baogao* (Hong Kong: Oxford University Press, 1994).

Wang, Yuzhao, *Dabaogan yu daqushi* (Beijing: Guangming ribao chubanshe, 1987).

—— *Zunzhong nongmin de jueze: nongcun gaige de shijian he tansuo* (Shanghai: Shanghai renmin chubanshe, 1989).

—— 'Woguo jingji tizhi gaige de yi xiang lishixing juece', in State Science and Technology Commission (ed.), *Zhongyao juece shijian yu sikao* (Beijing: Zhongguo shehuikexue wenxian chubanshe, 1992), i. 1–10.

White, Lynn T., 'Local Autonomy in China during the Cultural Revolution: The Theoretical Uses of an Atypical Case', *American Political Science Review*, 70/4 (1976), 479–91.

White, Tyrene, 'Postrevolutionary Mobilization in China: The One-Child Policy Reconsidered', *World Politics*, 43/1 (1990), 53–76.

Wiarda, Howard J., 'Toward A Nonethnocentric Theory of Development: Alternative Conceptions from the Third World', in Howard J. Wiarda (ed.), *New Directions in Comparative Politics* (Boulder, Colo.: Westview, 1985), 127–50.

Wildavsky, Aaron, 'Choosing Preferences by Constructing Institutions', *American Political Science Review*, 81/1 (1987), 3–21.

Williams, Walter, *et al.*, *Studying Implementation: Methodological and Administrative Issues* (Chatham: Chatham House, 1982).

Winckler, Edwin A., 'Policy Oscillations in the People's Republic of China', *China Quarterly*, 68 (1976), 734–50.

Woetzel, Jonathan R., *China's Economic Opening to the Outside World: The Politics of Empowerment* (New York: Praeger, 1989).

Wolfinger, Raymond E., 'Nondecision and the Study of Local Politics', *American Political Science Review*, 65/4 (1971), 1063–80.

Wolman, Harold, 'Decentralization: What It Is and Why We Should Care', in Robert J. Bennett (ed.), *Decentralization, Local Governments, and Markets: Towards A Post-Welfare Agenda* (Oxford: Clarendon Press, 1990), 29–42.

Wong, Christine P. W., 'Between Plan and Market: The Role of the Local Sector in Post-Mao China,' *Journal of Comparative Economics*, 11 (1987), 385–98.

—— 'The Maoist "Model" Reconsidered: Local Self-Reliance and the Financing of Rural Industrialization', Joseph, Wong, and Zweig (eds.), *New Perspectives on the Cultural Revolution*, 183–96.

Woodward, Dennis, 'A New Direction for China's State Farms', *Pacific Affairs*, 55/2 (1982), 231–51.

World Bank, *China: Agriculture to the Year 2000*, annex to *China: Long-Term Development Issues and Options* (Washington: World Bank, 1985).

Wu, Guoguang, 'Command Communication: The Politics of Editorial Formulation in the *People's Daily*', *China Quarterly*, 137 (1994), 194–211.

Wu, Xiang, 'Nongcun gaige weishenmo cong Anhui kaishi?' *Zhongguo renli ziyuan kaifa*, 2 (1994), 24–35.

—— 'Kaichang xinjumian de wuge yihao wenjian', *Zhongguo renli ziyuan kaifa*, 3 (1994), 32–40.

Wunsch, James S., 'Institutional Analysis and Decentralization', *Public Administration and Development*, 11 (1991), 434–43.

Xia, Zhenkun, 'Shilun nongye jixiehua de jingji fenxi', *Nongye jishu jingjixue wenxuan* (Beijing: Nongye chubanshe, 1981), 74–80.

Xiang, Xiyang and Shen, Chong, *Shinianlai lilun zhengce shijian: ziliao xuanbian* (Beijing: Qiushi chubanshe, 1988), 2 vols.

Xiao, Mugong, 'Shixing shuangbao buyao shunhai jiti suoyouzhi', *Fendou*, Mar. 1982, 39.

—— 'Zhengque renshi nongye jitijingji de youyuexing', *Fendou*, Sept. 1982, 18–19.

Xu, Bu, 'Guanyu Heilongjiangsheng tuixing nongye jixiehua jige wenti de tantao', *Nongye jishu jingji*, June 1983, 19–22.

Xu, Jingyong, *Zhongguo nongye jingji lilun yu shijian* (Fuzhou: Fujian renmin chubanshe, 1986).

Xu, Shiqi, 'Cong Anhuisheng Liuan diqu sannian de shijian kan shuangbao zerenzhi', *Nongye jingji wenti*, 3 (1982), 3–7.

Xu, Yong, *Baochan daohu chenfulu* (Zhuhai: Zhuhai chubanshe, 1998).

Yan, Jiaqi, *Lianbang zhongguo gouxiang* (Hong Kong: Ming Pao Publisher, 1992).

Yang, Dali L., *Calamity and Reform in China: State, Rural Society, and Institutional*

Change Since the Great Leap Famine (Stanford: Stanford University Press, 1996).

Yang, Xun and Liu, Jiarui, *Zhongguo nongcun gaige de daolu: zongti shuping yu quyi shizheng* (Beijing: Beijing daxue chubanshe, 1987).

Yang, Yuyuan, Liu, Zheng, and Chen, Wuyuan, *Nongcun jingji tizhi gaige yanjiu* (Chengdu: Sichuan shehuikexueyuan chubanshe, 1986).

Yanshou xianzhi (Harbin: Sanhuan chubanshe, 1991).

Yanzhe maozhuxi zhiyin de nongye jixiehua daolu qianjin (Beijing: Renmin chubanshe 1972).

Yao, Zhenyan, *Zhongguo touzi tizhi gaige* (Beijing: Zhongguo caizheng jingji chubanshe, 1994).

Ye, Zhengzhi, 'Woguo nongye jixie chanpin jiage wenti tantao', *Nongchanpin chengben yu jiage lunwenji* (Beijing: Zhongguo kexue chubanshe, 1983).

Yi'anxian zhi (Beijing: Zhongguo qingnian chubanshe, 1989).

Yin, Robert K., 'Studying the Implementation of Public Programs', in Walter Williams *et al.*, *Studying Implementation: Methodological and Administrative Issues* (Chatham: Chatham House, 1982), 36–72.

——*Case Study Research: Design and Methods* (Beverly Hills: Sage Publications, 1994), 2nd edn.

Young, John D., 'Implementation: Key to Reform', *The Bureaucrat*, 12/1 (1983), 35–40.

Yu, Guoyao, Cao, Mengxiang, and Lo, Yousheng, 'Jilinsheng Yushuxian nongyue jixiehua diaocha', *Nongye jingji luncong*, June 1982, 253–8.

Zang, Xiaowei, 'Provincial Elite in Post-Mao China', *Asian Survey*, 31/6 (1991), 512–25.

'Zenyang chengbao nongye jixie', *Fendou*, Mar. 1983, 37–8.

'Zenyang shixing nongji zhuanyedui chengbao', *Fendou*, July 1983, 37–8.

Zhang, Desheng, *Anhuisheng jingji dili* (Beijing: Xinhua chubanshe, 1986).

Zhang, Furu, Fan, Weichang, and Shen, Xingfa, 'Sunke nongchang jingji xiaoyi diaocha,' *Xuixi yu tansuo*, 1 (1984), 71–6.

Zhang, Guangyou, 'Guanyu shuangbao zerenzhi fazhan qushi de tantao', *Nongye jingji wenti*, 7 (1982), 24–6.

——*Lianchan chengbao zerenzhi de youlai yu fazhan* (Henan renmin chubanshe, 1983).

——*Wan Li zai yijiuqiwu dao yijiubaliu* (Hong Kong: Qiwen Publishing House, 1995).

Zhang, Lin and Wang, Qiang, 'Yejidadui shixing baogan daohu de luogan tedian', *Jingji yanjiu*, July 1983, 66–70.

Zhang, Zhongcheng, *Zhongguo shuishou zhidu gaige* (Beijing: Zhongguo caizheng jingji chubanshe, 1994).

Zhaodong xianzhi (Zhaodong, 1985).

Zhao, Guoliang, *Zhongguo nongcun jingji tizhi gaige dashiji* (Beijing: Qiushi chubanshe, 1988).

Zhao, Suisheng, 'From Coercion to Negotiation: The Changing Central–Local Relationship in Mainland China', *Issues and Studies*, 28/10 (1992), 1–22.

Zheng, Yong-nian, 'Perforated Sovereignty: Provincial Dynamism and China's Foreign Trade', *Pacific Review*, 7/3 (1994), 309–21.

Zhonggong Heilongjiangsheng weiyuanhui, 'Zuohao tuixing jiating lianchan cheng-bao zerenzhi gongzuo', *Nongye jingji wenti*, Febr. 1984, 18–22.

Zhonggong sanzhong quanhui yilai zhongyang shouyao jianghua ji wenjian xuan-bian (Taibei: Zhonggong yanjiu zazhishe, 1983).

Zhongguo fenxian nongcun jingji tongji gaiyao (Beijing: Zhongguo tongji chuban-she, 1989).

Zhongguo gongchandang renming dacidian (Beijing: Zhongguo guoji guangbo chubanshe, 1991).

Zhongguo guding zichan touzi tongji ziliao 1950–1985 (Beijing: Tongji chubanshe, 1987).

Zhongguo jingji nianjian (Beijing: Jingji guanli chubanshe, various years).

Zhongguo nongye dashiji (Beijing: Nongye chubanshe, 1982).

Zhongguo nongye nianjian (Beijing: Nongye chubanshe, various years).

Zhongguo nongye yinhang, *Zhongguo nongcun jinrong tongji 1979–1989* (Beijing: Zhongguo tongji chubanshe, 1991).

Zhongguo tongji nianjian (Beijing: Tongji chubanshe, various years).

Zhongguo tongji zhaiyao (Beijing: Zhongguo tongji chubanshe, various years).

Zhonghua renmin gongheguo fensheng dituji (Beijing: Ditu chubanshe, 1977).

Zhonghua renmin gongheguo xingzheng quhua jiance (Beijing: Ditu chubanshe, 1983).

Zhou, Haile (ed.), *Suxichang fazhan baogao* (Beijing: Renmin ribao chubanshe, 1994).

Zhou, Kate Xiao, *How the Farmers Changed China: Power of the People* (Boulder, Colo.: Westview, 1996).

Zhou, Qiren, *Nongcun biange yu zhongguo fazhan 1978–1989* (Hong Kong: Oxford University Press, 1994), 2 vols.

Zhou, Yueli, *Jiating chengbaozhi tantao* (Hefei: Anhui renmin chubanshe, 1985).

Zweig, David, 'Opposition to Change in Rural China: The System of Responsibility and People's Communes', *Asian Survey*, 23/7 (1983), 879–900.

—— 'Strategies of Policy Implementation: Policy 'Winds' and Brigade Accounting in Rural China', *World Politics*, 37/2 (1985), 267–93.

—— 'Peasants, Ideology, and New Incentive Systems: Jiangsu Province, 1978–1981', in William L. Parish (ed.), *Chinese Rural Development: The Great Transformation* (Armonk, NY.: M. E. Sharpe, 1985), 141–63.

—— 'Context and Content in Policy Implementation: Household Contracts and Decollectivization, 1977–1983', in David M. Lampton, (ed.), *Policy Implementa-tion in Post-Mao China* (Berkeley: University of California Press, 1987), 255–83.

—— 'Agrarian Radicalism as A Rural Development Strategy, 1968–1981', in Joseph, Wong, and Zweig (eds.), *New Perspectives on the Cultural Revolution*, 63–81.

—— 'Rural People, the Politicians, and Power', *China Journal*, 38 (1997), 153–68.

Index